WONDERS
of the
SEA

WONDERS
of the
SEA

ROBERT BURTON
CAROLE DEVANEY
TONY LONG

Exeter Books

NEW YORK

First published in USA 1983
by Exeter Books
Distributed by Bookthrift
Exeter is a trademark of Simon & Schuster
Bookthrift is a registered trademark of Simon &
Schuster New York, New York

ISBN 0-671-05964-5

Printed in Singapore by Koon Wah Printing Pte.,
Limited

Contents

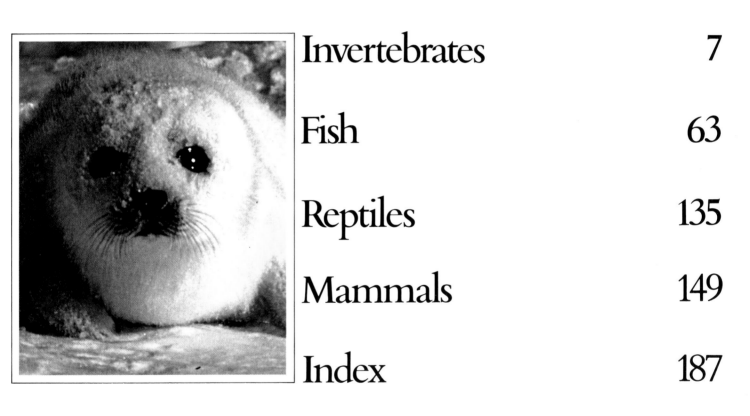

Invertebrates
primitive marine animals

Above: siphonophores, relatives of the jellyfish, drift at the surface where they are largely at the mercy of tides and currents.
Left: the sea anemone is similar in structure to a jellyfish, but lives attached to the sea bed

There are well over a hundred thousand species of marine invertebrate. This total represents the vast majority of animals in the sea, both in terms of the number of species and in terms of the number of individual animals. However, while all vertebrate animals are distinguished by the possession of an internal skeleton of cartilage or bone, the invertebrates are a much broader assemblage of animals, many of which have few features in common. Some groups of marine invertebrate are closely related to one another, but many have no clear relationship to other groups. They display a great range of structure and adaptation to different ways of life, and the difference between individual groups of marine invertebrate may be as great as that, say, between fish and mammals.

The diversity of marine invertebrates becomes more apparent when we take into consideration

that, of about twenty 'phyla' in the animal kingdom recognized by zoologists, the vertebrate animals of both land and sea constitute only a part of one single phylum. The remainder of it and all the remaining phyla contain species of invertebrates.

Many marine invertebrates are not immediately recognizable as animals at all. Creatures like the sponges and sea anemones spend all or most of their lives rooted to the sea bed. On rocky shores shellfish, like barnacles, cement themselves to rock surfaces to resist the force of the waves, or even onto mobile surfaces like the back of a whale. Other kinds of marine invertebrate, such as octopuses and lobsters, find their food by moving about the sea floor. Still other invertebrates drift or swim in the open sea. These include jellyfish and squid. The latter are among the great rivals of the sea fishes for midwater and deep-sea existence and, over short distances, can achieve faster speeds than almost any other animal in the ocean.

The creations of one tiny invertebrate animal, the coral polyp, play an especially important role in the ecology of the sea. Corals shape, not only their own environment, but also that of a great many other marine animals, both vertebrate and invertebrate.

A distinguishing feature of the invertebrate animal life of the sea is the absence of all but a handful of insect species. Since insects make up about three quarters of the animal species on this planet, their absence from the sea is particularly notable. Crabs, lobsters and their relatives, however, are related to the insects and they have a similar body plan.

The first forms of animal life to appear on earth were marine invertebrates. But, although their modern forms are primitive compared with the more recently evolved vertebrate animals, each one has been evolving for hundreds of millions of years. As they exist today, marine invertebrates, are the product of this long evolution and they are, in fact, highly specialized.

Sponges

The sponges occupy a position on the border of the animal kingdom, between animals and plants. To the casual observer they look like plants and for centuries biologists considered them as such. Sponges spend their lives rooted to the sea bed, they grow in an upright, branching formation and they display no perceptible movement. All these features seem to indicate a vegetable rather than an animal way of life.

However, in 1765 an English naturalist, John Ellis, demonstrated the sponge's animal nature. He observed that currents of water were drawn in through the tiny pores in the sponge's skin, carrying nutriment and oxygen to all the cells in its body. But other biologists were less convinced and sponges at present occupy a subkingdom of their own, within the animal kingdom, called the Parazoa, meaning 'like animals, but not true animals'. Some zoologists nonetheless credit the sponges with close affinities to the coelenterates, a group which include jellyfish, corals and sea anemones, but this relationship is still the subject of controversy. Within the Parazoa sponges are classified in the Phylum Porifera.

Whatever their relationship to other animals, the sponges are obviously a primitive group, with a simple body plan. They made their first appearance very early on in the Earth's history, during the Cambrian period, over 500 million years ago, and since that time they have lived in an evolutionary cul-de-sac, not being the ancestors of any other group of animals.

Two kinds of sponge, *Spongia* and *Hippospongia,* are better known than any other. These are the soft yellow bath sponges which were once a familiar household accessory.

Cosmopolitan creatures

There are about 5,000 species of sponges, living in all seas of the world. From the seashore to depths of more than 24,000 feet, sponges usually attach themselves to hard objects and remain fixed throughout their lives. They may grow by themselves or in large colonies, covering several

Below left: sponges from a coral reef in the Bahamas. The sponges of shallow tropical waters are brightly coloured and irregular in shape. Below: a branched sponge showing the large opening or 'osculum' at the top of each part of the colony through which water, containing oxygen and food, is discharged after it has passed through the body. Also visible are the many smaller pores, or 'ostia', through which water is taken into the sponge. These pores have given the group its scientific name, the Porifera or 'pore-bearers'

square feet in area. The colour is very variable. Sponges that live in shallow tropical seas are especially brightly coloured, being red, blue, yellow, purple, white or orange. Deep-sea sponges are of a more sombre shade, generally brown, grey or green. The shape of sponges varies greatly, even among individuals of the same species. Sponges of the seashore, for example, are affected by the shape and depth of the crevice or rock pool in which they live, or by their degree of exposure to the tides and waves.

Many sponges grow as flat encrusting masses, soft and slimy to the touch, and others assume a vase or urn shape, ranging from less than an inch tall to eight feet or more. The purse sponges, common on British shores, look like flattened brandy glasses or bunches of bananas, and they hang downwards from the undersides of rocks or weeds. The orange or yellow breadcrumb sponge, called *Halichondria*, is very abundant on the lower shore. It often grows as a flat mat, its surface patterned with miniature volcano-like craters; these are the water-exit pores of the colony. The beautiful Venus's flower basket,

found in the deep waters off the Philippines, has a delicate glass-like structure. It grows to a height of about one foot and, during the late nineteenth century, was the prized possession of many a Victorian household.

Sponge structure

A sponge consists of a bag of cells arranged about a central cavity called the spongocoel. On the outside of the body, there is a layer of cells, protective in function, perforated at intervals by pore cells which open into the spongocoel and form a system of canals running from the outside to the inside of the body. This feature has given rise to the scientific name of the phylum to which the sponges belong – the Porifera, meaning the 'pore-bearers'. Lining the spongocoel are special cells, characteristic of sponges, called collar cells. Each cell has a long, whip-like thread, called a flagellum, arising from it. These flagella beat together and draw a current of water into the body through the pores that riddle its surface. Tiny animals and plants, bacteria and particles of organic matter are brought into the sponge with the water and these form its food. The collar cells engulf the food and digest it within their cell bodies. The water and waste products are evacuated through a large opening, called the osculum, at the top of the body.

This simple body plan is called the asconoid type of sponge. There are two other grades of construction seen in sponges, varying in complexity, called the syconoid and the leuconoid body types. Both involve a folding of the body wall into finger-like growths, forming numerous radial canals leading into chambers lined with collar cells. The leuconoid type of sponge body is the most complex of all – thousands of canals opening into innumerable flagellated chambers. Such sponges can filter a great amount of water and some species can pump a volume of water equal to the volume of the sponge through their bodies each minute.

In between the outer layer of cells and the collar cells, there is a jelly-like layer called the mesoglea. Hundreds of cells wander freely within the mesoglea, unspecialized in function. They are like a reserve pool of labour, and can be called upon at any time to assume a digestive function as a collar cell, a protective function on the surface of the body or a reproductive role as a sperm or egg cell. These unemployed cells also produce the rods or spicules that form the internal skeleton so typical of sponges. These spicules may be composed of calcium carbonate, silica or a fibrous protein substance called spongin, whose fibres interlock to form an intricate latticework in certain sponges.

Classification of sponges

Sponges are divided into three classes according to the type of skeleton they possess. The Calcarea have a skeleton made of calcium carbonate spicules. Members of this class, such as the purse sponges, inhabit shallow seas to depths of

about 2,000 feet. The Hexactinellida have siliceous skeletons, made of six-rayed spicules, as the name suggests. The Venus's flower basket belongs to this class whose members occur in the deeper waters of the oceans, down to depths of 25,000 feet. The Demospongiae may have skeletons of silica spicules or of spongin fibres, or both may be present within their bodies. The commercially important bath sponges and the breadcrumb sponges are members of this class.

A complicated classification system of sponges has been based on the size and shape of the spicules that make up the skeletons, and on the number of axes or rays of each spicule. Identification of sponges is thus a difficult task and a high-powered microscope and a good identification book are essential tools to dispel doubts about the identity of most species of sponges collected.

Reproduction and regeneration

The most common method of reproduction among sponges is by budding or fragmentation. Small buds form all around the parent sponge's body and drop off to form new adults. During fragmentation, the sponge may become constricted in the middle and pinch off the upper part of its body, which then settles on the sea bed to form a new individual. Asexual cells called gemmules are frequently formed too. They are laden with fat and protein food reserves and may be surrounded by a tough spongin coat. They are resistant to adverse conditions and may not develop for many months, but lie dormant and exist on their food reserves until times are favourable once again.

Sponges have remarkable powers of regeneration. If a sponge is squeezed through fine bolting silk so that all its cells are dissociated, the individual cells will team up again in small clumps, each of which will become a new sponge. The collar cells swim about, lashing their flagellae, and the mesogleal cells creep around like tiny amoebae. When two cells come in contact, they either pair up or move apart to find other partners. If two species of sponge are thus broken up, the cells of each species will not mix. They seek out their own kind and form numerous new sponges of the two original species.

Sponges can also reproduce sexually. A sponge may be hermaphrodite, possessing both male and female cells, or it may be either male or female. The sperms are brought to the female cells in the water current. A fertilized egg cell develops into an embryo, embedded in the collar-cell layer of the parent sponge. When it is fully developed, the embryo bursts out of the parent's body and turns itself inside out, so that the flagella of the collar cells are on the outside of its body. It now becomes a free-swimming larva, searching for a home. After a short time it settles down, and turns part of its body inside out again, the result being that the collar cells are now in the adult position, lining the central body cavity.

Sponges are harvested from the eastern Mediterranean, the Gulf of Mexico, the West Indies and the Philippines. They may be harpooned from boats with long forked poles or taken by skin divers. The sponges are cured by leaving them to rot in the air. Then the soft tissues are washed away with sea water, leaving the soft fibrous skeleton, which is then left to dry in the sun. Synthetic plastic sponges have largely replaced the natural sponges nowadays. But in ancient Greek and Roman times, *Spongia* was a familiar household object, being used as a paint brush, mop and even as a drinking vessel for the men of the house.

A sponge from the Bahamas. About 5,000 species of sponge are found in all the seas of the world but the greatest number and variety are found in the tropics.
Bottom: a man trimming bath sponges. These familiar items belong to the two genera Spongia *and* Hippospongia

Jellyfish

Jellyfish and their relatives, such as the Portuguese man-of-war, are placed in the Phylum Coelentrata. In the same group we find corals and sea anemones. Sponges were once classified in the Coelentrata and, since their exclusion, it has acquired another name, Cnidaria. Within the Cnidaria, or Coelentrata, jellyfish are placed in the class Scyphozoa.

Jellyfish are among the most unpopular of sea creatures. Notices bearing such messages as 'Beware sea wasps', 'Men-of-war today' and 'Stinging nettles coming' are displayed along the beaches of Florida and northern Australia maybe two or three times a year, warning the holiday maker to keep clear of the water.

A public nuisance

Carried inshore by local currents and winds, shoals of jellyfish may invade the shallow coastal waters, terrifying bathers and, on occasions, causing excruciating pain and even death. The box-shaped sea wasp haunts Indo-Pacific waters. A man stung by one of these creatures often dies within eight minutes. Less noxious, though still extremely dangerous, is the Portuguese man-of-war, a relative of the jellyfish. The luckless swimmer who blunders into its violet-tinted curtain of tentacles is injected with a poison seventy-five per cent as potent as that of the king cobra. Victims have described the experience as like being attacked by a swarm of angry bees or being bombarded with searing hot darts. The lesions resulting from such a sting may last for months and some fatalities have been reported. Even a beached man-of-war retains its virulence; the tentacles are still capable of stinging. Laboratory tests have shown that the man-of-war's venom retains its potency even after being frozen for six years.

Jellyfish are so called because of the very thick layer of jelly-like material sandwiched between the outer, protective layer of cells and the inner layer of cells making up the body organs. Jellyfish share this feature with their relatives, such as the sea anemones and corals. The two-layered arrangement of cells, enclosing the jelly layer, is

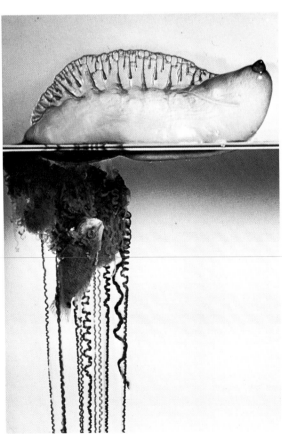

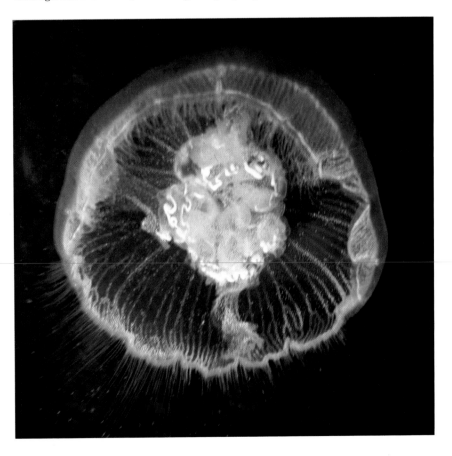

Left: Cotylorhiza, a type of jellyfish which has arms around the mouth, each one of which has a mouth at its tip.
Below left: Portuguese man-of-war with a fish that has been paralyzed by its stinging cells. Men-of-war are not single animals, but colonies of different animals, playing different roles in the life of the colony.
Below: underside of a typical bell-shaped jellyfish with its mouth at the centre

a characteristic of the coelenterates. But sea anemones and corals do not have the jelly developed to such an extent as the jellyfish. This is probably because the former are sedentary animals, living attached to a solid surface for most of their lives, whereas the jellyfish drift and swim in the sea and the thick jelly layer helps them to stay afloat.

Stinging cells

Another characteristic of all coelenterates is their stinging cells, called nematocysts, which are scattered all over the body surface but especially concentrated on the tentacles surrounding the mouth. Nematocysts are not found in any other group of animals, which makes biologists think that the coelenterates as a group are an evolutionary dead-end, a side branch off the main tree of life.

Each stinging cell consists of a capsule inside which is a long, hollow, coiled thread, variously armed with spines, hooks or barbs. When the cell is stimulated – either by an animal touching it or by chemicals liberated into the water by the prey – the thread explodes to the outside, penetrating the skin of the victim. It is a matter of debate whether the explosion of the thread is due to excess water pressure inside the capsule or to contraction of the muscles surrounding the stinging cell. A poison is injected through the hollow thread and acts as a neurotoxin, deranging the nervous system and paralysing the muscles. Thousands of these stinging cells, all discharging their harpoon-like threads, can immobilize relatively large prey and dissuade even the most persistent predator.

Jellyfish feed on all kinds of animals, from tiny one-celled creatures in the plankton to large fish. Several ploys for catching food are used. The jellyfish may swim to the surface, by languid pulsations of muscles in its 'bell', and then sink slowly down, trapping prey in its tentacles. Instead, the tentacles may be spread out under the body like a giant spider's web – the blue or orange sea blubber, *Cyanea*, with its eight tufts of long tentacles hanging from the bell, employs this method. Other jellyfish, such as the common *Aurelia*, found around the coasts of the British Isles, do not rely on their tentacles to such an extent. A layer of slimy mucus coats the body surface and the tiny plants and animals of the plankton become trapped in it, like flies on sticky fly-paper. Millions of tiny hairs, called cilia, sweep the food along channels to the mouth.

The largest of British jellyfish, *Rhizostoma*, whose bell reaches a diameter of some two feet, uses a feeding method akin to that of a sponge. There are no tentacles around the bell; instead the mouth tube is drawn out into long, elaborately folded arms, perforated by a prodigious number of little mouths. *Rhizostoma* has the general appearance of a large white mushroom with numerous cauliflower-like appendages hanging from it. Water containing plankton is sucked into the mouths and the minute plants and animals

are digested. A tropical relative of *Rhizostoma*, called *Cassiopeia*, has developed a most peculiar feeding method – it lies flat on its bell on the sea bed with its shrub-like arms extended upwards into the water, sucking in the drifting plankton.

Polyps and medusae

Coelenterates exhibit two characteristic body forms, called the polyp (from the Greek words for 'many feet', though referring to the tentacles) and the medusa (named after the mythical Gorgon Medusa whose snaky tresses killed mortals). The structure of both is very similar. The polyp's body consists of a hollow cylinder, through the middle of which runs the gut, opening at the mouth. The latter is surrounded by food-catching tentacles. The flat, disc-shaped base of the body enables the polyp to attach itself to hard surfaces by suction. Polyps, therefore, are sedentary animals, and adult sea anemones and corals are obvious examples of the polypoid plan.

The medusa, on the other hand, swims about and acts as a dispersal stage in the life cycle of many coelenterates. It is simply an upside-down polyp. Jellyfish exhibit the medusoid structure. The upper surface (the base of the polyp) is greatly expanded into an umbrella shape. The mouth is now on the underside, situated at the end of a long tube, sometimes extended into oral arms. The whole body looks rather like a bell with its clapper hanging in the centre. The tentacles hang downwards, like a curtain, fringing the margin of the bell. The gut is not a simple cavity as in the polyp – the medusa's mouth opens into the stomach from which radiate many canals, joining up with a ring canal, encircling the bell.

During a jellyfish's lifetime, the medusa is the familiar body form. But the polyp has an important part to play in the life cycle. A tiny free-swimming larva hatches out from each fertilized egg. The larva settles to the seabed and changes into a sedentary polyp, which feeds and stores food during the winter months. At the onset of spring, the polyp's body becomes constricted by a series of transverse grooves; it looks like a pile of saucers on top of a stalk. One by one, the saucers break off from the parent and swim away as tiny medusas, which will then develop into adult jellyfish. Some species have done away with the sedentary polyp stage, their larvae developing directly into young medusas. The tropical *Cassiopeia*, mentioned earlier, has come full cycle – breaking away from a polypoid parent, it becomes a free-swimming medusa and then reverts to the lazy life of a polyp, though retaining its medusoid form.

Relatives of the jellyfish

The Portuguese man-of-war, so called because early mariners likened it to a sailing galleon, is not a true jellyfish. It belongs to the closely related group, the Siphonophores. These animals are, in fact, colonies of individuals – both polyps and medusas – all co-ordinated into a single unit.

Right: jellyfish swim by pulsating movements of their bell-shaped bodies, but they are not active in pursuit of their food which consists largely of whatever animals or plants come within their reach

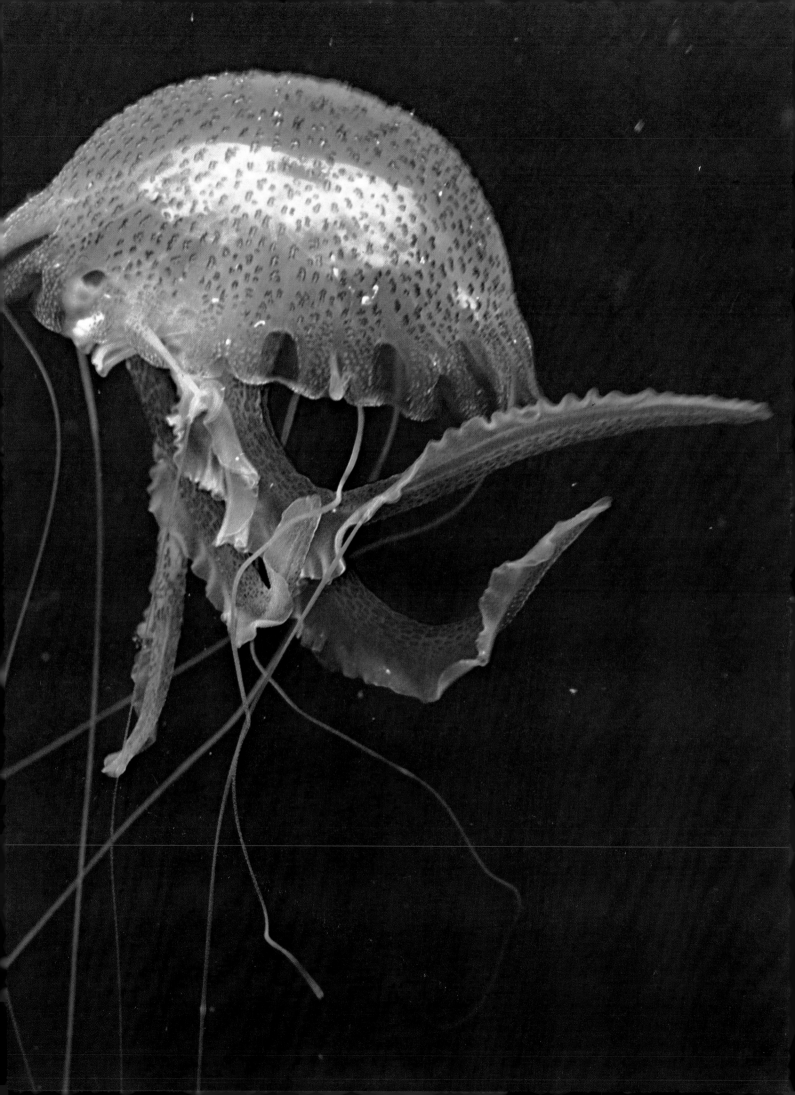

The vivid blue, crested float of the man-of-war is a modified medusa. The float is filled with gas, and some species can regulate their gas content so that the colony can sink beneath the surface of the sea in stormy weather. Beneath the float, which has an average length of eight inches, hang feeding, reproductive and stinging polyps, the latter being equipped with tentacles up to a hundred feet long – a formidable drift net. Other modified medusas serve as leaf-like flaps or bracts to shield the other parts of the colony. The salmon-pink bracts of the tropical siphonophore *Physophora* are a sight to behold, looking like an exotic water lily floating just below the surface. Strangely, some fish are the constant companions of the man-of-war. The yellow jack and the silver *Nomeus* dart unmolested among the tentacles of their overlord, sharing their host's food.

The medusoid individuals of other siphonophores are modified into powerful swimming bells, which propel the colony through the sea. The by-the-wind sailor, *Velella*, which looks rather like a small man-of-war, has a float topped by a prominent sail. This sail catches the wind and drives the animal along. There is evidence to show that *Velella* that live in the Northern Hemisphere have their sails set at a different angle from those that live in the Southern Hemisphere – the two populations are mirror images of each other. This is nature's way of coping with the reversal of the wind system experienced north and south of the equatorial zone.

Below: this beautiful jellyfish comes from the Pacific Ocean. Jellyfish occur in all seas from the tropics to the poles, although there are more different species and greater numbers in tropical waters. They are also more numerous in coastal waters than in the open ocean, probably because of the better feeding conditions there

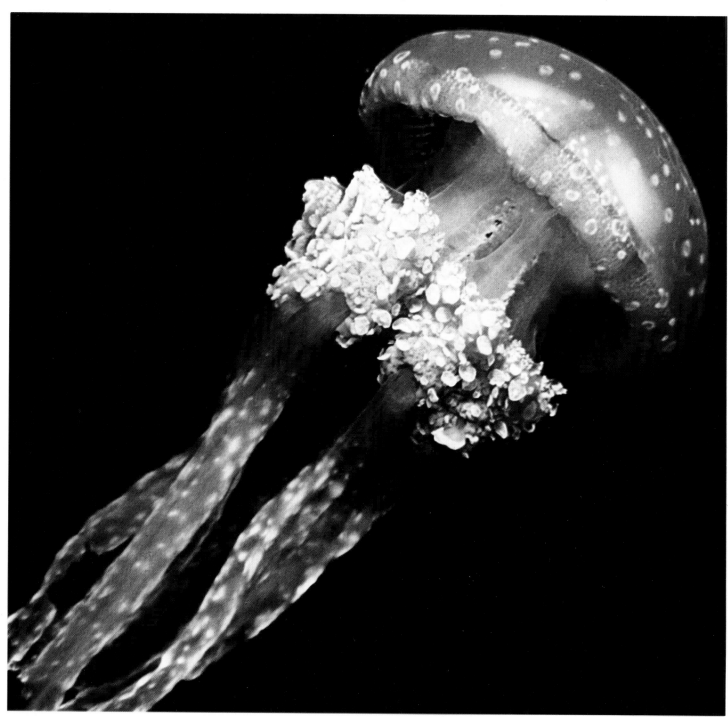

Left: the jellyfish Pelagia noctiluca is one of the most intensely luminescent species. It lives in warm waters, but is occasionally swept to the cooler waters of northern Europe and America. This is a jellyfish in which the single egg, after fertilization by sperm, develops directly into a free-living medusa. In most jellyfish, the medusa's eggs each develop into a minute larva. This becomes anchored to some firm support and grows into a tiny polyp. This in turn buds off a number of medusas. When mature, these reproduce sexually to form the polyp stage, and so the 'alternation of generations' continues

Corals

The massive offshore barrier reefs and the circular atolls of tropical seas have always given mariners cause for caution in navigation, and they have long been the subjects of study and speculation for scientists, as they are of great ecological and economic importance. They are created by tiny, soft-bodied creatures called coral 'polyps'. Each polyp is similar in structure to the sea anemones.

Like jellyfish, both corals and sea anemones are members of the Phylum Coelenterata or Cnidaria. Characteristic of this group are the batteries of stinging cells, or nematocysts, that arm the tentacles and general body surface. The nematocysts are used both in defence and offence. Although anemones and corals usually feed on the tiny animals of the drifting plankton, their stinging cells are powerful enough to paralyze larger animals such as fish.

Most species of coral are found in the warm waters of the tropics. They generally live at depths of less than 200 feet. This is connected with the fact that the corals contain within their tissues tiny one-celled organisms, called dinoflagellates. These minute creatures need light to make their food by the process of photosynthesis. Most biologists think that there is a symbiotic relationship between the coral and its 'lodgers', that is, a partnership in which the organisms benefit each other. Besides being protected against the outside world, the dinoflagellates use the carbon dioxide gas, a by-product of their host's respiration, to make their food by photosynthesis. The dinoflagellates also process other waste materials produced by the coral, such as nitrogen and phosphorus, in some way that is useful to the host. The dinoflagellates release oxygen as a by-product of photosynthesis; this is available to the coral's tissues for respiration. Finally, it seems that the presence of the dinoflagellates is necessary for the formation of the coral's calcareous skeleton, the tiny organisms accelerating its development in some way.

Although this symbiotic relationship is a great advantage to corals it has certain limitations and some corals are devoid of algal partners. Because photosynthesis of the algae requires light of a certain intensity, coral reef formation cannot take place at depths below which sufficient light penetrates. This is why active reefs are restricted to those areas of the seas where the water is not more than 160–200 feet (50 to 60 meters) deep and where the temperatures of the water is around 68 to 86 degrees Fahrenheit (20 to 30 degrees centigrade).

This, then is the reason why active coral reefs are all to be found in warm seas. In colder seas we find solitary or very simple colonial corals without algal partners and lacking the ability to form the spectacular reefs of warmer climes.

As mentioned, corals are carnivorous. The polyps are most active at night, and catch their prey with their tentacles. A planktonic animal of suitable size is held in the tentacles, then stung and paralysed by the nematocysts. It is then pushed into the mouth with the tentacles, passed through the tube-like gullet, and thence into the gut or enteron. Here, specialized body cells carry out the digestion and absorption of the food. In some species, the capture and transfer of food is assisted by the currents set up by the tiny hairs, or cilia, covering the tissues of the polyps.

Stinging carnivores
Corals have a simple construction. Like sea anemones, they live attached to hard surfaces, such as rocks. They anchor themselves to the substrate by means of their sucker-like basal discs. The body of a coral polyp consists of a hollow sac, through the centre of which runs the 'blind' gut, so described because it has only one opening, through which food is taken in and waste products expelled. The mouth is surrounded by the tentacles. Thin walls of tissue, called mesenteries, divide the gut into several compartments. The mesenteries contain nematocysts and also enzyme-producing cells, which break down food in the gut. Other cells absorb the products of this breakdown. The mesenteries can sometimes be extended out of the mouth of the polyp to digest food particles that have fallen onto the outer surface of the animal.

There are two major types of coral – those with an external skeleton (the stony, or madreporian,

Left: a colony of madreporian corals, showing the individual polyps, some of which are contracted and others of which are extended and feeding. Below: in some species of coral there is a division of labour between individual polyps. Some play a digestive role, while others, such as these, catch prey

corals) and those with an internal skeleton (the eight-armed, . or octocorallian corals). The madreporians include the most important reef-building species, consisting of individual polyps living together in huge colonies of minute individuals, each measuring from one to three millimetres in diameter.

The sex organs, or gonads, of the coral polyp are attached to the mesenteries. They release their sex cells, or gametes, into the gut. After the female gametes are fertilized by the male ones, they develop into larvae, called planulae. These are discharged into the sea through the open mouth of the polyp. The larvae are very small and surrounded by fine cilia that wave to and fro, like tiny oars, and row their owners through the water. At this stage, the corals are part of the zooplankton of the sea, and run great risks of being eaten by other animals. Soon they settle on a hard surface and attach themselves to it by means of their basal discs.

Skeletons of lime

Cells in the lower part of the body, and in the disc itself, produce calcium carbonate (limestone). This is secreted in such a way that it forms a cup-shaped skeleton around the lower

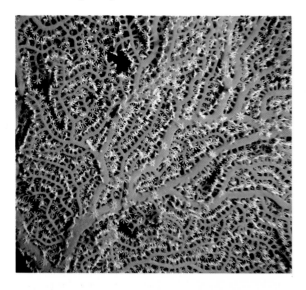

half of the animal. Just above the lip of the cup the body wall folds out and joins with the body walls of adjacent polyps. A continuation of the gut extends through each fold, and in this way, all the polyps of a colony are connected together, each drawing nourishment from the others. When the polyps die, new individuals grow on top of them from asexual buds that arise from the connecting membranes. The dead corals with their skeletons provide the necessary hard substrate for their successors.

The colonies of stony corals grow in an endless variety of forms, from the flat rounded colonies of the brain coral (Meandrina) to the knobbed, leaf-like bodies of the lettuce coral and the upright, branching 'antlers' of the stagshorn.

The octocorallian corals have an internal skeleton, in contrast to their stony relatives. When alive, the soft coral of tropical seas, called Alcyonium, or dead man's fingers, is a bloated-looking rubbery mass. When the animal dies, however, the calcareous spines, or 'spicules', embedded in the body become evident. In some octocorallians, such as the gorgonian corals (including whip corals, sea fans and sea feathers), there is a central axis of horny material, called gorgonin, running through the middle of the colony. Spicules of various shapes, sizes and colours are scattered throughout the coral tissues, and these determine the overall colour of the colony. The red gorgonian coral Corallium, found in the Mediterranean and off the coast of Japan, has a central axis of fused red spicules. This skeletal rod is made into coral jewellery.

Thirty-five cubic feet of active living coral may contain more than a million polyps. As a coral colony grows and develops upwards, the lower parts gradually die away, leaving accumulations of the calcareous skeletons to add to the reef. At the same time, the calcareous parts of the associated animals which have died add their increment to the reef mass. Very little information is known concerning the rate of growth of coral but, in any case, this must be greatly affected by climatic and other environmental conditions. It is probable that a coral grows by only a couple of inches each year. Light, temperature, the amount of movement of water over the colony, the degree of silt formation and the salinity of the water have a considerable influence on growth. Growth of the reef is also offset by the destructive effect of boring animals and the waves.

Coral formations

Ever since Charles Darwin wrote his book 'Coral Reefs' in 1842, based on observations he had made during his famous voyage on HMS Beagle, there has been great discussion and considerable difference of opinion concerning the precise manner in which the different types of coral formations have arisen and developed.

Three types of coral formation are generally recognized – fringing reefs, barrier reefs and atolls. Fringing reefs are found rather close to the shores of land masses so that there is only a

Top left: looking rather like a plant, with its main 'trunk' and side 'branches', this is in fact a gorgonian coral colony, popularly known as a 'sea fan'. Bottom left: the gorgonian, or soft, corals have an internal skeleton of needles, or spicules, of lime, in addition to their central core of horny gorgonin. The lime spicules are of various colours, giving this colony its delicate rainbow-like coloration. Above right: this madreporian coral colony forms part of a barrier reef off the island of Lealta in the southern Pacific Ocean. Corals are unable to form reefs unless the temperature of the water is above 65° F. Above far right: part of the Australian Great Barrier Reef, showing madreporian corals, gorgonian corals and sponges. A tropical reef may be the home of several thousand different animals. Right: close-up view of the polyps of the 'precious red coral'. Its skeleton is used to make coral jewellery

narrow, shallow channel between them and the shore. Wave action breaks off pieces of coral on the seaward side and deposits them in front of the reef. This debris provides a platform for colonization and further growth of the corals. On the shoreward side, behind the narrow channel, beaches of sand composed of eroded coral together with other debris are deposited.

Barrier reefs are probably formed in a somewhat similar way, but at a much greater distance from the shore. The intervening channel may be many miles wide and several hundred feet deep.

The Great Barrier Reef of north-eastern Australia, which borders the Coral Sea, is the outstanding example of a land mass formed by the activity of corals and associated plants and animals. It extends for more than 1,200 miles and varies in width from 10 to 40 miles. It has a total area of approximately 80,000 square miles.

Several hundred small islands of coral origin, often called atolls, occur in the tropical zone. Most atolls are more or less circular and have a deep lagoon in the centre. They are usually great distances from any mainland. The origin of atolls is not always certain, but most of them seem to have been formed on top of volcanic peaks which have subsided. In recent years this theory has been strengthened as a result of deep borings on atolls. Some theories which have been advanced are less concerned with the effects of land subsidence and suggest that a change in sea-levels following the melting of the ice caps after the last great Ice Age has been a significant factor in the formation of some atolls.

In spite of the diversity of shape, size and colour of the stony corals, of which there are more than 2,000 species, only a limited number are commonly found in reefs. Among the more important species are *Madrepora* (now generally known as *Acropora), Favia, Orbicella, Porites, Fungia* (the well-known mushroom coral), *Meandrina* (the brain coral), *Dendrophyllia, Eusmilia,* and *Galaxea.* Reefs are by no means composed entirely of corals and their dead skeletal remains, for there are many other organisms present which are also able to deposit calcium carbonate. Such associated, but totally unrelated, organisms frequently play an important part in the formation of reefs: In fact there are areas of 'coral reef' where the bulk of material present has been laid down by organisms other than corals. Coralline seaweeds of various kinds, single-celled foraminifera, molluscs, crustaceans and others are all important reef builders. It is, however, the stony corals which provide the basis for reef formation and development.

The huge masses of coral provide a great range of suitable habitats for a rich variety of plant and animal life. Cavities and depressions in the coral mass give shelter and feeding grounds to marine worms, sponges, sea-slugs, sea-fans, molluscs, crabs, prawns, sea-anemones and many other kinds of animals in huge numbers. In this environment, swarming with life, there is a ceaseless struggle for self-preservation, food,

shelter and oxygen. This fascinating and rich living community provides the marine biologist with wonderful material for the study of food chains, special adaptations to the environment and the complex patterns of ecological interdependence which profoundly affect the growth and development of coral reefs.

One member of the coral-reef community is the gall crab *(Hapalocarcinus marsupialis).* The young female crabs enter cavities in the stony corals, and in the course of their growth produce irregular gall-like growths of the coral around them. Once inside, the crabs cannot leave the cavities, but they are able to live on planktonic food carried in by the water flowing through the apertures in the wall of their coral prison. The male crabs are entirely free-living and do not make galls. They are much smaller than the females, and so they can enter the corals to fertilize their mates. The young crabs are released to become part of the plankton.

Right: Acropora, *one of many corals which assume an upright branching formation. Below: among the many other animals living within and around the corals are numerous species of fish. Many are brightly coloured, their colours often blending subtly with their coral background. Some fish root out prey hiding in the coral; others eat the coral. Bottom: this close-up of a madreporian coral colony shows the ring of tentacles surrounding the mouth of each polyp*

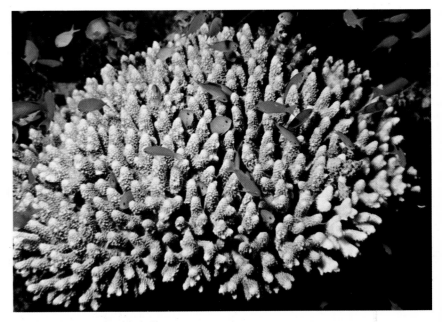

Corals in danger

Like most animals, corals are vulnerable to predators. One of the most serious threats is posed by the crown-of-thorns starfish, another marine invertebrate, which has shown a dramatic increase in numbers during recent years. One of the reefs endangered by the ravages of this predator is the Great Barrier Reef.

Various commercial pressures constitute an added threat to coral reefs. In some areas, permission is being sought to quarry the reefs for limestone, to make trial borings for oil, and so on. Any such disturbance, however localized, could be a danger to reefs because of the silting which could result; corals can only live in clear water.

Coral reefs provide a specialized type of habitat for a wealth of marine life. They also provide endless fascination to the skindiver fortunate enough to enter their exquisitely coloured world. Damage to the great coral formations could deprive the world of a great subject for both study and enjoyment.

Left: A crown-of-thorns starfish browses on living coral. During recent years, this animal has increased greatly in numbers, and in some areas has destroyed large areas of reefs. It is capable of turning a thriving reef, such as that off Fiji (below), into a wasteland of dead coral

Sea anemones

Like jellyfish and corals, the sea anemones are members of the Cnidaria. In particular, they are closely related to certain kinds of coral. Anemones are creatures of remarkable beauty, their delicate tentacles and range of vivid colours inviting comparison with the flowers that share their name. Indeed they have been called 'flowers of the sea', but their flower-like appearance belies sea anemones' true nature which is animal and predatory.

Sea anemones display a fascinating diversity in their methods of feeding, movement and reproduction. Certain species are also remarkable because they maintain unique symbiotic relationships with totally dissimilar sea creatures. All these features make the anemone a popular choice for the marine aquarium, and it is underwater that the beauty of the sea anemone can best be appreciated. Its tentacles are extended and drift gracefully in the current or backwash of the waves breaking on a rocky

shore. However, sea anemones are perhaps more commonly encountered after they have been stranded by the rising tide. In this state an anemone draws in its tentacles and resembles a round lump of jelly. The inert appearance is deceptive, because anemones are active and voracious.

Flowers of the sea

Anemones are among the commonest of marine animals, inhabiting coastal waters throughout the world and being particularly numerous in tropical seas. The tropics also boast the largest species. Anemones vary in size across the body (excluding tentacles) from a mere half-inch to as much as two feet in the case of individuals of *Stoichactis*—the largest anemones ever recorded —on the Great Barrier Reef of Australia. Along rocky shores of the British Isles, many common anemones can be seen in rock pools at mid-tide or low-tide level. The beadlet anemone (*Actinia equina*) and the dahlia anemone (*Tealia felina*) are widely distributed, and the snakelocks anemone (*Anemonia sulcata*) may often be seen

Below: the beautiful beadlet anemone, common dweller on the seashore, showing off its array of stinging tentacles surrounding the protruding mouth. At the base of the thick body column, a flat muscular disc enables the anemone to attach itself to any surface by suction

clinging to the fronds of brown kelp. The snake-locks is unusual in not being able to draw in its long tentacles as other anemones can. Another common dweller on the sea shore is the plumose anemone (*Metridium senile*) which has a large number of feathery tentacles.

Anemones eat animal food, live sea creatures such as shrimps and fishes, which they trap in their tentacles and paralyse with their stinging cells. These cells work somewhat like the sting of a nettle. Jellyfishes and corals exhibit similar properties and it is for this reason that the phylum to which all these animals belong is known as the Cnidaria, which means 'nettle animals'. (The older name for the group, Coelentrata, means 'animals with hollow stomachs'.) Within the Cnidaria sea anemones are classified in the class Anthozoa, which means 'flower animals'.

Simple animals

The structure of an anemone is extremely simple. It has no skeleton, heart or blood vessels, and only a simple network of nerve cells. Its body is a hollow cylinder with a flattened basal disc on its underside, fixed to the ground partly by muscular contraction, partly by a secretion of sticky mucus. On the upper side is another disc with a mouth at the centre, which is surrounded by rings, or 'cycles', of tentacles. The mouth leads into a throat, below which is the stomach or 'enteron', occupying the whole interior of the body and divided into sections by thin tissues, known as 'mesenteries'. These mesenteries project in pairs from the body wall and hang like

Top left: when disturbed a sea anemone withdraws its tentacles and contracts into a tight ball. The inert-looking blob of jelly to the right of this dahlia anemone is the same animal in the contracted state.
Above left: although often considered to be sedentary, sea anemones can move about. This snakelocks anemone is walking upside down on its tentacles, its base partly inflated with air.
Left: the anemone fish is so called because it has a special relationship with the anemone. The fish hides unharmed among the stinging tentacles, protected by a mucus secreted from cells in its skin

that mechanical, often preceded by chemical, stimulation alerts the nematocyst. The capsule wall becomes more permeable and water rushes into it so that the lid is forced off, and the coiled thread abruptly everts. A nematocyst can only be discharged once. Special cells in the skin of the anemone produce new ones within a matter of hours.

There are other cells in the tentacles called 'spirocysts' with the aid of which the anemone holds onto its prey. The thread inside the spirocyst contains delicate spiral bands which readily absorb water, causing the thread to swell. If the bands touch anything they stick to it and spread out in fine web-like strands, increasing their grip.

While the usual method of feeding is to wave the tentacles around, or merely to spread them, like a drag-net, to catch anything floating or swimming by, other methods may be used. The mouth may be pushed out like a tube to search for food; or one or several tentacles may be extended well beyond their normal length, like probing fingers. Tracts of cilia on the skin of the anemone may carry small particles of food to its mouth. Once the anemone has secured its food the holding tentacle bends over towards the mouth and pushes the food in, assisted, in the case of larger morsels, by neighbouring tentacles.

Motion and multiplication

Most sea anemones tend to stay in the same place for long periods, provided circumstances are favourable; others move about readily in search of food. The method of locomotion varies, but the commonest is powered by movements of the

Left: a deadly embrace. The stinging cells in the tentacles inject a toxin, paralyzing the prey, which is then pushed into the mouth by the tentacles.
Below: a co-operative venture. This hermit crab Pagurus *receives the benefit of protection from the anemones, called* Calliactis, *which it carries on its back. The anemones benefit from this 'symbiotic' relationship by getting a free ride to new feeding grounds and also by picking up scraps of food dropped by the crab*

curtains in the enteron, their free ends bearing digestive filaments which secrete enzymes to break down the food for absorption through the stomach lining.

Respiration is an equally straightforward business. Two grooves lined with minute hairs called 'cilia', the 'siphonoglyphs', lie one on either side of the throat. The concerted beating of the cilia sets up an incoming current of water, from which oxygen is extracted by the body tissues. In the enteron itself are two pairs of ciliated 'directive' mesenteries, which circulate the water for further oxygen absorption.

The stinging cells in the tentacles are called 'cnidoblasts'. Within the cnidoblasts are stinging structures called 'nematocysts'. A nematocyst consists of a capsule with a lid, containing a long coiled hollow thread, often bearing barbs at the base. Many cnidoblasts have a trigger or 'cnidocil', a small spike projecting outwards. When a small animal, such as a shrimp or fish, brushes against the cnidocil the lid of the capsule comes off and the nematocyst explodes outwards. The coiled thread springs out of the capsule and pierces the skin of the prey. A poison is injected through the thread into the prey, which is paralysed and held by the tentacles.

The mechanism by which the nematocyst is discharged is not yet well understood. It seems

Friends and enemies

Such prolific reproduction often indicates that an animal has many enemies. This is true of the anemone. Fish feeding on the plankton take a large proportion of anemone larvae, while a wide variety of creatures ignore the stinging cells and make meals of the adults. Starfishes, sea spiders, whiting, cod and haddock take their share, and the flounder is often caught with a stomach full of anemones. The foremost predators are the 'nudibranchs' or sea slugs, shell-less marine molluscs that not only ignore the stinging cells but, in some tropical species, actually make use of them for their own defence. So copious is the slime secreted by their digestive tracts that the nematocysts fail to discharge their venomous darts. The sea slug incorporates these cells into its own tissues, usually in finger-like growths on its back, so that any predator striking from behind gets stung by the sea slug's last dinner. Furthermore, cannibalism is another threat to the small or weak anemone, which may be devoured by its neighbour.

In spite of these hazards, some anemones attain a great age, possibly even hundreds of years—there are certainly authentic records of anemones living in aquaria for up to ninety years.

However, unremitting hostility between the anemone and its environment is not universal. Some species are characterized by their habit of striking up special relationships (known as symbiotic relationships) with various sea creatures, to the benefit of both parties. Tropical anemones are often seen with small, brightly-striped fishes, known as anemone or clown fishes, hiding unharmed among their tentacles. How does the clown fish avoid being consumed by the anemone like any other fish? The answer is partly a slime on the scales of the fish, which inhibits the action of the nematocysts, and partly to a particular friendship between fish and anemone. The clown fish darts in and out of the tentacles, staying a little longer each time until the anemone seems to be used to its presence and does not sting. In return for providing protection, the anemone probably makes a meal of any predator that pursues the clown fish too close to its home.

Another sea creature which makes use of the protection of the anemone is the hermit crab, which occupies empty sea shells to protect its own soft, vulnerable body. The hermit crab introduces itself to an anemone of the right species (usually known as the commensal anemone, for this reason) by stroking the anemone until it is amiable enough to be lifted up by the crab and placed on the back of its shell. Thus the crab gains both protection and camouflage, while the anemone probably picks up food scraps and gets a free ride into the bargain. The crab may even transfer the anemone when it moves to a new and larger home. Similarly some species of tropical crabs utilize certain anemones in an astonishing manner—grasping two with their front claws and using them like boxing gloves for both protection and attack.

Above: three little anemones watched over by their parent. 'Budding' of new individuals off an adult is a common method of asexual reproduction among anemones. The budding young are connected to the parent's stomach until they are ready to detach themselves and lead independent lives.

Right: view of a sea anemone from above, showing the central mouth and the rings of tentacles surrounding it. The stomach of an anemone has only one opening and so waste products are expelled through the mouth

basal disc, similar to those of the foot of a snail. A few species drag themselves along by means of ridges running along the sides of the body, or perform a series of somersaults using their tentacles. Some release their hold on the seabed, inflate the body and are carried about by the currents. Others float head downwards at the surface of the sea. Some anemones walk on their tentacles or make movements similar to jumping or swim by lashing their tentacles. On the other hand, a few species burrow into sand, leaving only the mouth and tentacles above the surface.

This variety of methods of locomotion is rivalled by the many different ways in which anemones reproduce themselves. First there is the usual sexual method of multiplication. Anemones may be hermaphrodite (a single individual producing both ova and sperm) or the sexes may be separate. The ova and sperm are shed into the water through the mouth, and sink to the sea bed. There the fertilized ovum develops into a ciliated larva called a 'planula', that swims away and becomes part of the teeming world of plankton, ultimately settling again to form a new anemone. In some species, however, the ova are fertilized, and the larvae mature, inside the parent's body. Some species have a limited breeding season; others breed all the year round.

There are also several forms of asexual reproduction. Some anemones are known to split longitudinally, producing two perfect individuals where there was previously one. Others split horizontally, the splitting being preceded by the growth of a ring of tentacles from the body wall, just below the line of the eventual rupture. In some species young individuals are 'budded off' from the edge of the basal disc, and it has been known for anemones to move about leaving pieces of their basal disc behind, each piece growing into a new anemone. An anemone doing this may be seen to be moving over sharp edges of rock, as if cutting bits off itself.

Moss animals

Moss animals, or sea mats, are a group of marine creatures, comprising some 4,000 species, that form plant-like colonies and look for all the world like seaweeds. They belong to the Phylum Bryozoa. The name 'bryozoan' is from the Greek words for 'moss animal'. Bryozoans are to be found on seashores from the tropics to polar regions, growing on any object that will provide firm anchorage, such as rocks, seaweeds, driftwood, pilings or shells. They are notorious as fouling organisms, about 130 species being commonly found growing on ships' hulls. They grow in a variety of forms, from flat encrusting colonies, often measuring several feet in diameter, to erect branching types, reaching a height of a foot or more. A single species may incorporate both growth styles, growing first as a flat mat and, on encountering some obstruction, continuing its growth upwards.

Many individual animals, called zooids, make up a sea mat. This fact is reflected in the name Polyzoa, meaning 'many animals'. Each zooid, usually less than a fiftieth of an inch long, is encased in a little compartment or 'house', which may be box-like, oval, vase-shaped or tubular, depending on the form of the colony. The house is made of an outer layer of horny chitin (the same material that forms the shell of a crab), underlain by a thick layer of calcium carbonate or lime. The whole skeleton is reminiscent of that of a barnacle or a coral. There is an aperture at one end of the house through which a structure called the lophophore protrudes. This is the food-catching organ, characteristic of all moss animals. It is part of the digestive tract and consists of a ring of delicate tentacles, numbering between eight and thirty-four, encircling the mouth like a fan.

When the animal is feeding, the lophophore is extended out of the body. The beating of tiny hairs, or cilia, on the tentacles creates a current of water. Small plants and animals of the plankton are swept towards the tentacles where they become trapped in mucus, which is then moved towards the mouth. Any disturbance in the vicinity causes the lophophore to be retracted with lightning speed. This is effected by muscles attached to its base. The danger past, the lophophore is protruded again by hydrostatic action – the action of muscles working against the fluid contained in the spacious body cavity.

In many species of bryozoans, the front wall of the zooid has a thin membranous area, less calcified than the rest of the body wall. Muscles are attached to the underside of this membrane and to another part of the interior. When these muscles contract, the frontal membrane is pulled down, exerting a pressure on the body fluid which forces the lophophore out of the zooid. Other species, whose bodies are completely calcified, have another method – a tiny sac, near to the aperture, can be opened by muscles. Sea water rushes in to fill the sac, increasing the pressure inside the zooid and thus causing the lophophore to be protracted.

When a colony grows as a mat, some zooids act as suckers to attach it to the substrate, others are root-like; in erect shrubby colonies, some serve as stolons, like the runners of a strawberry plant. In most colonies, regardless of form, certain zooids are involved in offence and defence. These are the avicularia, so called because they look like birds' heads, which are armed with a sharp beak and a movable jaw. Often they are set on stalks and perform pecking movements, snapping up any intruder and holding it in a vice-like grip. Other, long, whip-like zooids sweep any debris from the colony's surface.

Bryozoans reproduce asexually by budding off new individuals from the body wall. In this way, a colony can increase in size at a rapid rate. Sexual reproduction also occurs; each zooid is usually hermaphrodite, that is, it contains both male and female organs. The eggs and sperm are released into the body cavity. After the eggs have been fertilized, they may be retained until they hatch. Often, however, the fertilized eggs are shed into the water. A tiny larva breaks out of each egg and swims about for a time, looking for a suitable place to settle. Once it has found its intended home, the larva secretes a sticky fluid, which secures it firmly to the substrate, and it then changes into an adult. Almost immediately, it assumes its duties as founder member of the future colony and starts to bud off new individuals, which reproduce again and again, until a sizeable colony has formed.

Right: moss animals are often found living on plants and other animals. In order for them to be attached in this position there is a division of labour within the colony. Some zooids act only as suckers, deriving their nourishment from the other members of the colony

Colonies of moss animals assume an astonishing variety of shapes and forms. Many look like plants (bottom right) while others resemble the branching formations of coral (far right). Some bryozoans form lumps or balls on the sea bed (bottom), sometimes more than a foot high. The tiny animals are only visible on close inspection (middle right)

Marine worms

There are several groups of marine worm. Flatworms, roundworms and ribbonworms all belong to different phyla of the animal kingdom. However, common marine worms like the lugworm and the ragworm are members of another group, the Phylum Annelida, to which the earthworm also belongs.

The body of an annelid is divided into many segments, each segment being equipped with its own muscles, nerves, blood vessels, section of gut and excretory organs. The head bears eyes, antennae and a pair of sensory palps on the underside near the mouth. All the senses are thus concentrated at the front end of the worm. The most characteristic feature of marine annelids is the fleshy, paddle-like lobe that is attached to both sides of each body segment. These lobes, called 'parapodia', have stiff bristles at their tips. Sometimes the parapodia are very large and leaf-like, as in the paddleworms, and act as swimming organs. The bristles of the tropical fireworms, which live among coral, are poisonous and are used for defence. The parapodia also serve as feet with which the worm can move itself along. Progress is visible as a series of waves rippling along each side of the worm's body, augmented by alternate contractions and expansions of the muscles of the body.

Basically, marine annelids, or polychaetes, are divided into two types – the errant or crawling worms and the sedentary or tube-dwelling worms. The ragworms are examples of the active errant type. They are carnivorous predators, armed with a pair of jaws at the tip of an eversible organ called the proboscis which can be shot out of the mouth at great speed. At rest, the proboscis is retracted inside the mouth. *Nereis virens*, commonly growing to a foot in length but sometimes reaching three feet, is a common ragworm of the seashore. Its overall colour is green but its back exhibits shades of purple and its belly is an iridescent pink. The large jaws are capable of giving the unwary bait-collector a sharp nip. The three- or four-inch *Nereis diversicolor* is generally yellowish-brown but it is readily identified by a red line, the dorsal blood vessel, that runs down the centre of its back.

Certain relatives of the ragworm have forsaken the sea bed and become free-swimming. *Tomopteris* is one of these. Its parapodia are much enlarged, presenting a large surface area to the water to help support its body. This is small, fragile and transparent, but the worm is a voracious feeder, preying on young fish and crustaceans of the plankton. When it swims, it moves like a centipede running along the ground.

Not all the errant types are as active as the ragworms and paddleworms. Some burrow and eat their way through mud or sand, digesting the organic particles it contains. The scale worms are typical burrowing errants. These worms have

a series of overlapping scales on their backs and look like sea slaters. The sea mouse, *Aphrodite*, growing to about four inches, has a fur of fine bristles covering the scales, giving it its popular name. It lives just below the surface and grinds up carrion with its muscular mouthparts.

Lugworms are examples of sedentary polychaetes. The coiled casts produced by their activities are a common sight on a muddy foreshore at low tide. Near each cast there is a circular depression. These features mark the two ends of the U-shaped burrow in which the lugworm lives. Mud is drawn in through the mouth, creating the shallow depression at one end of the burrow, and expelled through the anus, giving rise to the cast on the surface at the other end.

Left: serpulid worms make limestone tubes with secretions from glands in the mouth. Below: the two ends of a lugworm's burrow are visible as a cast and a shallow depression. These sedentary worms feed by drawing sand or mud in at one end of the burrow and expelling it at the other

The polychaetes that live permanently in tubes in mud or sand are modified for this way of life. The head is generally pointed to facilitate burrowing and the sensory palps and antennae are reduced. The parapodia too are small and the bristles are hook-like for clinging to the walls of the tube. There are often special structures on the head, such as strong bristles for digging, as in *Pectinaria* which lives head-down in a conical tube made of sand grains.

These tube-dwelling worms do not have a proboscis or jaws. There are two principal methods of feeding namely filter and deposit feeding. The fan or feather-duster worms, for example, have a crown of tentacles which protrudes from the top of the burrow and food particles are filtered out of the water and trapped in the sticky mucus that covers the tentacles. Other tube-worms, such as the terebellids and redthreads, feed by spreading their tentacles over the ground outside the burrow. Food deposits stick to the mucus on the tentacles which are then drawn back to the mouth. The particles are wiped off on the lips and then swallowed.

The sedentary worms can be grouped according to the material out of which they construct their tubes. There are the serpulid worms that form limestone tubes with secretions of calcium carbonate produced by glands in the mouth. The coiled tubes of *Spirorbis* are commonly seen on weeds and rocks. The honeycomb worms, such as *Sabellaria*, make tubes of sand on rocks. Colonies of these worms live together and their tubes build up to form massive reefs, with the consistency of sandstone – the temperate equivalent of the tropical reef-building coral animals.

The peacock worm, *Sabella*, makes tubes of mud or sand, up to a foot long. This worm's tentacles are brightly coloured with bands of brown, red and violet. They are not only used for filter-feeding but also act as gills, being richly supplied with blood vessels to aid gaseous exchange. Medium-sized sand grains are carefully sorted and stored by the worms in pouches below the mouth and are used to construct or repair the tubes when necessary.

Reproduction in polychaetes involves a major change in the bodies of the adult males and females. In the breeding season, the hind part of the body becomes packed with the sexual cells, or gametes, and the parapodia there become greatly enlarged. At certain times of the year, influenced by the phases of the moon, the worms swarm to the surface of the sea and perform nuptial dances, swimming around each other in tight circles. The females secrete a chemical which attracts and stimulates the males to release their sperm. The most spectacular display of swarming is seen in the palolo worm of the West Indies which swarms in October or November of every year, during the third quarter of the lunar cycle. The fertilized eggs, often covering acres of sea, develop into planktonic larvae which soon settle to the seabed and assume the lives of their parents.

Above: fan worms feed by filtering food from the surrounding water with the aid of their tentacles.
Left: ragworms are errant polychaetes. Characteristically, there is no separation of the body into abdomen and tail sections, as in sedentary types

Sea snails and sea slugs

Sea snails and slugs belong to another important group of marine invertebrates, Mollusca. Within this phylum they are included in the class Gastropoda and they and their relatives are commonly known as gastropod molluscs. Also molluscs, but belonging to different classes, are the oysters, clams and mussels, and the cuttlefishes, squids and octopuses. The sea snails and sea slugs range from the familiar limpets and whelks to the exotic sea butterflies and the beautiful nudibranch sea slugs. In size, too, they vary, from tiny snails measuring only one thirtieth of an inch to the giant Californian sea hare which may reach a weight of as much as sixteen pounds.

Gastropod molluscs exhibit a wide variety of different structures. They also differ in their choice of habitat and their environments range from wave-beaten shores to the depths of the ocean.

The most obvious feature of a snail – indeed often the only part of the animal that can be seen – is its shell. Unlike another large group of molluscs, the two-shelled bivalves (such as the oysters and mussels), all gastropods except for one small group have 'univalve' shells that are made up of one piece only. The shell is spirally coiled, although this feature may be lost when the animal changes from its larval to its adult form so that some adult snails have tube-shaped, cup-like or almost flat shells, or none at all.

Twisted bodies

During the development of the young snail, the body organs become twisted into a loop, forming a figure-of-eight shape. This twisting, or 'torsion', is accompanied by the loss of the organs of the right side. Torsion also affects the mantle, a layer of specialized tissue that secretes the shell and encloses the mantle cavity within which the body organs are suspended.

As the mantle becomes twisted during the development of the snail larva, so does the shell it secretes. The shell is made mainly of calcium carbonate, the substance that makes up chalk and limestone. The shell typically has three layers, the outer one being covered by a horny protective coating or periostracum.

In nearly all snails with spiral shells, the spiral is right-handed or dextral. A few species normally have left-handed, or sinistral, spirals and in some others, the odd abnormal individual has a left-handed shell. The shell coils around a central pillar called the columella – this may be solid or hollow. The animal is attached to its shell by a muscle attached in turn to the columella. When the muscle is relaxed, the animal's body is extruded from its shell; contraction of the muscle,

together with the fluid pressure of the blood in spaces within the head and foot, cause the snail's body to withdraw into its shell. In nearly all marine snails, the shell opening can be closed by a horny, or sometimes limey, plug called the operculum, borne on the upper surface of the hind end of the foot.

A snail moves over the ground on its muscular, fleshy foot, by means of continuous waves of muscular contractions. The head projects well ahead of the shell when the animal is moving, and bears a pair of long tentacles which are the snail's organs of touch and taste. At the base of each tentacle is an eye, borne on a short stalk.

Internal anatomy

The parts of the body concealed and protected within the shell are suspended within the mantle cavity. The gill or gills are made up of triangular-shaped leaves, each supplied with numerous small blood vessels. On the surface of the leaves are many tiny hair-like cilia; these beat so that they drive a constant current of water over the gill surface, bringing in oxygen for respiration,

Top right: looking like a futuristic underwater vehicle, an ormer Haliotis tubercula *creeps across the sea bed. Together with limpets and topshells, ormers are the oldest and least specialized gastropods. They are a warm-water species and are common in the Mediterranean, but one species is found as far north as the Channel Isles.*

Above right: this sea snail Fasciolaria tarentina *shows well the spirally-coiled protective shell*

which passes into the blood vessels, and carrying away waste products. A few snails have other methods of breathing – some marine snails can breathe in air for some time, and all snails can respire through their entire body surfaces under adverse conditions.

Because of the twisting of the snail's body during its development, the rear part of the gut lies above the head, and the anus is situated above the snout-like mouth, which is usually equipped with lip-like folds and horny jaws. The mouth leads into the buccal cavity, which contains the radula – a long ribbon of tissue studded with teeth. The radula teeth are used by plant-eating gastropods to rasp away at seaweeds or lichens, and by carnivorous species to tear at the flesh of their prey. The radula also acts as a conveyer belt, carrying the food back into the snail's gut. Snails feed in many different ways and on a variety of foods. As well as the two important types just described, there are snails that feed on dead and decaying food, scavengers, and a small number of parasites; the latter have lost the radula and feed by sucking the body juices of their hosts through modified mouthparts. Other gastropods filter tiny plants or animals from the water with their modified gills, as do the bivalve molluscs. Yet others use traps of sticky mucus to ensnare their prey – the captured food is pulled back into the mouth by the radula.

Snail reproduction

In most marine snails the sexes are separate, unlike the land and freshwater snails, which are hermaphrodite. The eggs and sperm may be shed into the water, but in the more highly evolved snails fertilization is internal. The eggs may be deposited in gelatinous strings or capsules. The

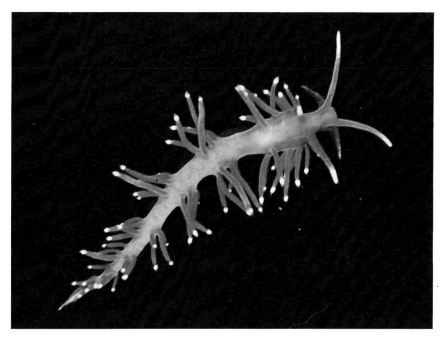

tiny larva, known as trochophores or veligers, may swim feebly but freely in the sea, living as members of the plankton, or remain enclosed within an egg capsule.

The Class Gastropoda is divided into two Sub-Classes, the Prosobranchia and the Opisthobranchia. The Sub-Class Prosobranchia is divided into three orders. The first is the Archaeogastropoda. These are the limpets and topshells. Limpets are probably the most successful of all molluscs in adapting to the often harsh conditions of life on rocky shores. They live on the lower shore, their conical shells perfectly adapted to withstand the full force of the waves. The shell profile of a limpet is directly related to the amount of battering it receives from the waves.

Above: a nudibranch sea slug, Hervia peregrina. *These beautiful creatures lack shells. At the front end are two pairs of tentacles, while the body bears delicate outgrowths that serve as gills. Sea slugs have a wide range of feeding habits, but most are carnivores. Below: a sea hare* Aplysia limacina *from the Mediterranean browses on sea lettuce. This is one of the 'tectibranch' sea slugs, with a very small flattened shell*

Right: Lunatia heros, *one of the carnivorous snails in the family Naticidae, commonly known as moon shells. The moon shells are placed in the great group Mesogastropoda. The shell barely covers the large foot, which is used both for locomotion and for grasping prey, which is then dealt with by the teeth on the snail's ribbon-like radula.*
Below right: two limpets Patella vulgata *cling tightly to their rocky home*

The tenacious limpet

A limpet weathers heavy breakers by pulling its shell firmly down around its body, gripping the rock surface tenaciously with its foot. When the tide is out, it sits hugging the rock tightly, always in exactly the same spot. The rim of its shell becomes ground down so that it matches any irregularities in the rock, just as if limpet and rock were moulded together.

At high tide however, and especially at night, the limpet forsakes the security of its rocky home and wanders about in search for food. Limpets feed on the carpet of green seaweed that covers many of the rocks. The extent of a limpet's wanderings can be seen clearly from the bare trail it leaves, where it has rasped away the seaweed with its toothed radula. No matter how far a limpet wanders, it always returns to its own home, but it is not known how the mollusc can find its way back with such unfailing accuracy.

The related topshells also live on the lower part of rocky shores, as far down as the edge of the sea itself. They have tentacles on the sides of the foot and a single feathery gill. The shell is broad-based, rounded or conical.

The winkles and their relatives

The second order within the Prosobranchia is the order Mesogastropoda. This includes such familiar marine snails as the periwinkles (or winkles), spire shells, slipper limpets and

their strong radula teeth. Many neogastropods, including the whelks, have a breathing tube, or siphon, which they can extend into the water above them when they are burrowing through mud or sand.

Sea slugs

The Sub-Class Opisthobranchia contains the sea hares, the sea slugs or nudibranchs and the sea butterflies or pteropods. Most have a very reduced shell, often internal and fragile, or no shell at all. The gills are either behind the heart or lacking entirely, the animal carrying out respiration over its whole body surface.

The bullas or bubble shells generally have an external shell and a large shield on the head for ploughing through sand or mud. They are all carnivores.

The sea hares have a reduced shell, mostly or completely internal or lacking completely. They graze on seaweeds and can change their colour to match that of the seaweed on which they are feeding.

The exquisite pteropods or sea butterflies have their feet modified into a pair of large wing-like parapodia which they use for

Left: two nudibranch sea slugs Calma glaucoides from the Indian Ocean.
Below: this periwinkle, like the moon shell (opposite), is a mesogastropod, but it is a herbivore, rasping seaweed and lichens from the rocks. Different species of periwinkle live in well-defined zones on rocky shores – where they live is determined mainly by the degree of exposure to the air

cowries. The shell is usually spirally coiled, but is very variable in shape, some species having tall pointed shells, others squat rounded ones.

The winkles are among the most familiar snails of British rocky shores. They are found all over the world, from ice-bound rocks on the coast of Greenland to sun-baked tropical shores. One species of periwinkle may occur at a density of about 10,000 individuals per square yard. Winkles are herbivores, grazing seaweeds or lichens from the rocks.

Other mesogastropods are the cowries, many of which are renowned for their beautiful shells. These are widespread in warm and tropical seas, most species occurring in the Indo-Pacific region. Most cowries are carnivores, feeding on such animals as bivalve molluscs and sea urchins.

The Naticidae, including the moon shells and necklace shells, are carnivores that live in mud or sand, burrowing after their bivalve prey. Other mesogastropods live in the open ocean, swimming rapidly after their prey – crustaceans, jelly-fish and even small fish.

The whelks and their kin

The third order of prosobranchs, the Neo-gastropoda, is entirely marine, and entirely carnivorous. Most of them, including the familiar whelks, have a long tube called a proboscis which they evert into the bodies of other animals to suck out their contents, often digesting them first with the aid of powerful chemicals called enzymes. Many neogastropods, such as the whelks, feed on other molluscs, such as limpets and bivalves. They may force the proboscis through a chink in their prey's armour, or they may bore a hole through its shell, using

swimming. Some have transparent shells which reveal the body organs inside, others have no shells at all.

The largest order within the Opisthobranchia is the Nudibranchia or sea slug. These are among the most beautiful of all marine creatures with often brilliant coloration and flowing form. Most species live in tropical or subtropical seas, but a small number are found in cooler waters. They have no shells, and possess elaborate outgrowths from the body that may be used for respiration – they lack gills. Some species use the whole body surface for respiration. They are mostly carnivores, feeding on a wide range of marine animals, from sponges to sea anemones and corals.

Oysters, clams and mussels

Within the Phylum Mollusca, between the gastropods and the cephalopods, we find the oysters, clams, mussels and their relatives. These species make up the class Pelecypoda within the molluscs and they are commonly known as bivalve molluscs. They are called bivalves because their shells consist of two sections, or valves, which the animal is able to open in order to move or feed but which, when closed, protect the soft body of the animal from injury. They have also evolved other means of defence. Without them these slow-moving animals, lacking the weapons for active retaliation, would be extremely vulnerable to the depredations of other animals. As it is, bivalves are preyed upon extensively and form the principal diet of some marine predators.

Bivalve molluscs

There are thousands of species of bivalve, ranging from the small tellinid of the sandy shore to the giant clam, *Tridacna*, of the south Pacific. This leviathan of the group can attain a length of over four feet and weigh some five hundred pounds. Bivalves are favourite items of sea shell collectors and the conchologist has a vocabulary dealing with his seashells almost equal to the number of species. There is an infinite variety of shell size, shape, colour and surface sculpturing, and each character is important in identification. The names of some bivalves testify to their exquisite beauty, such as the wedding cake *Venus*, the jewel box, the elegant basket *Lucina* and the striped setting-sun shell.

Bivalves are found throughout the seas of the world, living on or in sandy or muddy bottoms. Some bivalves, such as the oysters, live permanently attached, with one valve of the shell

cemented to the ground. Others, like the mussels and pen shells, anchor themselves to hard objects such as rocks, other shells or wharf pilings. The anchorage is provided by tough horny threads, called byssal threads, which are secreted from a gland in the animal's foot. (This organ is characteristic of the molluscs as a group; the slimy foot on which garden snails and slugs crawl is a familiar sight to many people.) The byssal threads emerge as a sticky fluid and harden on contact with the water. They are planted one at a time until the animal is attached by a diverging mass of threads, like the guy ropes of a tent.

For hundreds of years, the 'byssus industry' flourished in Taranto, southern Italy. The long fine threads of the noble pen shell, *Pinna nobilis*, found in the Mediterranean and growing to a length of about sixteen inches, were collected and made into attractive and durable garments. However, since each bivalve produced only a single gram of byssus, it is not surprising that the industry declined rapidly with the advent of modern synthetics.

Mother-of-pearl shells

The shell of bivalves, like that of other molluscs, is secreted by the mantle, a thin membrane of tissue that surrounds the soft body of the animal. Layers of calcium carbonate are laid down to

form the shell. The inner layer is called the nacreous layer, better known as mother-of-pearl. The mantle is attached to the shell by muscle but sometimes a grain of sand can lodge between the mantle and the shell. The animal reacts to this irritant by surrounding it by layers of nacreous material. In this way pearls are formed. The finest natural pearls are formed by the pearl oysters *Pinctada*, of the warm Pacific. But all bivalves can produce pearls, including the fresh-water clams.

The two valves of the shell are attached by an elastic ligament along the hinge line. Small teeth and opposing sockets also aid in locking the valves together. One or two large muscles, called the adductor muscles, act against the hinge ligament in closing the valves. These muscles stretch between the valves and their scars can be seen on the inside of an empty shell. It is the single large adductor muscle of scallops that serves man as food.

Most bivalves burrow into soft mud or sand, living well below the surface. Two long tubes, called siphons, connect the animal to the water above, providing oxygen for respiration and tiny animals and plants as food. The laterally compressed body and shell, together with the pointed blade-like foot, endow the bivalve with unique

Opposite top: the scallop, showing the tiny 'eyes' around the edge of the mantle. The single adductor muscle, prized by man as food, is relaxed, allowing the valves to gape. By sudden contraction of this muscle, the scallop can propel itself along with water jets. Opposite left: the cockle, showing the red fleshy foot. This bivalve usually burrows into sand, drawing water containing plankton food through the siphons which extend to the surface. Opposite right: the giant clam Tridacna, of tropical seas. Millions of tiny plants (algae) live in the clam's greatly expanded mantle tissues, giving them a greenish tinge – a symbiotic association. Left: the beautiful file shell, Lima, swimming, surrounded by its long sensory tentacles. Related to the scallops, Lima builds a nest made of byssus threads on the floor of tropical seas

37

adaptations for burrowing. The foot is thrust into the sand or mud and becomes distended by a sudden rush of blood forced into it from the rest of the body. The tip of the foot swells out into a bulbous disc, and grips the sand like a mushroom anchor. Then, muscles in the foot contract and the body of the animal, with the valves closed, is pulled down into the ground. At the same time blood is forced out of the foot back into the body, increasing the downward movement.

In order to burrow deeper, the valves of the shell are opened, wedging the animal firmly in its temporary position. Once again the combination of blood pressure and muscle action in the foot pulls the animal downwards. The razor shells *Ensis* have perfected the art of burrowing. Long, narrow, smooth and either straight-edged or slightly curved, these animals can disappear from the surface of the sand with remarkable speed, as anyone who has tried to collect these shells well knows to his frustration.

Most bivalves feed by filtering plankton out of the surrounding water. In addition to respiration, the gills have assumed the role of food acquisition. Tiny hairs on the gills, called cilia, filter out the animals and plants of the plankton which are then transferred to food grooves leading to the mouth. The food particles are further sorted by the palps, two flaps of tissue near the mouth, and in the stomach, so only the very finest of material is actually digested.

Wood and rock borers

Some species of bivalve have taken up the unusual habit of boring into hard rock, wood or shell. These boring animals have undergone a number of modifications for this way of life. The shell, for example, is equipped with cutting teeth and sharp ridges which accomplish the abrasion of the hard material. Since the valves of the shell must be freely movable during boring, the elastic ligament has been reduced or is absent. The shipworm, *Teredo*, is well-known for the destruction it can cause to wooden ship bottoms and piers. The piddock, *Pholas*, and the red nose

bivalve, *Hiatella*, are other bivalves that bore into rock by abrading it with their tough shells. The date mussel, *Lithophaga*, is unusual in using chemical means to penetrate rocks. It attacks limestones and sandstones, secreting an acid which dissolves the rock.

Not all bivalves lead such a sedentary existence as the oysters, mussels and boring species. The scallops, for example, swim about in a jerky manner, flapping their valves. The jet of water expelled from the shell as the valves are slammed shut propels the animal forward. Correlated with this active life, thousands of tiny bright blue 'eyes' are arranged around the margin of the mantle. These eyes possess a retina, lens and cornea and, although they cannot form an image like our eyes can, they detect changes in light intensity, which may indicate the presence of an obstacle or a predator ahead.

The beautiful file shells of tropical seas also include some swimming types, such as *Lima*. A mass of long sensory tentacles adorn the edges of the mantle and hang from the shell like a bunch of colourful streamers. To watch *Lima* swimming is an unforgettable sight.

For hundreds of years man has made use of bivalves as food, currency and ornaments for his home and person. The window-pane oysters of the Indo-Pacific have small translucent shells which the natives of the Philippines make into windows, verandah roofs and table lamps. The quahog clam of the western American seaboard was used by the Amerindians as coinage and food, and this bivalve is now familiar to many Americans as clam chowder or clam-on-the-half-shell. Oysters have been acclaimed as the rarest of delicacies by gourmets of classic and modern civilizations. They are farmed in many parts of the world today. In Japan, for example, one acre of oysters is capable of an annual production of 46,000 pounds of protein food. Sea food, in the form of oysters, mussels and scallops, may, in the years to come, no longer be regarded as a gourmet's delight, but may become one of the main items of diet for the world's population.

Far left: a pearl being removed from the pearl oyster Pinctada *of the warm Pacific. Most of the world's cultured pearls are produced in Japan, where they are known as 'tears of the moon'. A pearl of marketable size is obtained after about four years growth. Left: a cluster of mussels. It has been estimated that an acre of mussels yields more, in terms of protein food, than an acre of beef pasture land*

Cuttlefish, squids and octopuses

The most advanced and specialized of all the molluscs are those belonging to the class Cephalopoda. The members of this group include the cuttlefish, squid and octopus. As molluscs, the cephalopods are related to animals like the snail and the oyster. However, the relationship is by no means obvious at first sight and it took biologists some time to recognize it. All molluscs have evolved from a snail-like ancestor, but the cephalopods have been transformed in the course of their evolution more radically than others. The most highly evolved of the cephalopods, and of all molluscs, is the octopus. However, close examination of the octopus, or any of the cephalopods, reveals the same basic structure, albeit much modified, as is found in all members of the Mollusca.

The curious appearance and behaviour of the cephalopods, and, in at least one case, their gigantic size, automatically arouse our interest and curiosity. Imaginative writers, such as Victor Hugo and Jules Verne, have endowed these animals with a ferocity that has since become a part of popular legend. A myth has grown up around octopuses and the giant squid, in particular, similar to that which surrounds maneating sharks. They are attributed with premeditated and unprovoked attacks on men and ships. In the case of the giant squid, at least, there may be some foundation for such a reputation in reality, although most stories seem to be the products of mere fantasy.

Powers of perception

The great development of their nervous system and their superior powers of movement place the cephalopods far above any of the other invertebrate, or backboneless, animals of the sea. Their method of swimming by jet propulsion enables them to move at a great rate and squids are

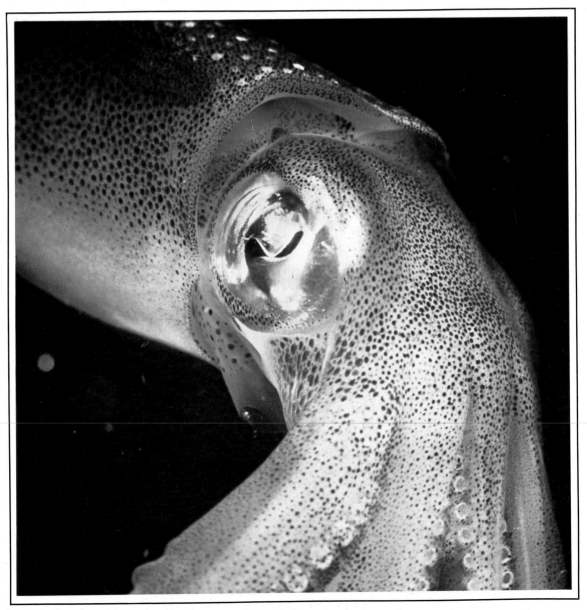

Right: like other cephalopods, this northern squid, Loligo forbesi, *has two large and highly efficient eyes, which are very similar in structure to our own eyes. It is likely that they can see colours. The squid can also find out about its surroundings by interpreting the messages from the sensory cells on its tentacles, which are sensitive to touch and to chemicals in the water*

Above right: a small cuttlefish from a coral reef in New Caledonia. Below: two cuttlefish, Sepia officinalis, *lurk among coral on the Mediterranean sea bed. These inhabitants of European coastal waters spend the day on the sea bed, often partly buried by sand; at night they rise to hunt their prey – crustaceans, small fish and sometimes even each other*

among the fastest of all marine animals over short distances.

The eyes of cephalopods have a striking similarity to those of mammals. In fact, the cephalopod eyes are theoretically more efficient than our eyes, due to the arrangement of the retina, the light-sensitive layer which lines the inside of the eye. It is possible that cephalopods have a wider field of clear vision than do humans. It is also likely that they are able to perceive colours.

The brain is well developed in cephalopods and the nervous system contains 'giant' nerve fibres that transmit nervous impulses at speeds comparable to those in some mammals. Cephalopods have remarkable powers of learning and memory; for example, they can learn to discriminate between objects of different sizes and

shapes. Their ability to change colour is well known. They are the quickest colour-change artists in the animal kingdom, even outdoing the chameleon. Colours of every hue flow over their bodies in rapid succession, allowing them to intimidate their enemies or avoid them altogether by blending in with their surroundings. And if all these colour tricks fail, they are able to deter their enemy by releasing a cloud of ink into the water and escaping in the ensuing confusion, unnoticed and unharmed. The ink was once used for writing purposes.

The cephalopods are a very ancient group of animals. They first appeared in late Cambrian times, over 550 million years ago. Two main groups flourished in the seas of the world – the nautiloids and the ammonites. Both forms had shells surrounding their soft bodies. Many nautiloids and all ammonites had coiled shells, wound round in a tight spiral. The nautiloids dwindled in number and variety during the Mesozoic era of the earth's history. The ammonites died out at the end of that era, about 70 million years ago, disappearing from the seas as inexplicably as did the dinosaurs from the land. Today, only one form of nautiloid survives – the pearly nautilus which lives in the warm seas around the East Indies. Being the sole representative of a long extinct group of animals, it is often called a 'living fossil'.

Losing a shell

The third group of cephalopods includes the octopuses, squids and cuttlefish. They evolved from a straight-shelled nautiloid ancestor. As they

did so, there was a general trend for the shell to become internal and reduced in size. *Spirula* is a cuttlefish which lives in the deep waters of tropical seas. It has a small coiled shell buried within its body at the hind end. The chambers of the shell are filled with gas, which is secreted by the animal. The amount of gas can be regulated and the whole shell acts as a buoyancy organ. Other cuttlefish, such as *Sepia* (commonly found in British waters), have a straight shell inside their bodies which acts as an internal supporting skeleton. This 'cuttlebone' is often washed up on beaches; it is also often put in the cages of pet canaries or parrots to give them a supply of lime and salts. The squids have gone a stage further. The shell is reduced to a horny strip, called the pen, which lies deeply embedded within the leathery skin. The octopuses lack a shell altogether; a few calcareous grains inside the body are all that remain to testify to the former existence of their internal skeleton which has otherwise disappeared.

The cephalopods get their name from two Greek words meaning 'head' and 'foot'. This name refers to the close association between these parts of the body. The foot is a characteristic organ of all molluscs. It is the flat muscular base of the animal upon which it moves. The foot of cephalopods has been modified into the arms, or tentacles, that extend from the head and encircle the mouth. Squids and cuttlefish have ten arms, including two extra-long tentacles which can stretch out and grasp prey. The flat sides of the arms have powerful suckers which have horny rims and are armed with sharp hooks.

Octopuses have eight arms, all of equal length, studded with suckers which, however, lack horny rims and hooks. The difference in the number of arms provides the basis for dividing these cephalopods into two groups. The cuttle-fishes and the squids are described as decapods, which means that they are ten-footed, while the various different species of octopus are octopods, meaning 'eight-footed'.

Jet propulsion

Swimming by jet propulsion is unique to the cephalopods. The body of a squid is long and torpedo-shaped; that of an octopus is bag-like. Whatever the shape, there is a spacious cavity inside the body called the mantle cavity. The walls of this cavity are muscular. When the muscles are relaxed, water flows in at the sides and fills the cavity. When the muscles contract the water is forced out of the cavity through a tubular funnel on the underside of the animal. The funnel is also muscular and very flexible. It can be moved in all directions. Depending on the position of the funnel at the time when the water is shot out of the cavity, the animal is propelled by reaction in the opposite direction. The speed of movement depends on how forcibly the water is expelled. Squids can back away from trouble at an astonishingly rapid rate. Some squirt the water out of their funnels with such force that they shoot clean out of the sea. It is such animals that give rise to accounts of 'flying squid'. By spreading the fins at the sides of their bodies, they can glide for considerable distances. There have even been reports of squids landing on the decks

Below: the common octopus of Europe, Octopus vulgaris, *is widely distributed in coastal waters as far north as the English Channel. Much more sluggish than the squids or cuttlefish, it hides in rock crevices, occasionally pouncing on its unsuspecting prey, which consists mainly of small fish and crustaceans*

Above: although it remains immobile for long periods in its rocky lair, the common octopus can move about on the seabed using the eight tentacles from which it gets its name. It can also swim rapidly by 'jet propulsion' when alarmed

of ships twelve feet above the sea's surface.

Squids live in the open sea. Generally they are small, the common squid *Loligo* being, on average, about ten inches long. As already mentioned, they are among the fastest of marine animals. The body is beautifully streamlined. Two small fins project from the sides of the body and act as stabilizers, though they can also propel the squid forward by their slow undulations. Squids feed mainly on fish and crustaceans. Darting backwards into a school of fish, a squid will grasp one of the fish with its long tentacles. Then, holding its chosen victim with its other arms, it bites into its neck, severing the nerve cord. A poison may be injected into the wound from glands in the squid's mouth. Squids, like all other cephalopods, have two powerful horny jaws, which look rather like the beak of a parrot. The unwary fisherman handling a live squid caught in a trawl may receive a nasty bite from these jaws.

Titans of the ocean

It is among the squids that we find the largest invertebrate animals. The mythical 'kraken' of Norwegian legend probably refers to the giant squids of the genus *Architeuthis*. These formidable creatures can grow to lengths of over sixty feet, including the tentacles. They inhabit the depths of the ocean, living between 900 and 18,000 feet. One fifty-five-foot-long *Architeuthis* which was found off Newfoundland in 1878 had a body with a girth of about four feet and an estimated weight of some three tons. The sperm whale seems to be the only animal brave enough to tackle these monsters. Evidently, fierce battles occur between these titans of the ocean, because the head and jaws of dead sperm whales frequently bear large round scars, left by the horny suckers of giant squids. A squid's eye

measuring fifteen inches in diameter was found inside the stomach of a sperm whale.

Cuttlefish have a squat, rounded body. They are not open-sea dwellers like the squids nor are they such rapid swimmers. They live in relatively shallow waters, resting on the seabed during the day. They usually settle on sandy seabeds and, like flatfish, cover themselves with sand, camouflaging their upper surfaces so that they can rest in peace. They become active at night when they hunt for fish and crustaceans. The cuttlebone inside their bodies is filled with gas: the amount of gas that is secreted determines the animal's level of buoyancy. In turn, the intensity of light is a prime factor in regulating the secretion of gas. When the light decreases as night falls, gas is released, making the shell lighter so that the animal can rise off the seabed.

When searching for prawns or shrimps, the cuttlefish uses an ingenious approach. It moves slowly along, blowing soft jets of water into the sand where the shrimps hide. If a shrimp is disturbed, it makes desperate efforts to bury itself again. The cuttlefish sees the movement and seizes it in a flash with its long tentacles.

Octopuses are more sedentary in their habits than squids or cuttlefish. They have forsaken the active swimming life and taken to crawling and lurking among the rocks of the seabed in shallow coastal waters. They can swim by jet propulsion, trailing their eight arms behind them. Certain deep-sea octopuses have abandoned this method. Instead, their arms are united by a web of skin which stretches almost to the tips, forming an umbrella or parachute. These octopuses swim like jellyfish, allowing their arms to pulsate slowly.

Tales of giant octopuses are pure fiction. One of the largest species lives off the Pacific coast of North America. The length of its body rarely exceeds one foot, although the arms may be sixteen feet long. Generally, octopuses are shy animals, hiding within their dark lairs to lie in wait for passing fish and crustaceans, especially lobsters and crabs. Bivalve shellfish are also a favourite food. Using the adhesive suckers on its arms, the octopus wrenches the shells of a clam apart by brute force. Sometimes octopuses can become a major pest on oyster or mussel beds.

To escape from a predator (such as a moray eel) the octopus, like the squid and cuttlefish, throws out an inky fluid through the funnel. The ink was formerly thought to act simply as a smokescreen but it is now believed that it also dulls the sense of smell of the predator. Several minutes may elapse before the anaesthetic effect of the ink wears off, by which time the octopus is far away.

Courtship and mating

Reproduction is an elaborate affair in cephalopods. Hundreds of squids and cuttlefish congregate at certain times of the year to mate and spawn their eggs, after which both sexes die. At the time of mating, the males assume their nuptial colours – striking patterns of white and purple stripes ripple over the surface of their bodies. This colour display is not to attract females but to intimidate other males. Copulation occurs while the animals are swimming, the male grasping the female head-on. The sperm are wrapped in a gelatinous coat before being deposited in the female's mantle cavity. The cephalopod transfers the sperm by using one of its long arms which is modified specially for this purpose. In octopuses, for example, the tip of this arm is spoon-shaped and the sperm are carried in the hollow. Sometimes, the whole arm may be wrenched from the male and left inside the female. Biologists used to think that the arm was a large parasitic worm, found only in females, until it was correctly identified.

The next stage in reproduction is when the female releases the eggs from her ovaries, whereupon they are fertilized by the sperm in the mantle cavity. The eggs, surrounded by their thick coats of jelly, are laid in long strings which are attached to weeds and rocks on the seabed. A tiny replica of the adult emerges from each egg. It spends a few weeks drifting with the plankton in the surface waters. Soon it becomes independent of the ocean currents and assumes the adult life style.

Below: an octopus's eight arms are well supplied with suction discs. The animal uses these to pull itself along, to anchor itself to the rocks and to seize its prey; this it kills and eats with its horny 'beak' after injecting poison into the wound from modified salivary glands

Barnacles

The barnacles are other animals which posed problems of classification for the zoologist. They are in fact crustaceans, like prawns and lobsters, and as such they are part of the Phylum Arthropoda. However, the barnacle's sedentary way of life, its way of cementing itself onto rocks and the piles of wharves and piers, and the tough calcareous shell which encloses the body, all suggest affinities with animals like the limpet. Consequently, until the early nineteenth century biologists considered that barnacles were molluscs.

It was in 1830 that an English biologist, Vaughan Thompson, discovered the free-swimming 'nauplius' larvae of the barnacle, which is a form typical of arthropods of the class Crustacea. In this way biologists discovered their mistake. On close examination it can be seen that barnacles do not bear more than a superficial resemblance to the snail-like molluscs. The Swiss biologist, Louis Agassiz described them in the following terms: 'nothing more than a little shrimp-like animal, standing on its head in a limestone house and kicking food into its mouth'.

As well as other crustaceans, the arthropods include insects. This group, which incorporates the majority of animal species found in the world, is scarcely represented at all in the life of the ocean.

Within the class Crustacea barnacles are placed in the subclass Cirripedia. The name is a reference to the barnacle's curly feet. The limbs of the barnacle are curled up inside the animal's shell when it is closed and cannot be seen when the barnacle is out of the water. However, when the tide returns and the shell is opened, the limbs are unfurled into the water and they serve the barnacle as a means of catching its food.

There are three main families of barnacles – the common acorn barnacles, the stalked goose barnacles and the parasitic barnacles. The acorn and goose barnacles are found throughout the world attached to any solid surface, be it wood, metal or rock. Their habit of attaching themselves to buoys, piers and the hulls of ships renders them among the most serious of fouling organisms. Special anti-fouling paints can be used to deter the larvae from settling, but many boat owners know the frustrations of careening their vessels and spending many long hours scraping the resident barnacles from the bottom.

The acorn barnacles, clustered in their thousands on the rocks of the seashore, are familiar to most people. Glands in the base of the animal secrete a cement which attaches the young barnacle to the rock when it first settles after its free-swimming youth. The shell, consisting of several overlapping plates connected to each other by living tissue or rows of interlocking teeth, is secreted by the mantle – a feature found in other animals.

The goose barnacles are so called because in

Far left: goose barnacles feeding underwater. Large colonies attach themselves to all kinds of floating objects by their long flexible stalks.
Centre: acorn barnacles cemented to a scallop shell. The cement obtained from these animals may be used to stick false teeth in position.
Left: with forked legs forming a drift net, the acorn barnacle strains tiny planktonic organisms out of the water. During feeding, the legs open and close about 140 times a minute.
Below left: the most common species of barnacle, Balanus balanoides, *crowded on the shore at low tide. The upper plates of the shell are tightly closed to prevent the animal drying out. The free-swimming larvae of barnacles usually settle in areas where other barnacles live, attracted by a chemical substance secreted by the adults*

the Middle Ages it was a popular belief that birds miraculously emerged from them. Adult geese were thought to lay their eggs at sea on pieces of driftwood. The long stalk of the barnacle was likened to the neck of a young goose and the shell to the beak. After a while, the creature supposedly changed into a goose. These barnacles usually attach themselves to floating objects such as ships or flotsam, and form large colonies, hundreds of them hanging one from the other.

Barnacles feed by opening the upper plates of the shell and extending the six pairs of biramous legs, or 'cirri', which are modified as feeding appendages. The waving movement of the cirri creates a current and small planktonic organisms are swept towards the basket-like net which the cirri form. Tiny hairs arranged along the length of each cirrus sort out the food particles which are then passed to the mouth. The action of the cirri is analogous to the opening and closing of the fists when placed together at the wrists.

Barnacles are hermaphrodite. Each animal contains both male and female sex organs. However, self-fertilization is not the rule. The penis is protruded out of the body into the mantle cavity of another individual alongside and sperm is deposited to fertilize the eggs. These are incubated inside the body for about four months, at which time nauplius larvae hatch out and swim away. After six months, they change into cyprid larvae, which look like tiny mussels. This is the settling stage. Having found a suitable surface, the larvae settle on their heads, secreting a cement from the first antennae. The swimming legs turn into feeding cirri and the limestone shell develops within a matter of days. Barnacles always settle in the vicinity of other barnacles, or where others have lived before. Research has shown that a protein called 'arthropodin' is secreted by barnacles and this substance attracts others to the site.

There are numerous species of parasitic barnacle either living on or in other animals. Associations are formed with all sorts of marine creatures, from crabs to whales. Many of these barnacles have undergone degeneration, losing their legs, shell and alimentary canal.

Prawns and shrimps

Shrimps and prawns are crustaceans, closely related to crabs and lobsters. All these commercially important shellfish belong to the crustacean group called the decapoda, which means ten-footed. This name refers to the five pairs of walking legs attached to the thorax, or trunk, of the body. The first pair of walking legs in a crab or lobster are large and armed with heavy pincer-like jaws. These are the claws, a distinctive characteristic of these shellfish. Prawns and shrimps do not have such well-developed claws. However, in common with crabs and lobsters they have a soft and delicately flavoured flesh which provides the basis for numerous well known and highly esteemed food dishes in many parts of the world.

Unfortunately, the popular names 'prawn' and 'shrimp' are applied indiscriminately; often the names are interchangeable and, in some cases, clear misnomers. Thus 'pink shrimps' are, in fact, little prawns whose bodies are transparent until boiled in water. The so-called Dublin Bay prawn, the source of scampi, is really a species of marine crayfish, sometimes called the Norway lobster. There are many other kinds of crustacean in the sea that look like shrimps and are given this name. In America the term 'shrimp' is widely used to describe animals of both kinds.

To many people, prawns and shrimps look very much alike. There are a few structural details that distinguish them. However the real difference lies in their habitats. Prawns are active swimmers and during the summer months they are commonly found in pools on the seashore, hidden amongst the weeds or rocks. In winter they move offshore to warmer, deeper waters, returning to the shore in the spring to breed. Shrimps, on the other hand, are not as good swimmers as prawns and tend to stay close to the seabed, burrowing into the sand or mud during the day and coming out to feed at night. Shrimps are much hardier than prawns and can tolerate great extremes of temperature and wide fluctuations in the salt content of the water. Several species of shrimp live readily in the brackish waters of estuaries, burying themselves beneath the soft muddy river bed.

Segmented structure

Shrimps do not grow to a great size. The common shrimp, *Crangon vulgaris*, found all around the British coast, is about three inches long. However some prawns are quite large, especially tropical species. The banana prawns of north-western Australia can attain lengths of about eleven inches, although they usually average seven inches. A Pacific prawn, named *Penaeus monodon*, grows to thirteen inches.

The body of a prawn, like those of its decapod relatives, is made up of nineteen segments – five in the head, eight in the thorax and six in the abdomen. The head and thorax are fused together and covered by a tough carapace or shell. This projects out from the front of the head as a rostrum, often armed with sharp spines. A distinguishing feature of many shrimps is the absence of a rostrum. The eyes of prawns and shrimps, which are compound like those of insects, are carried at the tips of stalks. The carapace must be shed periodically to allow the animal to grow. During the summer months

Far left: a mantis shrimp. These colourful crustaceans live in burrows in shallow tropical seas and may attain a foot in length. Left: Gnathophyllum, a shrimp found in the Mediterranean. Below: Periclimenes. This delicately coloured shrimp enjoys a special relationship with sea anemones, such as that on which it is resting, which would kill other species of shrimp

Above left and right: these beautifully coloured shrimps come from the Straits of Messina between Italy and Sicily. Clearly visible are the long, slender antennae; these are the shrimps' sense organs. At the rear of the animals are the paired limbs called swimmerets, which propel the shrimps through the water, and also bear the eggs in the female

prawns moult, or shed their shells, once every two or three weeks. Sometimes, in rock pools on the shore, you may see the ghostly skeletons of prawns with a soft prawn nearby, waiting in some hideout for its new shell to harden, in a day or two. Until then, the animal is very vulnerable, with no protection from enemies.

Attached to the segments of a prawn's body are nineteen pairs of appendages. Those of the head consist of two pairs of sensory antennae and various mouth parts, including jaws. The eight appendages of the thorax are divided in function. The first three pairs are accessory jaws. The other five pairs are the walking legs, typical of all decapods. The first two pairs of walking legs bear pincer-like claws which aid in catching food. In the shrimp, only the first pair of these legs has claws, but they are often more sturdy than those of a prawn. The snapping or pistol shrimp, *Alpheus*, has one claw much larger than the other. This claw is used mainly for defence. It is rather like the hammer of a gun, having a moveable finger that can be cocked when the claw is open. The finger is released with such speed and force that it slams home with a loud pop, like the retort of a gun, hence the shrimp's common name. *Alpheus* has been seen to stun small animals swimming past with its pistol claw.

The pistol shrimp spends most of its time hiding in the burrow that it makes in the sand, using its pistol claw to catch its prey – including relatively large fish, up to six inches long – and to frighten off its enemies. The sound of the snapping claw carries a long way; once a pistol shrimp placed in a glass jar shattered the glass with the shock wave that was produced when it fired its pistol.

The abdomen of the prawn bears six pairs of feathery limbs called pleopods or swimmerets. They beat in series and move the animal gently through the water. The sixth pair of abdominal

limbs make up the broad swimmerets of the tail fan. If attacked, the prawn can take immediate action. The tail fan is opened wide and the whole abdomen is flicked under the body with such rapidity that the prawn shoots backwards, its long antennae and legs streaming out in front of its body. Lobsters employ similar escape tactics. Sometimes the prawn flexes its abdomen with such force that it leaps clean out of the water.

Into the jaws of death

Prawns and shrimps are predators, eating all kinds of small animals such as baby fish, other crustaceans and the eggs of oysters and clams. They are also scavengers, picking up any scraps discarded by more discerning predators. Many shrimps that burrow into sand leave their antennae sticking up above the surface. Any small animal that brushes past is immediately sensed and the shrimp leaps out of the sand and grasps it with its pincers. Some species of swimming shrimp, such as *Sergestes*, have very long antennae, often four or five times the length of the body. Hook-like hairs on the antennae entangle the prey which is then hauled in by long whip-like appendages.

Certain species of shrimp have interesting associations with other animals. *Alpheus* fashions long tubes for itself from a filamentous seaweed. It lies on its back and pulls the weed around it like a cloak. Then it sews up the edges of the tube, using one of its slender pointed legs as a needle and the weed's filaments as thread. Other shrimps live in the spacious body cavity of sponges. The continuous flow of water through the sponge provides the shrimps with planktonic food. The beautiful glass sponge known as the Venus flower basket is often found with a male and a female shrimp imprisoned inside it. The shrimps enter the sponge when they are young. As they grow larger they cannot escape and spend the rest of their lives trapped in a glass prison. This sponge used to be presented as a wedding gift in Japan to symbolize the concept of 'till death us do part'.

The boxer shrimp and Pederson's shrimps of tropical seas are known as the cleaner shrimps. They perform the invaluable service of removing parasites from fish. These cleaner shrimps are usually brightly coloured and advertise themselves at particular spots on the seabed. A fish in need of attention swims up to one of these cleaners and hovers gently in the water while the shrimp works over the surface of its skin. The cleaner can even enter the mouth of the fish unharmed, to pick off little parasites clinging to the gills. The fish will tolerate the shrimp making small incisions into its flesh to remove well-rooted parasites.

Coastal chameleons

Shrimps and prawns are well known for their ability to change colour. This is a protective device which allows the animals to blend with their surroundings and remain unnoticed by predators. The chameleon prawn, *Hippolyte varians*, is common in rock pools around the coast but it is difficult to find because, when resting during the day, it takes on the colour of the weeds to which it clings. If a green prawn is placed on red weed, it will have changed its colour within a few days. Irrespective of their surroundings, all prawns and shrimps change to a translucent blue colour at night.

The ability to change colour is due to small colour cells, called chromatophores, scattered throughout the skin of these crustaceans. Each chromatophore contains granules of red, yellow, blue and white pigment. By contracting or expanding the colour cell, all other colours can be produced from these four pigments. The whole system is controlled by chemicals called hormones which circulate in the blood. The hormones are released from glands at the base of the eye stalks. The stimulus to change colour is received by the eyes, which then activate the glands to release the appropriate hormones.

Below: the common prawn Leander serratus *is widely distributed in rock pools on the lower shores of temperate waters. Like many other crustaceans, prawns are mainly scavengers, feeding on small pieces of dead flesh*

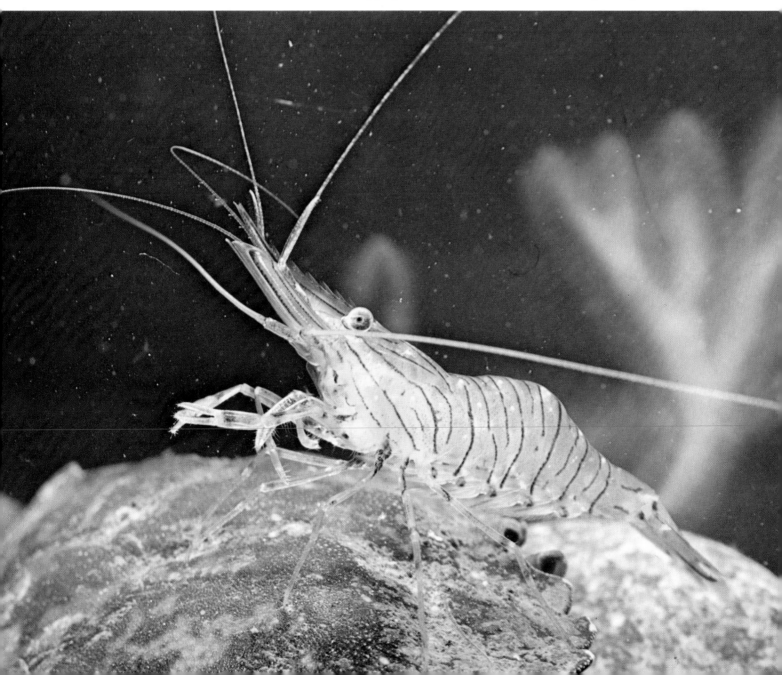

Above: this gaily-coloured prawn, Stenopus hispidus, *comes from a coral reef in Florida*

Deep-sea prawns

Like some of the prawns found in tropical waters, many deep-sea prawns are large – some almost a foot long. Like many other animals of these regions, most of them are a rich scarlet or orange in colour; for a deep-sea animal, there is a distinct advantage in having colours at this end of the spectrum. In the deep waters in which these prawns live, only violet, blue and green light can penetrate. The colour of any object is determined by the colour of the light that is reflected from its surface. So a deep-sea prawn, though it appears brilliant scarlet when fished out of a net at the surface, will appear black in its natural environment, because there is no red light at these depths to be reflected by the animal. The advantage to the prawn is clear; its black appearance against the gloom of its surroundings makes it virtually invisible to unwary prey and hungry predators alike.

Some deep-sea prawns bear light organs, which give out a greenish-yellow light. One species known to scientists as *Sergestes prehensilis*, bears about 150 light organs along its sides, rather like the lighted portholes of a ship. The prawn can flash these lights on and off; it has been seen to switch them all on and then all off, and also to switch them on and off one by one in sequence, from head to tail, remarkably like a neon sign.

Carrying on the line

Reproduction generally takes place in the spring. In the male the first two pairs of swim-merets are modified into finger-like appendages which aid in the transfer of packets of sperm to the female's body. When the eggs are laid, they may be liberated directly into the water, or they may be brooded underneath the female's abdomen, cemented to her swimmerets and secured by long hairs which she bears only during the breeding season.

In those shrimps and prawns with the most complex life history, each egg hatches into a tiny larva called a nauplius, with three pairs of limbs. This, and the following larval stages, live in the surface waters as members of the multitude of drifting plants and animals making up the plankton. The nauplius can swim feebly by moving its antennae. Soon it develops trunk segments, at which stage it is called a meta-nauplius larva. This soon changes into a proto-zoea, with seven pairs of limbs. The protozoea still swims using its antennae. The next stage is the zoea, which develops movable eyes and swims using its thoracic limbs. These thoracic limbs soon become bifurcated, and the abdomen increases in size, producing the mysid stage. Finally, the abdomen develops swimming paddles called pleopods and the animal grows to its adult form.

At each of these stages, the creature must shed its shell and grow a new one, as it still must do to increase its size when adult.

These larval stages often bear little or no resemblance to the adults, so that many of them were classified as different animals before their true relationships were discovered.

There are variations on this plan; for example, the two nauplius stages may be 'missed out', when the eggs hatch directly into protozoeas or zoeas.

Shrimps are farmed on a large scale in Japan and in the United States. They are reared from the egg stage in indoor tanks and when they reach a certain size, they are housed in outdoor pools. *Penaeus japonicus*, bred in Japan, is ready for market in six to ten months, by which time it is a full ten inches long.

Shrimp fishing on a commercial scale is done in many parts of the world. Bottom trawls are towed along sandy seabeds and large numbers of shrimps, together with many other bottom dwellers (called 'trash' by the shrimpers), are caught. Sometimes a small electric current is passed through the net, making the shrimps leap out of the sand. 'Fixed engines' are used on sand and mud flats, from the Severn Estuary to Singapore. The engines consist of large conical nets or baskets which strain shrimps out of the water as the tide ebbs. Often there are so many of these engines in one place that they form a solid wall of netting, allowing few animals to escape their meshes. Beach shrimping is a more leisurely pastime. Like a miniature trawl, the shrimp net, with its wooden cross bar, is pushed through the top few inches of sand, and, hopefully, at the end of the day, the keen shrimper will be rewarded with a fine catch of little shrimps.

Lobsters, crayfish and crabs

Lobsters, crayfish and crabs are crustaceans belonging to the same order, Decapoda, as the prawns and shrimps which are their near relatives. As mentioned before, crustaceans are members of the Phylum Arthropoda and these decapod, or ten-footed, crustaceans should not be confused with decapod molluscs, like the squid and the cuttlefish, which belong to quite a different group, the Phylum Mollusca. In appearance it would be difficult to confuse them since the bodies of these crustaceans more closely resemble those of giant insects, to which they are in fact related.

Many crustaceans, including lobsters, crabs and crayfish, are a valuable source of food. With bivalve molluscs, like the oyster and the scallop, crustaceans are commonly described as shellfish and command high prices in the fish markets. However, they may become less of a luxury when the possibilities of shellfish farming have been more fully exploited. At present lobsters and their relatives are fished commercially and by amateurs, to such an extent in some areas that the more sought-after species have become exceedingly rare where they used to be abundant.

Crabs, lobsters and crayfish are typically scavangers. For this reason they often rob baited fishing lines and are regarded as a pest by commercial fishermen as well as a valuable catch.

Crabs grow to an enormous size. The distinction of being not only the largest crab, but also the largest living arthropod, belongs to the giant spider crab, *Macrocheira kaempferi*, from Japanese waters. When fully extended the outstretched claws of this scarlet crab may be a full twelve feet apart and the shell may attain a width of eighteen inches. Another giant among crabs, the Tasmanian crab, *Pseudocarcinus gigas*, may weigh as much as thirty pounds and has a pair of seventeen-inch long pincered legs.

Lobsters, too, can reach a good size. An American lobster, *Homarus americanus*, recently weighed in at forty-four and a half pounds and measured three and a half feet.

Segmented bodies

Crabs and lobsters have bodies made up of rings or segments. The body is basically divided into three parts: the head, thorax and abdomen. There is a total of nineteen segments in the body – five making up the head, eight the thorax, and six the abdomen. This possession of nineteen segments is the one feature uniting all decapod crustaceans and distinguishing them from other crustaceans. At a glance the division of the body into segments is not apparent. When seen from above the body of a crab is covered by a single continuous shell, while in a lobster or crayfish only the six segments of the abdomen are visible. This is because the head and thorax of these animals,

Below: a crab in the process of regenerating a claw which has been removed, perhaps during an attack by a predator or during battle with another crab. The ability to regenerate lost limbs is a feature of animals in this group

like those of other decapod crustaceans, are covered by the carapace. However, if they are turned upsidedown the segmentation of the whole body becomes visible.

Each body segment of a crab or lobster bears a pair of appendages, so there are thirty-eight appendages in all. They perform a variety of functions between them, including walking, swimming, respiration, catching and tearing up food, burrowing and producing sounds. In males, some of the limbs are adapted for copulation, and in females, the abdominal appendages form a protective brood pouch in which the eggs can develop until they are ready to hatch.

Some appendages have become strikingly modified. The first pair of walking legs in crabs and lobsters is large and has a moveable, pincer-like claw at its tip. These modified limbs are called chelipeds. They are used for defence and in catching prey, and may be extremely powerful, as many an uninitiated or unwary crab-hunter well knows. The claws of some large crabs and lobsters are capable of badly injuring or even amputating a man's finger. Even those of smaller crabs are surprisingly strong.

The gills are housed within chambers on either side of the body, between the body and the carapace. At the front of each chamber, a modified limb part beats back and forth, causing water to flow through the gill chamber. The dissolved oxygen is extracted by the gills. As the water flows out, it removes waste products from the excretory organs situated behind the gills.

Shedding a limb

The casting off of a limb and its subsequent replacement are common phenomena among crabs and lobsters. It is a very effective, albeit dramatic, way to escape from predators. The break occurs along a predetermined line, usually at the base of the second segment of the limb. When the animal is about to shed a limb, it contracts a set of muscles spasmodically. A membrane of tissue in the joint seals the fracture and a blood clot forms rapidly. A small bud of tissue appears at the next moult and several moults later the limb has been regenerated. It is indistinguishable from the original one. Some crabs are able to cast off all five pairs of limbs; others can only rid themselves of the first three pairs, while lobsters are able to break off only the first pair.

This ability to regenerate limbs was exploited by Spanish fishermen who would catch crabs, tear off their claws (the only marketable portion), and throw the unfortunate crabs back into the sea. In time, the crabs' claws would grow again and the animals would be subjected once more to the same treatment.

Like man, some crabs wrest off the claws of other crabs for food. The tropical robber, or coconut, crab, *Birgus latro*, which lives on land, does just this to another land crab, *Cardiosoma*. The latter is chased to its burrow by *Birgus* and once inside sticks out its large cheliped in a gesture of defence. Seemingly, this is just the reaction *Birgus* is waiting for, because it attacks and wrenches off the claw of its relative and rushes off with its tasty prize.

New shells for old

The head and thorax of lobsters and crabs are fused together and covered by the hard carapace which is made of a horny substance called chitin. The chitin at the joints is thin and soft and allows the body to bend. This tough suit of armour has the obvious advantage of protection, but also has one major disadvantage. It is incapable of expansion, and so the animal cannot increase in size within the same shell. Instead, it must shed its shell periodically throughout its life and replace it with new larger ones. This process of shedding a shell is called moulting.

The period of moulting is a very dangerous time for the animal; most crabs and lobsters hide away until their new carapaces have hardened. For some time before the actual moult, food is stored in the cells of the body in preparation for growth. A lot of water is also absorbed. This provides the necessary internal pressure for the shell to split along a line between the thorax and abdomen, in the 'waist-line' area. Enzymes dissolve away the inner layers of chitin, facilitating the split, and the animal simply slips out of its old shell. Crabs withdraw backwards, abdomen first; lobsters emerge head first. The new shell is already formed on emergence, but it is soft and pliable. Crabs are often caught at this stage for the table delicacy known as soft-shelled crab.

In this pliable condition, the animal stretches and rapidly increases in size. But its freedom is short-lived, for soon (forty-eight hours in the case of the edible blue crab) the new shell hardens to form the characteristic inflexible coat. Crabs and lobsters eat their discarded shells immediately after the moult. This seems to be Nature's way of providing the lime salts that are essential for the rapid hardening of the new shell.

Long and short tails

In the decapods, there is a general trend towards reduction of the abdomen and its appendages. The two major groups – the long-tailed lobsters and crayfish, and the short-tailed crabs – illustrate this trend. A third group, represented by the hermit crabs and their relatives (such as the porcelain and land crabs and the squat lobsters) show the transition between the functional abdomen of the lobsters and the non-functional one of the typical crabs.

The well-developed abdomen of a lobster is covered with hard chitin, and tipped by a powerful fan-like tail. Lobsters can swim rapidly by stretching the abdomen behind the body and then flexing it inwards, resulting in a fast backward movement. The force of these flexures is so great that it can even drive the lobster out of the water and into the air.

The much reduced abdomen of true crabs is

Right: the common lobster is found on the Atlantic coasts in shallow rocky waters. It is armed with formidable claws and is caught in baited pots or creels. When alive the lobster is blue; the familiar red colour appears only as a result of cooking

carried tucked well beneath the thorax. It is an extremely vulnerable part of the body. Rapping the abdomen sharply is one sure way of discouraging a crab that has got hold of you with one of its pincers from holding on any longer.

Crabs generally do not swim, but spend their time crawling over the seabed or the seashore, picking up pieces of food and debris. The swimming crabs, however, such as the blue crab *Callinectes* and the velvet crab *Portunus*, are the most agile and powerful swimmers of all the crustaceans. The abdomen of these crabs is reduced and tucked away, like that of other crabs, but the swimming crabs have found another way of getting about – the fifth pair of thoracic legs have become modified into large, flattened paddles. These describe a figure-of-eight in the water, propelling the crab along at considerable speed; some species even chase and catch fish for food.

Hermits and sponge bearers

The hermit crabs and their relatives show different stages in the reduction of the abdomen and towards a crawling way of life. The squat lobster, *Galathea*, is the least modified. It looks rather like a small lobster. Like that of a crab its abdomen, though well developed, is normally tucked under the body, but if the animal is startled it flicks its abdomen backwards and swims away. In the tiny porcelain crabs, whose shells measure only a few millimetres across, the reduction is carried a stage further. As in the true crabs, the abdomen is tucked beneath the thorax, but the tail fan is retained in these tiny crabs, betraying their affinities with the lobsters.

Hermit crabs are fascinating animals. Their bodies are wonderfully adapted for their strange way of life. They live in the discarded shells of marine snails, such as those of whelks and periwinkles. The crab's soft, unprotected abdomen is twisted so that it fits neatly into the empty mollusc shell. The last pair of abdominal appendages are modified for anchoring the body by hooking themselves on the central pillar of the mollusc shell. Only the first two pairs of thoracic legs are used for walking. The other pairs are used to grip the sides of the shell and brace the crab inside. The crab blocks the opening to the shell with its chelipeds when danger threatens.

Hermit crabs often strike up friendly relationships with other animals. Many hermit crabs allow sea anemones to grow on their snail shells. Some anemones are found on hermit crab shells and nowhere else. The crab may pick up an anemone and place it on its shell. There may be several anemones on a single shell. The anemone protects both itself and the crab with its battery of poisonous stinging cells, which are scattered on its tentacles. The crab is immune to the anemone's poison, which may be fatal to other hermit crabs. There are benefits for the anemone too; not only does the crab gain protection, but the anemone, which could not otherwise move, is carried to new feeding grounds. When the hermit feeds the anemone sweeps the ground before it with its tentacles picking up morsels of food dropped by the crab. The crab, in its turn, may pick up food dropped by its living crown. In some cases, the anemone grows so that it keeps pace with the crab's growth. Then the crab does not need to find a new home.

A small marine worm often lives inside the hermit crab's shell. It probably cleans the shell, receiving in return a good supply of food and a safe home from the crab.

The Mediterranean sponge-bearing crab *Dromia* has the habit of cutting off a piece of sponge and placing it carefully on top of its shell, like a beret. The sponge continues to grow and eventually fits tightly over the crab, totally concealing it.

Lobsters

The common European lobster is found all around the Atlantic coasts, in shallow waters. Like crabs, it is caught in baited pots, or creels. The best bait is fish that is not quite fresh. Crabs and lobsters can be kept in their pots for weeks until they are wanted for market. Their large claws are usually tied up since they are extremely pugnacious and will attack their own kind when confined.

The Norway lobster or 'Dublin Bay prawn', which grows to a length of about eight inches, is the source of scampi. Both this and the common lobster are found in coastal waters from Norway to the Mediterranean.

The rock lobster is also known as the marine crawfish, spiny lobster or langouste. It does not have the large chelipeds of other lobsters, and its shell is very spiny. This lobster lives in deeper water than does the common lobster. It has a more southerly range than the other two species. It is used by man for food mainly in the Mediterranean region. It has a curious larval stage called the glass shrimp or phyllosoma larva. For a long time this was thought to be a completely separate animal, so different is it from the adult stage of the spiny lobster.

The eggs of most crabs and lobsters hatch into 'zoea' larvæ, each with a long spine projecting from the top of its head. After several moults, this changes into a 'megalops' larva, which looks like a tiny lobster with enormous eyes. Crabs usually migrate to deeper offshore waters in winter. Here the eggs are fertilised by the male sperm. This may occur shortly after mating, but in some crabs the mating takes place many months before and the sperm is stored in special receptacles which are sealed and plugged with the seminal fluid.

In most decapods the eggs are laid just after having been fertilized, and become attached to a specialized pair of limbs on the female abdomen, which lie within the shelter of the brood pouch. The eggs are attached with a sort of natural cement. In summer, the adults migrate to shallow, inshore waters. There, the larvæ hatch from the eggs and soon grow into adults.

Top far left: the edible crab which is found on the Atlantic and Mediterranean coasts. In the British Isles it is the only crab that is regularly fished commercially. Top left: a land crab on the east coast of Africa. Land crabs are found only in the tropics. They usually live in burrows, and are often nocturnal. They visit the water only to breed. In some, the chambers housing the gills have become modified to form lungs. Middle far left: the Norway lobster or 'Dublin Bay prawn', which is the source of scampi, is found in coastal waters from Norway to the Mediterranean. Middle left: the Mediterranean sponge-bearing crab. Dromia. It cuts out its protective cap of sponge with its claws and places it on its back. Below left: a crab on the Red Sea coast. Below: the crab, Eriphia spinofrons

Starfish and sea urchins

The animals of the Phylum Echinodermata are commonly known as echinoderms. In temperate waters the group is chiefly represented by the starfishes, sea urchins and brittle stars, while the feather stars and sea cucumbers are most commonly found in tropical seas. The majority of these creatures are strikingly symmetrical in form and many of them are beautifully coloured.

There are more than 5,000 different species of echinoderm now living and the group has left an impressive record in the form of fossil remains, dating back to the Cambrian period, 500 million years ago. Surprising though it may seem, zoologists believe that some of these animals may have been among the remote ancestors of vertebrates and of man himself. At any rate they represent an important stage in the history of evolution.

The name 'echinoderm' means 'spiny-skinned animal' and it was first used by a naturalist of the eighteenth century called J. T. Klein. He used it to describe the dried shells of sea urchins which are covered with hard spines. Not surprisingly we find that a similar name was applied to the hedgehog in earlier times. Klein's term was eventually extended to include all members of the phylum to which the sea urchins belong, since most of their relatives are in fact spiny-skinned. The main exceptions are the sea cucumbers which sometimes have spiny skins, but only rarely.

Stars of the sea

The echinoderm group have been highly successful in the exploitation of different marine habitats and various ways of life.

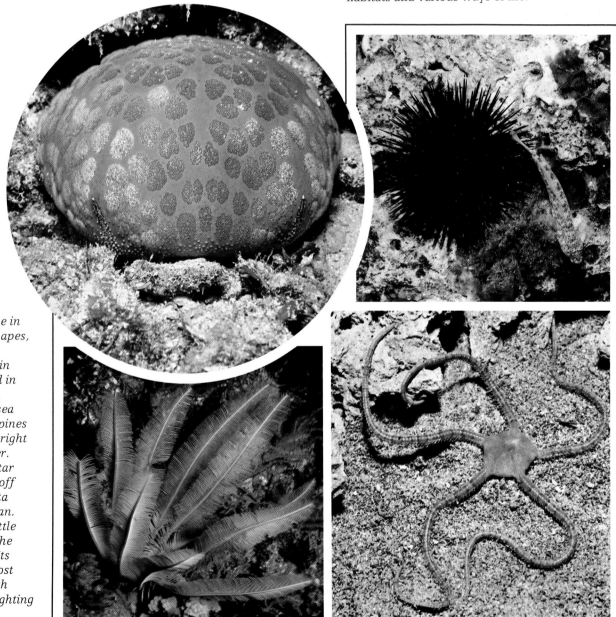

Echinoderms come in many different shapes, colours and sizes. Above: a sea urchin from Palau Island in the Pacific Ocean. Above right: this sea urchin has solid spines with which it can right itself if tipped over. Right: a feather star from a coral reef off the island of Lealta in the Pacific Ocean. Far right: this brittle star comes from the Sardinian coast. Its arms may be almost six inches in length Left: a starfish, righting itself after being turned on its back.

Although restricted to salt water, they are found in all oceans and at all depths. About 1,600 species of starfish are known to science. The common starfish, *Asterias*, which may be red, purple or orange, can be found on rocky shores of the Atlantic Ocean, in pools or clinging to the rocks at low tide. They are also often washed up onto the shore after storms or unusually high tides. Most starfish are, like *Asterias*, about four to eight inches in diameter, but the twenty-armed sun-star *Pycnopodia,* found in Californian waters, may be almost three feet across and weigh some eleven pounds.

There are about 800 species in the Class Echinoidea, containing the sea urchins, sand dollars and heart urchins. The empty test, or shell, of the sea urchin *Echinus* is commonly found washed up on the beaches of British coasts. The spiny skin which gave all echinoderms their name is most apparent in the sea urchins. The long, movable spines radiate from the globular body, ensuring protection on all sides. Some tropical reef urchins, such as the so-called hatpin *Diadema* have spines one foot long. Anything unfortunate enough to make contact with these spines is injected with a poisonous irritant, but, strangely enough, these same spines offer a safe shelter for three species of fish that retreat among them for protection. Other urchins, called the pencil slate urchins, have heavy blunt spines which, together with the powerful jaws, can drill holes into rocks, even into granite.

The brittle stars (about 2,000 known species) and the sea cucumbers (about 900 species) are animals of deeper waters, although some are found in the shallow coastal zone. Both are found in great numbers at depths of 18,000 feet, while in the deepest ocean trenches, the sea cucumbers may comprise as much as ninety per cent of the fauna.

The area of the world with the richest echinoderm fauna is the whole Indo-Pacific region, especially the area of sea around the Philippines, Borneo and New Guinea, and the West Indies. This is true for all groups except the starfish. They reach their greatest variety in the North-west Pacific region.

Anatomy of a starfish

Echinoderms possess some features that are unique among the invertebrate animals – those that do not have a backbone. The starfish illustrates the general structure of all echinoderms. There are many calcareous plates embedded in the soft flesh, forming a skeleton which is internal, like our own. This is unlike that of a crab, for example, whose skeleton is outside its body. (In sea urchins, the plates are fused to form a rigid test or shell.) The starfish body consists of a central disc from which radiate arms or rays. Five is the usual number of arms, though some species have more – the American sun-star *Heliaster* has as many as forty arms. There is no head as such, the mouth being on the underside of the body. So the starfish creeps along with its mouth to the ground. The anus is in the middle of the upper surface.

A groove runs along the underside of each arm. Movable spines flank the grooves and can fold over to protect the nerve cord that extends the length of each arm. Also contained within each groove are scores of little structures called tube feet. They are hollow, thin-walled cylinders and enable the animal to move, catch food and, to some extent, breathe. The tube feet are connected to a type of hydraulic-pressure system, called the water vascular system, found in echinoderms but in no other animals. The system consists of a series of fluid-filled canals. Water is taken into the body through a sieve-like plate on the upper surface, near to the anus. It flows down a short, vertical tube into the ring canal, encircling the mouth. From the ring canal, a radial canal extends into each of the five arms. From each radial canal, branch many lateral canals which connect to muscular sacs called ampullae. These sacs, in turn, connect to the tube feet. The system is an ingenious one. Water flows into the body to a lateral canal and from there into an ampulla. A valve shuts in the lateral canal, preventing water flowing backwards. The ampulla then contracts and the water is forced into the tube foot. This elongates and its sucker-like tip adheres to the hard ground beneath. To release its grip, the tube foot contracts, forcing water up again into the ampulla. One foot, acting by itself, is a feeble structure; but hundreds of feet, acting in a co-ordinated fashion, move the starfish about, though hardly at express speed.

Feeding habits

Though they move slowly, starfish have little difficulty in catching their chief prey, which consists of bivalve molluscs, such as the near-sedentary clam and the permanently fixed oyster. You may wonder how a starfish eats a clam, the latter being capable of closing its shell tightly if threatened. The starfish seems to win by sheer persistence and tenacity. Ambling up to a clam, the starfish mounts it and applies its tube feet to both valves of the shell. By using its feet in relays, the starfish eventually exhausts the clam's muscles that hold the valves together. When there is a gap in the shell, the starfish does an even more curious thing. It everts the lower part of its stomach out of its mouth and proceeds to digest the clam, whose soft parts are reduced to a thick broth. This is absorbed through the wall of the starfish's stomach, which is then pulled back into the body. Digestion is completed inside the body in the digestive glands, two pairs of which extend into each arm of the animal. In some starfish, the slightest gap in a bivalve's shell will admit the stomach, even a slit as small as 0.1 millimetre.

Not all echinoderms feed in this strange way. Sea urchins, for example, have a complex jaw apparatus, named Aristotle's lantern after the great Greek philosopher and scientist who included echinoderms in his studies of marine

Top left (opposite): a starfish caught in the act of killing a bivalve mollusc. The starfish grips the two valves of the mollusc with its arms, holding on fast by the suction of its tube feet. Then it slowly but steadily pulls the valves apart. Finally, the starfish everts its stomach and thrusts it between the now open valves to digest the mollusc's body within.
Top right: a strikingly-coloured starfish with six arms.
Middle left: this starfish has five very short arms that are little narrower than the central disc.
Middle right: one of the many-armed starfish called sun stars.
Bottom left: a starfish with long delicate arms on which the tube feet can be clearly seen.
Bottom right: like other echinoderms, starfish have rough skins covered with tiny spines or lumps

life. It consists of forty skeletal pieces, including five teeth operated by powerful muscles. Their lanterns enable the urchins to rasp off algae encrusted on rock.

The delicate crinoids

The crinoids can be divided into two types – stalked sea lilies, which live permanently attached to the sea bed, often at great depth, and the free-living, stalkless feather stars, which live in shallow waters, temporarily fixed to objects by a number of root-like hairs extending from the base of the body. The sea lilies flourished early in the earth's history, reaching their peak during the Carboniferous period, but today only eighty species survive. The stalk may be two feet long, but in ancient lilies it grew to considerable length – up to seventy-five feet in one species. At the tip of the stalk is the round, compact body from which arise arms, usually ten in number but, in some of the feather stars, ranging from 80 up to 200. Small side arms, called pinnules, branch out from the main arm, the whole structure looking like a feather, hence the common name. During feeding, the arms are held erect, forming a drift net in which are caught tiny animals and plants.

Bottom-living cucumbers

As the name suggests, sea cucumbers are cucumber-shaped. They have a definite head and posterior end. Unlike other echinoderms, with the exception of the burrowing heart urchins, sea cucumbers are bilaterally symmetrical – they have lost the radial pattern of organs which characterizes most other members of the phylum.

Right: a sea urchin, Echinometra, *perched on a coral formation. Below: a holothurian, or sea cucumber. Like sea urchins, sea cucumbers have no arms. Unlike other echinoderms they are elongated longitudinally and lie on one side rather than on their oral surface. In the Far East, some species of sea cucumber are regarded as delicacies after being boiled, smoked or dried*

Sea cucumbers have soft, leathery bodies, limp and slimy to the touch, for the calcareous skeleton, so typical of other echinoderms, is much reduced. In the deep-sea species, it is almost totally absent. The tube feet around the mouth are modified into numerous branching tentacles which collect food from in, or on, the mud or sand where these animals live. One group of sea cucumbers swims in the open sea. Curious modifications of the tube feet, into fins and sails, aid them in swimming. The pelagic cucumbers are beautiful creatures, in sharp contrast to their sluggish, worm-like, bottom-living relatives.

The breathing apparatus of sea cucumbers is unique. Two long branched tubes, called respiratory trees, lie on either side of the central gut. Water is pumped into the body through the anus, passes up the trees and the oxygen in the water diffuses into the body tissues. Attached to the base of the trees are a number of long, sticky threads, providing the cucumber with an excellent defence system. If attacked, the animal turns its anus towards the offender and shoots the threads out of the body with such force that they detach and entangle the unfortunate victim. The threads can be regenerated for future assaults. Another bizarre act that sea cucumbers periodically perform is throwing out their insides, a process called evisceration. The gonads, gut and respiratory trees can all be ejected and regenerated later. Why cucumbers do this is not too clear (it may be defensive) but it has been observed to occur only at certain times of the year, suggesting perhaps a natural seasonal phenomenon.

The coral eater

'Menace on the march', 'Paradise in peril' – such were the headlines in the late 1960s when the crown-of-thorns starfish, *Acanthaster planci*, began to ravage Australia's Great Barrier Reef and many other coral formations in the Indo-Pacific Ocean. Moving steadily, at rates of up to a few hundred feet each day, hordes of *Acanthaster* have decimated mile upon mile of living coral. One of the major causes of the plague, it is thought, is man's interference with the natural predator-prey cycle. A marine snail, called *Triton*, is one of the main predators of adult *Acanthaster*. Tourists' greed for the snail's beautiful shell has led to mass killings of *Triton*, so removing the starfishes' predator. Blasting channels through the living coral of the reef and dynamiting for fish have also played their part in this tropical drama. This is because the tiny coral polyps feed on the larvae of the starfish, as do many fish. So, by destroying the coral and killing the chief predator, man has upset the delicate ecological balance and removed the natural controls on the starfishes' population. Measures taken to attempt to reduce the numbers of the starfish to a more normal level include 'vacuuming' the sea bed, injecting massive doses of formaldehyde into the bodies of the starfish, and releasing hordes of *Triton* reared in special 'sea farms'.

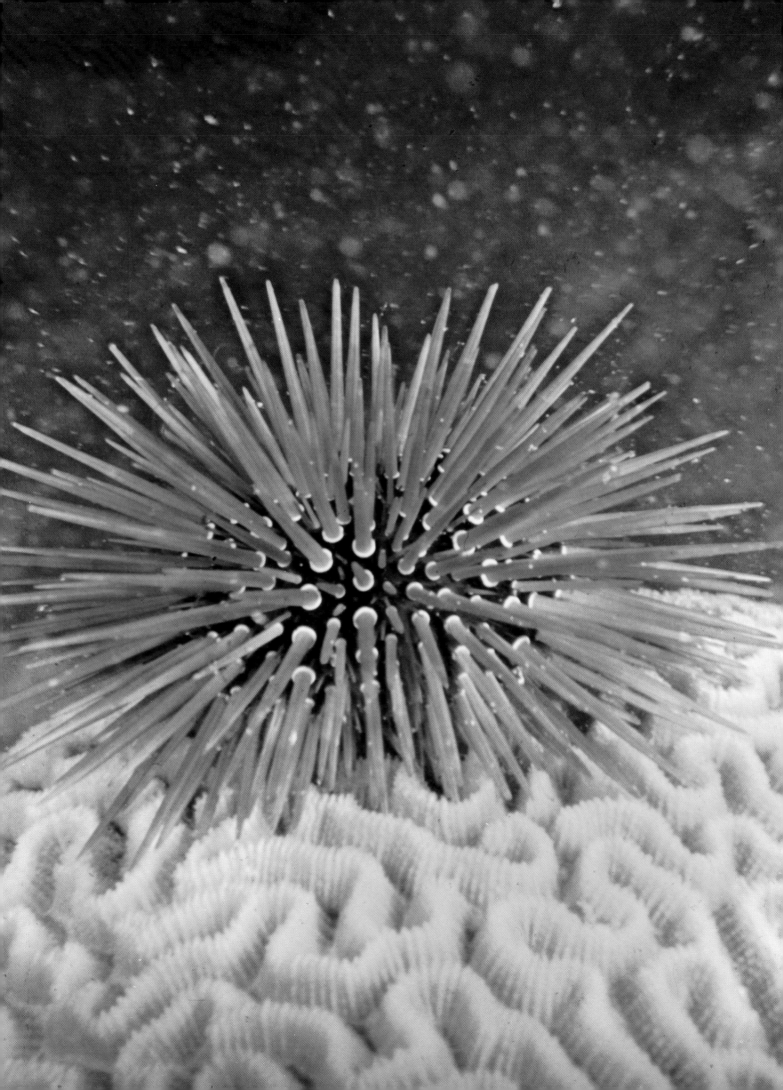

Fish
fish of the sea and sea bed

Above: skates and rays are cartilaginous fishes allied to the sharks. Left: bony fishes, like sweetlips and blue-striped snappers, differ from cartilaginous fishes in having a bony skeleton

Most of the twenty-five thousand species of fish known to science live in the sea, which also holds a much larger number of individuals than the waters of inland lakes and rivers. Moreover, most of the species that do live in fresh water are primitive and unspecialized by comparison with sea fish, which are more diverse in structure and behaviour because natural competition in the sea is more intense.

It is believed that almost all freshwater fish had sea fish among their ancestors. The colonization of fresh water may be observed in sea fish like the sharks which have taken up residence in Lake Nicaragua in South America. Many species of sea fish are notable for their extensive migrations. Particularly remarkable is that of the salmon which enters fresh water only to spawn and that of the common eel which enters the sea for the same purpose.

Zoologists divide the living species of fish into three classes. These are the Agnatha or jawless fishes, including hagfishes and lampreys, the Chondrichthyes or cartilaginous fishes, including sharks, skates and rays, and the Osteichthyes or bony fishes, which include sturgeons, herrings, tunas and the vast majority of sea fish encountered ·from polar waters to warm tropical seas.

Bony fish differ from the two more primitive classes of sea fish in a number of ways. For example, sharks and their allies do not have a swim bladder, the adjustable buoyancy apparatus which permits the bony fishes to maintain themselves at a given depth, in much the same way that a submarine does so with the aid of its buoyancy tanks. Another important feature of marine bony fishes is the fact that the proportion of salt in their body fluids is lower than that in the surrounding sea. By the process called osmosis, fresh water therefore tends to pass out of their bodies into the region of higher salt concentration outside. This process could continue until the concentration of salt within the fish was the same as that in the sea, making the fish dehydrated. Marine bony fishes have met this problem by modification of the kidneys to conserve water and also by absorbing sea water through the lining of the digestive tract, excess salt being eliminated through the gills.

Another important division, which cuts across those mentioned above, is that between bottom-dwelling fishes and open-sea fishes. The former are typically flattened in shape, while the latter are generally more streamlined. A third important category is that of the deep-sea species. These fish, having to contend with the perpetual darkness, crushing pressure and extreme cold of the sea depths, have evolved many of the most bizarre and specialized adaptations found anywhere in the animal kingdom. Typical of this group are the deep-sea anglerfishes which have luminescent organs, serving both to attract a mate and to lure their prey. Contrary to common opinion, most deep-sea fish are relatively small.

Lampreys and hagfish

Lampreys and hagfish are living representatives of the most primitive group of vertebrate animals ever to inhabit the sea. Unlike other vertebrates, they do not have moveable jaws and for this reason they are placed in a separate class, called the Agnatha. They have soft, scaleless, eel-like bodies and skeletons of cartilage. Unlike most fish, they have no paired fins and only one nostril – on top of the head in the case of the lamprey and at its tip in the hagfish. The gills are spherical pouches, not slits, arrayed along the sides of the body and opening directly to the surrounding water.

The fifteen species of hagfish are entirely marine, living and breeding in the temperate and tropical seas of the world. Some of the thirty or so species of lamprey live in the sea, mainly in coastal waters, and others live in temperate rivers and lakes. However, even the marine species enter fresh water to breed.

Some lampreys are parasitic, feeding on the blood and tissues of living animals, usually fish but sometimes even whales. The sea lamprey, *Petromyzon marinus,* is particularly unpopular because it attacks commercially important fish, such as salmon and cod. Averaging three to four feet in length, it is well equipped as a predatory parasite. It has a funnel-shaped mouth, lined with sharp, conical teeth, which acts as a powerful sucker. There are more teeth on two jagged plates inside the mouth and on the lamprey's muscular tongue. Prey is located by sight and the lamprey latches onto its victim with its mouth, puncturing and rasping away at the flesh with its teeth, using a piston-like action. Glands in the mouth secrete a saliva which dissolves flesh and contains a substance that prevents the victim's blood from clotting.

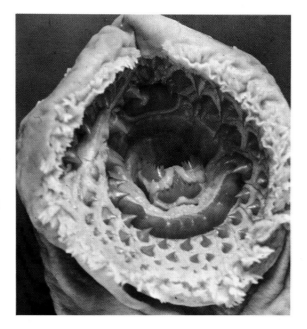

Not all lampreys are parasites. The river lamprey or lampern, *Lampetra fluviatilis* (misleadingly named since the adults live in the sea), feeds on molluscs, crustaceans and worms. Other species do not feed at all when they are adults.

Hagfishes are not parasites, but scavengers, feeding on carrion and injured or dying fish. Fishermen consider them pests because they often attack fish struggling on lines or in nets, reducing the catch to little more than skin and bones in a short time. Their eyes are degenerate and they find their prey by smell and touch. There are several short tactile tentacles around the mouth. The rasp-like tongue is equipped with plates of jagged teeth, with the aid of which hagfish bore into their prey.

Growing to about two feet long, hagfishes are sluggish animals, spending most of their lives buried in the mud of the sea bed, often in large numbers. If threatened or annoyed they secrete copious amounts of mucus from glands in the skin which makes them extremely slippery.

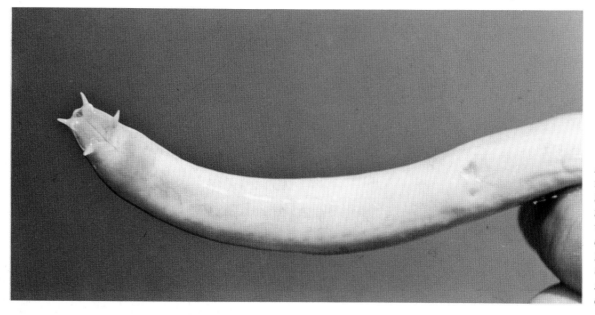

Above left: the jawless mouth of a sea lamprey, showing the rings of conical teeth with which it attacks other fish.
Left: a hagfish. The eel-like body is so sinuous that the fish can tie itself into a knot

Sharks and dogfish

Sharks stand out from almost all marine fish in their reputation for unbridled ferocity. This reputation, though not without some foundation in reality, is largely the product of man himself, who has fabricated a terror-laden folklore around sharks and their behaviour.

For the biologist, sharks and dogfish are distinguished in another way. Unlike the vast majority of fish in the sea, sharks and dogfish, like the skates and rays, do not have bony skeletons. Instead their skeletons are made of cartilage, the material of which the pliant tip of the human nose is made. For this reason they are placed in the class Chondrichthyes. Within this class, modern sharks are classified in the order Pleurotremi.

There have been sharks in the sea for a very long time. Today's sharks are the remanants of a group of fish which dominated the oceans during the Carboniferous period, some 300 million years ago. Since then sharks have changed comparatively little, although during this time they have seen countless other species of animal come and go.

The killing machine

The body of a shark is adapted as well as ever for the life of a roving predator. That it has survived for so long with so little change is a testimony to the success of the shark's original formula for survival. The shark has been described as a 'killing machine' and it is undeniable that its anatomy and nervous system are adapted with marvellous precision for the task of finding and killing its prey.

Typically the body is slim, muscular and streamlined, lending the fish great speed. However, the bottom-dwelling shark species do not conform to the conventional pattern, being more flattened in shape and more sluggish in behaviour than their open-sea relatives. Their diet consists of other bottom-dwelling animals which are generally slower-moving, though often heavily armoured.

Among open-sea sharks speeds in excess of thirty m.p.h. have been recorded during tests. The fastest sharks are generally considered to be the two species of mako, *Isurus paucus* of the Pacific and *Isurus oxyrhinchus* of the Atlantic. The members of the mako's family are characterized by an almost symmetrical, crescent-shaped tail. In other families, such as that of the grey or requiem sharks (Carcharinidae), the upper lobe of the tail is elongated. This development reaches an extreme form in the members of the thresher shark family (Alopiidae), where the huge scythe-like tail may account for half the total body length.

The thresher beats the water with its tail to drive small fish into a compact mass, then charges through them eating many and stunning others. However, a shark's lateral control of its bursts of speed is not good. The pectoral fins, unlike those of a bony fish, are fixed. Lying just behind the head, they stabilize the fish and help to

Below: a zebra shark (Stegostoma fasciatum) with a pilot fish (right) in attendance. Bottom-living species of shark are usually more sluggish in behaviour than their open-ocean relatives

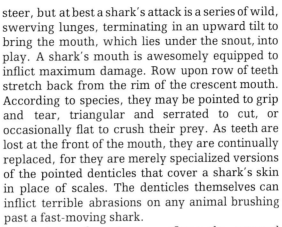

steer, but at best a shark's attack is a series of wild, swerving lunges, terminating in an upward tilt to bring the mouth, which lies under the snout, into play. A shark's mouth is awesomely equipped to inflict maximum damage. Row upon row of teeth stretch back from the rim of the crescent mouth. According to species, they may be pointed to grip and tear, triangular and serrated to cut, or occasionally flat to crush their prey. As teeth are lost at the front of the mouth, they are continually replaced, for they are merely specialized versions of the pointed denticles that cover a shark's skin in place of scales. The denticles themselves can inflict terrible abrasions on any animal brushing past a fast-moving shark.

The internal anatomy confirms the external appearance; it appears adapted simply to locate prey and digest it with a minimum of wasted internal space. A shark hunts mainly by smell. Its meagre brain is dwarfed by two massive olfactory lobes set well forward, enabling the fish to detect and trace food at ranges of over a quarter of a mile. The eyes are poor, although hardly as myopic as many items of shark-lore pretend. 'Hearing' – the means by which the shark detects changes in water pressure – is through small sense organs located at the bottom of a series of pits, concentrated on the head and trailing back on each flank to the tail: the equivalent of the lateral line of higher fish. Instead of a looped intestine, the sharks have a very short digestive tract. Its absorptive area is increased by a spiral valve that also slows the passage of the food.

Sharks differ from bony fishes in a few other characteristics. Their gills are separate, and are visible as slits behind the head. They lack a swim-bladder and are forced, quite literally, to sink or swim. Some of them alleviate their lack of buoyancy by swallowing air, and one or two of them possess oversized livers and can adjust the balance of oils in them according to depth. The most basic difference is in the reproductive mechanism, a system so organized that it must have made a significant contribution to the sharks' long history. The sexes copulate to ensure internal fertilization, and many species bear small broods of live young.

The hind edges of the male's pelvic fins are modified to form a pair of rods ('claspers', from the obsolete theory that they hold the female) which are grooved along the inner faces to form a tube and direct sperm flow. The eggs, whether laid or developed internally, are large and well supplied with nutrients. Some species lay flat, cushion-like eggs with tendrils on the corners, that tangle into seaweed. These, together with the eggs of some skates, are the familiar 'mermaid's purses' found on beaches. Sharks of the open sea tend to be viviparous, giving birth to live fully-formed young.

Carnivorous diet

The diet of sharks is entirely carnivorous, although the two largest species, the whale shark and the basking shark, feed almost entirely on

Left: the vast majority of sharks are not dangerous to man. Even man-eating species may be harmless when they are encountered outside the tropics. Inset: the head of a black-tipped shark, showing the extremely sensitive nostrils which can detect a single drop of blood over great distances

67

plankton. The large oceanic sharks feed on fish, turtles, small porpoises and even sea birds, as well as any terrestrial animal – including man – unfortunate enough to pass within range. Some, like the tiger shark, are inveterate scavengers and the extensive catalogue of incongruous objects found in their stomachs includes tin cans, chains, petrol drums, machine parts, and even the remains of an old bicycle.

The question of shark attack on man has been the subject of debate for many years. Unprovoked attacks documented since a Portuguese sailor died after an attack in 1580 until attacks in 1963 totalled only 866, of which 359 were fatal. Reports since average thirty to thirty-five a year, with the majority from Australian waters. Shark behaviour is notoriously unpredictable. All that is known with certainty is that blood in the water excites them to a state known as a feeding frenzy, in which they snap at anything, including one another. The various repellent actions often alleged to help the bather in the presence of sharks – shouting, splashing, clouting the shark on the nose and others – are as likely to infuriate as to deter. Shark repellent chemicals have worked on some occasions, but have been promptly eaten on others. The only sound defence seems to consist of attracting as little attention as possible, and beating a quiet retreat. Stupidity can bring on attacks; at least one hammerhead fatality has been recorded when a diver failed to abandon a bleeding fish on his spear. The combination of murky water and flashing equipment has also attracted attacks, possibly reflex strikes at what appears to be a fish.

Man-eating sharks

Of the twelve species of confirmed maneaters, the great white shark *Carcharodon carcharias* has been a highly consistent culprit. An impressive monster by any standards, it reaches a length of at least thirty-six and a half feet with an average size of about twenty feet. It is bluish to slate-grey above, fading to white below. Its teeth are an awesome array of serrated triangles, often the only evidence left in a body or boat attacked and abandoned. It roams the warm seas, occasionally venturing into colder waters, and may yet prove to be a casual visitor from great depths, for one was taken at 4,200 feet deep off Cuba. Research in Australia indicates that like other animals that eat men, the great white's reputation stems from 'rogue' sharks that through temper or infirmity take to attacking bathers and boats. Like the others of the mackerel shark family (Isuridae), the porbeagle and mako – both considered dangerous in warm waters – its normal diet is other fish and squid, usually far smaller than itself.

The hammerhead is another shark justly feared

Above: the formidable teeth of the great white shark (Carcharodon carcharias). *The great white is the most dangerous of all sharks and is frequently responsible for attacks on humans.*
Left: the bull huss or greater spotted dogfish (Scyliorhinus stellaris). *The dogfish are smaller relatives of the sharks*

as a man-eater. It gets its name from the lateral projections from each side of the head; their tips each bear an eye and a nostril and may be three feet apart in a twenty-foot shark. The function of this structure is unknown, but it appears to act as a supplementary stabilizer to aid manoeuvrability. The distance between the nostrils may aid the location of a scent, saving the zig-zagging trial-and-error movements made by other sharks to find the direction of food. An inhabitant of the warm seas, from the surface to 1,200 feet, it is an occasional visitor to temperate seas in summer. The cub, tiger and Australian whaler sharks are the most feared of the other confirmed maneaters.

Ironically, the two largest sharks are the only truly harmless ones. The fifty- to sixty-foot long whale shark of tropical seas and its temperate counterpart, the basking shark, which attains forty feet, sieve plankton from the upper waters like the baleen whales. Little is known, of these docile wanderers which are the two largest fish in the world. Basking sharks, having made a thorough nuisance of themselves, blundering in shoals through the drift nets off the south-west coast of Brittany, retire to deep water for winter, shedding their gill rakers and presumably, not feeding. They are of little commercial importance.

Big-game sport

Only four large sharks visit British waters regularly: the thresher, blue, mako and porbeagle. All but the thresher have, in the last twenty years, become a focus of interest for anglers seeking big-game sport. Around America larger species like the great white and the tiger shark are popular quarries. However, it is the seas around Australia which have so far yielded the largest catch – a great white, weighing well over a ton.

The blue shark is a pelagic species, reaching a maximum length of twelve feet in tropical waters but seldom exceeding about six feet in British waters. It is common at forty to sixty pounds, with the record at over 200 pounds. The blue shark is easily identified. It is slim, vivid blue when freshly caught, and has very long, slender pectoral fins. There is a constriction at the rear end of the tail stalk. It is a voracious feeder, harrying shoals of mackerel, herring, and spur-dog, sometimes taking cod and squid. In warmer waters it has an evil, though largely unconfirmed, reputation as a maneater. It is a late arrival among summer fish around British coasts, seldom appearing before late June, and leaving around October. Full information on its distribution is lacking, but any area washed by the rich North Atlantic Drift with a depth of 120 feet or more yields specimens. Although Cornwall is the traditional centre for all shark angling, blues are taken on the south and west coasts of Ireland and off the west coasts of Wales and Scotland.

The porbeagle shark, far larger than the blue shark, requires heavier tackle and larger baits. Although more portly, it can easily be confused with its close relative, the mako. The main differences are: the small secondary lateral keel on the lower lobe of the porbeagle's tail, lacking in the mako; leading edge of the second dorsal in line with that of the anal fin in the porbeagle, ahead of it in the mako; and the porbeagle has large eyes, the mako small ones. The porbeagle reaches around ten feet in length and 500–600 pounds, seldom exceeding 300 pounds in British waters. Evidence from commercial fishermen seems to indicate that it is present all the year round, seeking deeper water in cold weather. Porbeagles are concentrated around the south-west coast, but many are taken commercially for the Norwegian market from the North Sea. They are versatile feeders, combing the surface waters for mackerel, descending for squid, spur-dog and flatfish, but seldom operating in water of more than 450 feet. The mako shark reaches 1,000 pounds, and British fish of over 400 pounds have

Below: a black-tipped shark (Calcharhinus melanopterus). *Because they have no swim bladder, open-ocean sharks have to swim continuously to remain off the bottom*

Left: a mako shark. Tests have shown that these jaws may be capable of exerting a pressure of 50 tons per square inch.

Inset top left: the sand tiger shark is regarded as harmless in America, but in South Africa it is thought to be a maneater.

Inset above: a carpet shark, one of the most colourful members of the shark tribe. In Australia it is known as the wobbegong.

Inset left: two great whites which will not endanger bathers in Sydney Harbour. Netting has reduced the number of sharks in inshore waters

Above: sharks are found in waters where their prey are most concentrated. In the tropics they are attracted by the teeming forms of life that live around coral reefs

been taken. A warm-water species, it is found in the south-west in summer, often over rocky ground. The thresher shark is as yet an unexploited source of sport. Its habit of attacking shoals makes it difficult to attract attention to a specific bait, but some success has been achieved with slow trolling of a dead mackerel at the borders of shoals.

Very closely related to the blue shark, the tope is a long-standing favourite with anglers. Up to six feet long, it is common, hard-fighting and easily contacted. It could be confused with the smooth hound, but a glance at the mouth will show the many-pointed, predatory teeth of a tope or the flat, criss-cross crushing plates that the smooth hound uses to feed on shellfish and crabs.

Tope can be found anywhere where bait fish such as mackerel, whiting or herring are common with a good run of tide. They are most often taken over clean, sandy ground, but inhabit all types of bottom from quite shallow water to 300 feet. They are essentially summer fish; warm, calm weather is ideal, while after storms they seem to stop feeding for a few days. Generally, tope are most abundant in estuaries and over clean ground, larger but less plentiful over rocks.

Few others of the shark family have any commercial or sporting value. The dogfish find a place as huss or rock salmon in many fish shops, but as a rule, they are considered a nuisance by anglers and trawlermen alike. Spur-dog are a particular pest. Seldom more than eight to nine pounds in weight, they congregate into immense shoals. They are easily identified by the large, poisonous spines in front of the dorsal fins and a line of white spots on the flanks. They live from shallow water to 1,200 feet and can mar a day's angling by taking bait intended for better fish and spoil trawling by filling net after net with their spiky, almost worthless carcases. The two other dogfish common on British coasts are the greater and lesser spotted species. The greater nurse hound is stoutly built, with the nasal flaps on the underside of its snout not joined together and not extending as far back as the mouth. It is particularly common over sandy ground, where it feeds on small fishes, shellfish and shrimps. It averages eight to ten pounds. The lesser species is heavily spotted, very rough-skinned, and the nasal flaps are undivided and touch the mouth. Its average weight is only two to three pounds.

At the borderline between shark and ray, although belonging to a shark family, the monkfish is a curiously flattened, bulky bottom-dweller. It has large pectoral fins, and a squat ugly head. It winters in deep water, moving inshore to breed in summer. Seldom taken at less than forty pounds and reaching a maximum of over 150 pounds, it provides occasional sport at known marks, and its flesh is firm and sweet.

Skates and rays

The skates and rays are the other large group of marine fishes within the class Chondrichthyes and these unmistakable fish are closely related to the sharks and dogfishes.

With representatives in all but the coldest oceans, the skates and rays make up the order Batoidei. There are some 340 species, but the distinction between the two types is very loose; zoologically, 'skates' and 'rays' often belong to the same family. As a general rule, however, the skates have an elongated snout. And, seen from above, the skate's 'wings' are nearly concave, whereas those of a ray are more rounded. All skates and rays are cartilaginous fish, related to the sharks, but several characteristics differentiate the two groups. Typically, skates and rays appear flattened, because the pectoral fins are greatly enlarged and attached to the sides of the head. The tail is often much reduced; in some species it is merely a simple, whip-like appendage. The mouth is usually on the underside of the body, and the gill-slits are situated on the lower faces of the pectoral fins. Since many of these fish are bottom-dwellers, this combination has led to a modification of the breathing apparatus. Many skates and rays draw in water through large holes called spiracles on the upper surface of their heads. The water passes into the pharynx, or throat, and then through the gills below. This obviates sucking water through the mouth which would clog the system with mud or sand. The eyes are on the upper surface, and raised slightly so the fish has a good field of view. Skates and rays lack the free upper eyelid found in sharks.

Guitarfishes seem to lie at the border between sharks and rays; their bodies appear only slightly flattened, and they swim by sculling with the body and tail, rather than rippling the wings like a 'true' ray. The position of the gills on the underside of the pectoral fins, however, leads zoologists to group them firmly with the rays. Inhabitants of the shallow water regions of most tropical and temperate seas, they are a nuisance to sea anglers, a source of amusement to skin-divers, and of no commercial value. Mediterranean and American anglers resent these species because immense shoals of four- to five-foot long guitarfish arrive quite suddenly in a fishing area and pick up every bait on the sea bed. Docile and tractable, they give no fight at all on rod and line. These characteristics, however, endear them to skin divers, who can chase, catch and harry them with impunity. There is only one record of a guitarfish attacking man, off California, but the blunt, stone-like teeth, so well-suited to crushing molluscs, did no harm. There are some forty-five species, with the largest, *Rhynchobatos djiddensis* of the Indo-Pacific, weighing in at around 500 pounds and ten feet long.

Far more respect, or even fear, is justifiably accorded to the sawfishes, with their elongated snouts armed with a fearsome, double-edged saw. This adaptation of the snout occurs also in a shark family, the Pristiophoridae, but their gills

Below: skates and rays are symmetrical in shape, unlike flatfish. Their eyes are slightly protuberant, allowing them to see forwards. They draw in water through spiracles on top of their bodies, to breath, and expel it through gill slits on the under side

lie above the pectorals; the sawfish of fishermen's tales is a ray. Six species inhabit the warm seas, and grow to over thirty-five feet long and 5,000 pounds in weight. They are common in brackish water and estuaries, and there is a population in landlocked Lake Nicaragua in Central America. The saw is an all-purpose hunting tool. The fish uses it to dig for molluscs in softer sea beds, or slashes its way right and left through shoals of food fish, killing, stunning and impaling its victims. So deeply ingrained is their instinct to slash with their saws while feeding, that hand-feeding sawfish in research aquariums is not the most popular job among the divers. Like guitar-fish, sawfish are ovoviviparous, hatching their eggs internally to give birth to live young. The saw is soft at birth.

Electric organs

Far less straightforward in their choice of weaponry, the electric rays are a source of intriguing speculation and research. They were first recorded in early Greek and Roman times, when the application of their shocks was a standard cure for gout. Since the average voltage generated is around forty or fifty volts, such treatment would not have been comfortable and, with a big fish discharging over 200 volts, could have been nearly fatal. The power of the ray's electric organ runs down after successive shocks, and needs a few days to recharge.

The living 'batteries' of the electric ray family are situated in each wing root, close to the body. The individual electric cell is a disc filled with a gelatinous substance containing many nuclei. These discs lie in columns extending vertically through the wings, up to 400 cells deep, with fibrous tissue isolating each cell. As many as a thousand of these columns, according to species, may be linked in series to produce maximum current. An electric ray discharges positive electricity uppermost, negative on the under-surface. This flow is due to the plate arrangement: electric eels, for example, are positive on the head, negative on the tail; electric catfish are the opposite.

The most obvious functions of electricity in a fish are attack and defence. Nothing compares with a stiff deterrent jolt, particularly under-water, for blunting an intruder's appetite. When the ray is feeding, a stalking approach towards a small fish is followed by a quick pounce, and the prey is subdued by a swift shock. It is interesting, however, to speculate that the use of electricity for attack and defence is a side benefit acquired in response to other needs. The electric field of rays may well be comparable to the ultrasonic squeaks of bats as a method of orientation and detection. The water in which they live – in estuaries and over mud or sand – is often murky, and their eyesight is often poor; some species are even blind. If the ray produces a permanent, low-voltage field, it can probably detect interruptions in the lines of force caused by certain features in its surroundings or by

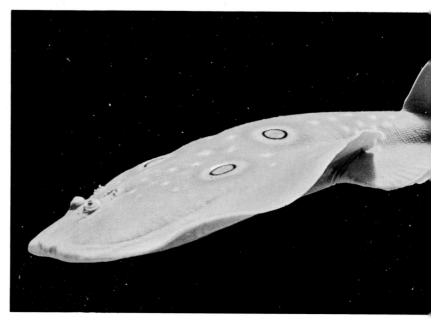

intruding fish. Pulsed discharges may also serve to communicate information between members of the same species.

About thirty-six species of electric ray exist, represented in all tropical and temperate seas. They are common, but the populations are well spread out, seldom forming the large aggregations typical of their relatives. Two species occur around the southern coasts of Britain, both members of the genus *Torpedo*. They have a well-rounded disc, a muscular tail and tail fin, and small eyes. The marbled ray *Torpedo marmorata* has a characteristic mottled upper surface. The Atlantic ray *Torpedo nobiliana* is red-brown, dark green or purple-black. *Nobiliana* is the largest electric ray, reaching over five feet long and possibly 200 pounds in weight. It occurs from the intertidal zone to a depth of 3,000 feet.

Electric organs are also found in the tails of many skates. Modified muscles lie on each side of the tail, but their supporting anatomy differs from that of the rays. The cranial nerves supply the rays' cells; the spinal nerves govern the skates'. Much research remains to be done. Close investigation by the specialist Dr Reizo Ishiyama has shown that all the skates in his home waters of Japan have electric organs, and that they generate larger outputs of current in shallower water. He suggests that all skates may prove to be mildly electric.

Skates

There are over a hundred species of skate, usually found on sand, gravel and mud sea beds at depths of less than 600 feet. A few species range very deep. *Raja abyssicola* has been caught at 7,200 feet in the Pacific. Typically, a skate has wide pointed wings, a stiff long snout and a narrow tail that mounts two nearly

Opposite top: the marbled ray Torpedo marmorata, well camouflaged against a pebbly seabed. One of the electric rays, it is found off the southern coasts of Britain.
Centre left: another electric ray, Torpedo torpedo, cruises through the water. This species is found in the warm Atlantic Ocean as far north as the Bay of Biscay.
Left: an electric ray from above. A large individual can discharge its 50-amp pulses of electricity at up to 200 volts – enough to give a careless bather a severe shock.
Opposite below: side view of a marbled ray.
Below centre: the electric organs on the underside of this torpedo ray are the oval areas of tissue on either side of the head

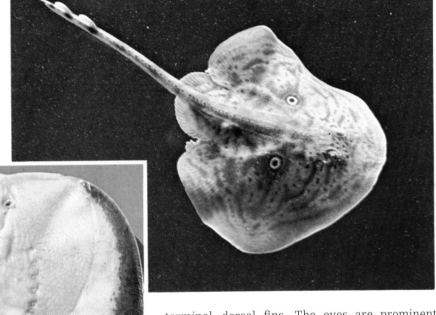

terminal dorsal fins. The eyes are prominent, with the spiracles nearby. Skates eat molluscs, crustaceans, worms and bottom-fish, but are slow-moving and usually lazy. They seem to prefer to have their food served to them by a good run of tide or the outflow of an estuary.

A dozen species frequent British waters, but identification of the smaller types can be very difficult. The largest, the common skate *Raja batis*, is also the most familiar to anglers and trawlermen. It is green to brown on the upper surface, sometimes with pale spots. The under-surface is grey, often with black or brown patterns. Its snout is elongated, two-and-a-half to three-and-a-half times as long as the distance between the eyes. Confusion with the long-nosed skate is possible, but the latter's snout is five to six times the distance between the eyes and the underside is white to light grey with dark spots. The common skate has variable numbers of sharp spines on its upper surface, according to age. Young ones have large thorn-shaped spines near the eyes and a single row of them along the tail. Older specimens lose the eye-thorns, but have two, sometimes three, rows along the tail. The largest Atlantic ray, the common skate reaches a maximum length of over eight feet and a weight in excess of 300 pounds, with the rod-caught record well over 200 pounds. It is found as deep as 1,500 feet, but smaller ones prefer shallow water and are often taken in the intertidal zone. The females lay very large eggs in autumn and winter. Encased in box-like, leathery capsules, with tendrils at the corners, these eggs can measure as much as six by eight inches. They hatch in three to five months.

Other skates in British waters include the pale ray, with its grey body and white belly, growing to six or seven feet; the shagreen ray, darker on the upperside with a white underside, reaching only three or four feet; the common thornback, with its obtusely-angled snout and nail-like thorns all over the upper surface, reaching three or four feet; and Fylla's ray, a northern type with a very rounded snout.

Stingrays

The remaining families of rays include the stingrays, some of the world's most dangerous fish. Armed with a spine (or spines) on top of the tail that can be brought into play with vicious agility, the larger specimens can inflict dangerous, sometimes fatal wounds. The spine itself is smothered in tiny barbs or teeth, and is often rendered even more deadly by a pair of venom glands set in grooves on either side. Although not all stingray cuts are poisonous, sandy and muddy areas which are known to harbour these potentially dangerous rays must be approached with caution.

The 118 species of stingrays fall into two main groups. In the dasyatid rays, the fins extend around the front of the head as a narrow shelf. In the second group, the holorhinid rays, this extension is a thick, fleshy lip. The dasyatid rays have long, tapering tails, and many replace their spines as they grow. Consequently, specimens with two, or even three, spines are not uncommon. They occur in shallow water, seldom venturing below 360 feet, with some preferring brackish or fresh water. Several species of *Potamotrygon* in South America never leave fresh water, and inspire considerably more respect

Below left: the underside of a skate reveals the U-shaped mouth; above it are the nostrils, and below it are the gill slits. This is a male, with finger-like 'claspers' (for placing sperm inside the female) along the inner edges of the pectoral fins.
Bottom left: one of the six species of sawfish, Pristis pristis, found in the Mediterranean.
Below: a tropical electric ray lies low among seabed plants.
Right: a giant manta ray gives a free ride to a group of remora fish, each attached to the ray by a suction disc on the top of its head. Mantas live in the open ocean in warm seas, feeding on plankton.
Bottom right: a thornback ray swimming, by undulating its winglike pectoral fins.
Bottom far right: an eagle ray

in the Indians than the local piranhas. Stingrays occur in all sizes, from the twelve-inch round rays to one Australian monster that spans six to seven feet and can weigh up to 750 pounds. The only common British stingray *Dasyatis pastinaca*, a blue to grey, acutely angled ray, averages two feet long, reaching a maximum of seven feet and fifty or more pounds. It haunts shallow sand beaches and estuaries.

The holorhinid stingrays, which include the eagle, bat, and cow-nosed rays, are more tropical in distribution, and often undertake migrations in vast numbers. Their taste for clams and oysters has ruined many American shellfish breeders. They are large, with some reaching seven feet across the wingtips, and their spines have served as spear-tips for many Pacific tribes.

Giant manta rays

The last group of rays is probably the best-known through myth and legend. The enormous mantas of the family Mobulidae have forsaken bottom-feeding for a pelagic life of plankton gathering in the warm seas. Like some surreal jet engine's air intake, their massive terminal mouth has guides pointing forward to direct water flow. These docile, massive fish simply sieve a living from the upper waters. The largest recorded was twenty-two feet across the wingtips, and turned the scales at 3,500 pounds. The danger presented by this fish is overrated, but understandable. It has a habit of jumping clear of the water, and the combination of seeing a huge bat-like silhouette clear the water, followed by the thunderclap of noise as it flops back is, to say the least, awe-inspiring.

Coelacanth

The bony fishes of the class Osteichthyes include the majority of fish in the sea and the remainder of those described in this chapter. The coelacanth, *Latimeria chalumnae*, is a representative of an extremely ancient order of bony fishes which occupy an important place in the history of vertebrate evolution. The members of this order were believed to have been extinct for seventy million years and were known only from their fossil remains. So when a living coelacanth was recovered from the nets of a trawler off South Africa in 1938 it caused a sensation in scientific circles and the coelacanth joined a select band of animals which are known as 'living fossils'.

It was not until 1952 that a second coelacanth was identified. This came from the Comorro Islands, north of Madagascar, where the sea bed plunges steeply down to the floor of the Indian Ocean. The area has since yielded several more coelacanths, so the first specimen may have been a wanderer from more northerly waters where coelacanths range at depths between a hundred and 1,200 feet.

Coelacanths grow to six feet in length and a weight of more than 200 pounds. They are heavily built, ugly creatures, strikingly dissimilar to other fish in several respects. The fins of the coelacanth are the most obvious indication of its exceptionally long lineage. They are modified into stalked flippers and have the appearance of rudimentary limbs. These they may well be, for a close ancestor of the coelacanth, *Eusthenopteron,* is thought to have been a forerunner of land animals. The coelacanth uses its fleshy fins to haul itself over the sea bed where it hunts other fish, probably by stalking and ambush.

Viewed from the side, the body of a coelacanth does not taper evenly towards the tail, like that of most fish. Instead it ends in a wedge shape. The upper and lower tail fins are located above and below this wedge and it terminates in a diminutive secondary tail, at the extreme end of the body.

Many of the internal organs are extremely primitive. The heart is little more than a simple S-shaped tube. In place of a swim bladder the coelacanth has a large, elongated structure filled with fat. The walls of the intestine are spiralled to increase their surface area, a feature not generally associated with bony fish, but found in sharks and their relatives. These features are of surpassing interest to biologists because they are too soft to appear among the fossil remains of ancient species.

It was not until seventy coelacanths had been examined that a female containing eggs was found. She bore only nineteen of them, the largest of which measured three-and-a-half inches in diameter. Such a small number of eggs may indicate that they are laid in a cluster and guarded by the fish. Alternatively, like the eggs of ovoviviparous sharks, they may hatch inside the fish's body.

The backbone of the coelacanth is no more than a tough hollow rod of cartilage. The hard spines of the fins are also hollow and made of cartilage, and it is from this feature that the coelacanth takes its name. The skull and scales, however, are made of bone, making the coelacanth the most primitive living bony fish known to science.

Below: the coelacanth (Latimeria chalumnae) has modified pelvic and pectoral fins that resemble rudimentary arms. The diminutive 'second tail' projecting from the end of the main tail is a link with the extinct fish which were ancestors of the first land animals and of man himself

Sturgeons

Like the coelacanth, the sturgeons are bony fish, but fall outside the ranks of the modern bony fishes. Of such primitive fishes, the sturgeons are the best known and by far the most important for commercial purposes. They form the family Acipenseridae, part of the order Acipenseriformes, which is shared with the paddlefishes of the family Polyodontidae. The latter are freshwater fishes found only in the great river systems of the Mississippi in North America and the Yangtze

pointed plates that run along the back and sides. The mouth lies underneath the almost shovel-like snout, and is protruded like a miniature trunk to pick up bottom-living invertebrates and, in larger individuals, fish. A sturgeon's eyesight is poor, but its sense of touch is highly developed; four highly sensitive tactile barbels precede the mouth, and the fish forages slowly over the bottom, testing its path and seeking out prey. Freshwater sturgeons seem to prefer a clean river bed, but ocean species find their food over mud – indeed, their name in some European languages means 'the stirrer', from their habit of

Kiang in China.

Sturgeons are inhabitants of northern temperate waters, both salt and fresh. There are about two dozen species, some of them attaining great age and size. The largest of all, the beluga sturgeon of the Caspian and Black Seas and adjacent rivers, has been recorded at 2,860 pounds weight and twenty-eight feet long. Although the age of this specimen was not recorded, a thirteen-foot specimen of 2,200 pounds was seventy-five years old. In the sea, the Atlantic species reaches 600 pounds and eleven feet long, although specimens measuring more than six feet in length are now very rare.

Ancient fish

The shark-like appearance of the sturgeon betrays the group's long ancestry. Like some link between the sharks and bony fishes, they retain extremely primitive characters, including the extended upper lobe on the tail, a spiracle to maintain a water current over the gills, a spiral valve in the intestine, and cartilaginous rays in the fins. The presence of gill covers and bony skulls, however, leads biologists to classify the sturgeons with the bony fishes. The body lacks scales, but for five longitudinal rows of heavy,

rummaging over the bottom with their snouts.

Most species of sturgeon spawn in spring. The freshwater types appear to prefer shallow water, and ascend to small streams. Their sea-going cousins move upriver to spawn in depths of eighteen to twenty feet, although the giant beluga favour holes as deep as 150 feet. The eggs take from two weeks to three months to hatch, according to species and temperature. The half-inch larvae have a pigmented groove in front of the mouth, a vestige of the sucking disc found in some other very primitive fishes such as the bowfins, gars, and lungfish. Initial growth is rapid, but it slows after some months. The beluga reaches fifteen inches in its first year, but a lake sturgeon needs twenty years to reach maturity at four feet long.

A prolific breeder

Female sturgeon are capable of immense egg production, shedding as many as five million eggs in a season. Such prolific breeding has been the downfall of the species, since for many years seemingly inexhaustible supplies of the fish have stimulated large fisheries. The flesh, oil, swim-bladder and eggs are all valuable. The swim-bladder supplies isinglass, almost pure gelatin

Above left: the common sturgeon, Acipenser sturio. *Sturgeon are relics of a primitive race of fish and have skeletons which are partly of bone and partly of cartilage*

79

used to clear wine and for specialized water-proofing. The name is derived from the Dutch *huisenblas, huisen* being a species of sturgeon and *blas* a bladder. The eggs are processed to give caviare of the highest quality. Although caviare can be obtained from many fish, the sturgeon suffers most from this form of exploitation.

Unripe eggs are carefully removed from a newly-killed female, or stripped from a living fish at the fish farms established to breed sturgeon. The eggs must then be freed of their membrane, by beating with fine twigs or pressing gently through a sieve. The free egg- are mixed with salt to remove moisture, drained, and lightly pressed into wooden casks.

Decline of an industry

Commercial exploitation, pollution and hydro-electric schemes blocking migration routes have caused great depletion in sturgeon populations everywhere. Once the Atlantic coasts of Europe all held sturgeon, but now they are confined to the mouth of the Gironde in western France, the Guadalquivir in Spain and Lake Ladoga in Russia. Overfishing in the Caspian and Black Seas – up to 15,000 fish were taken in a single day – has brought these populations to a dangerously low figure, and the same is true of the once flourishing sturgeon population in the New England states of America.

Crown property

The few sturgeon that occasionally appear in England are the property of the Crown, and all catches should be reported to the authorities. This dates from the early fourteenth century, when Edward II decreed that 'The King shall have the wreck of the sea, whales and great sturgeons.' Ironically, the fates of both these creatures now rest with industries and nations with no time for monarchy and little for marine conservation, and unless strict measures are applied the Eurasian sturgeons will be as rare as the 'royal' whales.

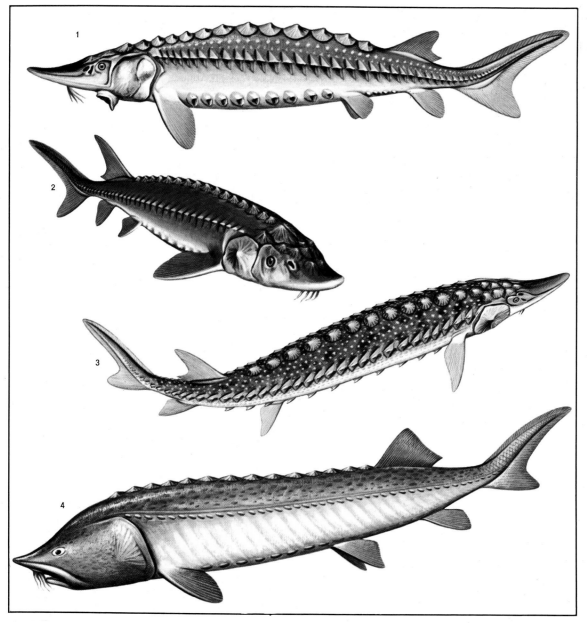

Left: there are 24 different species of sturgeon, most of which live in the sea and return to the rivers to spawn. 1. the common sturgeon, Acipenser sturio, *which is found from Scandinavia to the Mediterranean. The females, which are larger than the males, reach a length of at least twelve feet. 2. the sturgeon* Acipenser nacarri. *3.* Acipenser stellatus *occurs in abundance in the rivers of the Black and Caspian seas and the Sea of Azov. Its flesh is highly prized and its caviare commands high prices. 4.* Huso huso, *the Russian sturgeon or beluga inhabits the Caspian and Black seas and the Sea of Azov. Right: head of a sturgeon, showing the four barbels on the lower jaw. These are sense organs which the fish uses to find food by probing the sea bed*

Herrings

All the remainder of the fish described in this chapter belong to the Teleostei or modern bony fishes. The order Clupeiformes, to which the herring and its relatives belong, include the most primitive members of the Teleostei. These are mainly small, shoaling fish which occur in vast numbers in the surface waters of almost all the oceans of the world. As such, they provide food for a wide variety of marine predators, such as the various species of tuna. The course of tuna migrations is largely dictated by the movements of the herring shoals and the latter are a valuable source of a bait for commercial tuna fishermen.

However, the herring family are equally important, and perhaps best known, as a valuable source of food for man himself and they represent one of the most important of all the resources of the sea. The vast shoals of herring, sprats, anchovies and other members of the family, such as the shads, provide the world's commercial fishermen with a third of their total annual catch, about twenty million tons. Because the flesh is oily and easily preserved by smoking, these fish have been sought by fishermen for centuries. Cities have grown up near the fishing grounds and wars have been fought to defend a nation's right to the fisheries.

The herring family

There are some two hundred species in the herring family (Clupeidae), with many local races varying in size, rate of growth and migration routes. Slender, elongated fish, they seldom exceed eighteen inches long. They are green to grey-brown on the back, with silver flanks that lack a lateral line. The scales detach easily and the dorsal fin is short and located near the centre of the back. A standard 'rule of thumb' distinguishes herring, sprat and pilchard: suspended by the dorsal fin, a herring stays in balance, a sprat dips at the head and a pilchard dips at the tail. The majority of clupeids form enormous shoals, tending to circulate anticlockwise in the northern hemisphere, clockwise in the southern. They feed on animal plankton, sieving it from the water with a fine mesh of up to four hundred 'gill rakers' in the throat. Although primarily a marine family, many species enter brackish water. Some spawn in rivers (especially the shads), while others are entirely confined to fresh water, like *Pseudochirocentrodon* of the Amazon and *Stolothrissa* in Lake Tanzania. Clupeids inhabit most oceans from the polar seas to the tropics.

Commercially and politically the most important fish in the world is the northern herring (*Clupea harengus*). It moves in shoals that can contain thousands of tons of fish. It has been estimated that three thousand million herring are caught yearly in and around the Atlantic. About a foot long, the herring is identified by its lack of radial stripes on the gill cover, by the position of the base of the ventral fins (which lies behind the leading edge of the dorsal) and by its lack of a distinct sharp 'keel' of scales.

Although it was once held that herring followed a simple north-to-south migration route, more modern information suggests a slightly different pattern. Herring favour water temperatures of 43–59° Fahrenheit (6–15° Centigrade). When the Gulf Stream, moving north-east, successively warms the coasts of France, the British Isles, Scandinavia and Iceland, it drives the herring before it. When the warm water retreats in autumn and winter, the herring follow. Many races exist within the main species, of which the most important in the eastern range are the North Sea, Channel, Icelandic and Norwegian types, all of which spawn at different times of year and migrate over varying distances.

Pride of place must go to the Norwegian race, since this is the most important to the fishing industry. Its breeding cycle starts in the winter, when mature fish leave the North Sea for the coast of Norway. Where the brackish coastal water meets warm, deep, more saline water of the open sea, they form dense shoals at depths of between a hundred and two hundred feet. Norwegian herring spawn at random with little courtship behaviour, and the females lay between 21,000 and 47,000 eggs each, which sink and stick to shingle beds, rocks and shell banks. The relatively small number of sinking eggs, compared with the millions of floating ones laid by other types of fish, seems to indicate that they are relatively immune to predation, although haddock make a practice of following spawning herring. After eight or nine days at 50–57°F (10–14°C) the eggs hatch. Other races may shed eggs in water as cold as 32°F (0°C), developing much more slowly, but eggs fail to develop below this temperature. The larvae, at a quarter to a third of an inch long, rise to the light at the surface. They have no gills or mouth, feeding entirely on the remnants of their yolk sacs. A single fin runs down the back and over the tail. Initial growth is rapid and, at two or three months old and about half an inch long, they are feeding on planktonic plants and graduating to minute crustacean larvae. After a year they are two-inch replicas of their parents and assemble in shoals, often with young sprats. At two or three years old, having attained a length of eight inches, they leave the coast, joining the spawning migration at three to seven years old. After spawning, they scatter into deeper water to the north. Their movements are then closely followed by fishing vessels to the Arctic, into the Barents Sea, and back again. In contrast, the race which spawns at the entrance of the Baltic seldom strays far from this area.

Herrings and superstition

The movements of herring are notoriously capricious; they may disappear from once fruitful grounds for little apparent reason. Scottish highland tradition held that they abandoned waters where blood had been spilt. With the

advent of firearms, gunfire was blamed for dispersing the shoals and forbidden during the herring season. Then steamships bore the brunt of criticism for many years. Perhaps the most amusing story, recounted by the pioneer fish scientist Yarrell in 1842, tells of an Irish pastor who, considering his flock far too affluent on the proceeds of herring fishing, proposed a tithe on the catch. The herring failed to return to that part of the coast for many years.

Herring must be fished with various nets rather than baited lines, because they feed only upon the larger creatures of the animal plankton. All possible methods are employed – fixed 'keddle' nets of two to three-inch mesh are set on beaches, trawls by day and drift-nets by night take tons in the open sea, while whole shoals may be encircled by seine nets operated by one or more boats. Echo-location with sophisticated electronics is of great help, although seabird activity and local knowledge can help to find fish. A large shoal makes a dark patch in the water and 'boiling' water in the evening may betray a rising shoal below, because the herring release air from their swim-bladders in response to falling pressure. Nearly all clupeids follow the vertical migrations of the plankton, rising by night and going deeper by day. Experiments have been conducted whereby herring, once detected in sufficient quantity, are attracted to the mouth of a vast tube by the discharge of electricity, then simply pumped onto the deck of a factory ship. The total catch in the Atlantic and nearby seas is already two or three million tons per year, and shows few signs of falling off. Young herring are canned or ground for fish meal, while adults are cold- or warm-smoked, salted, canned, or sold fresh.

The herring and history
The herring fishery is centuries old and has at times exerted a considerable influence on the course of history. Many of the towns of the Atlantic and Channel seaboards coincide with the closest approaches of migrating herring to the shore. Hamburg, for instance, was founded as a herring port by Charlemagne in 809 AD. Ostend, Dunkirk, Etaples and Dieppe all followed, and some believe that the name Fécamp was derived from the Viking *Fisk havn* ('fish harbour'). These abundant fish have also been instrumental in starting wars: the Dutch war of 1652–54 was fought partly because the Dutch continually infringed what the English considered their own waters, in an attempt to capture the market left

Left: many sea fish swim in shoals, but those of certain members of the herring family are remarkable for their large size and extent. Herring shoals more than five miles long, containing hundreds of millions of individuals, have been seen in the North Sea. Forming shoals is instinctive behaviour in herrings and it gives each individual a better chance of survival from predators. It also means that each fish expends less energy in swimming than it would alone

open when the herring abandoned the Baltic in the fifteenth century. Even the Russo-Japanese war of 1902 was partly precipitated by the Japanese claim to the herring islands in Russian waters off Sakhalin Island.

Mass exploitation of a plankton-feeding fish need not trouble the sea angler since only two species of herring fall to rod and line in Europe. These are the allis and twaite shads, slightly larger than the herring, at up to two feet long, and displaying a variable number of black spots on the flanks. The twaite shad has six to ten spots, the allis shad one to six. A more definite means of identification is the number of gill rakers, which also shows the difference in their feeding habits. The twaite shad takes larger food, snapping at copepods and small crustaceans, as well as tiny fish. In consequence, it has only forty to sixty gill rakers in the first arch. The allis shad feeds on plankton and mounts a sieve of between ninety and 120 rakers. Both ascend rivers to spawn, but have become scarce in recent years owing to the pollution of inland waters. They are often taken on small ragworm and fragments of shellfish intended for mullet in estuaries.

The shads are what biologists call 'anadromous', from the Greek *ana*, upwards, and *dromos*, running, referring to their migration up rivers to spawn in fresh water. The North American shad (*Alosa sapidissima*) of the North Atlantic coast is unusually large for a clupeid – it can weigh as much as six pounds. It has been introduced by man into rivers of the Pacific coast. The Chinese herring (*Hilsa*) is the Oriental equivalent of the shads, travelling 1,000 miles or more up the Yangtze River to spawn. The gizzard shads of North America (*Dorosoma*) are found in muddy waters in rivers, estuaries and the sea. Their muscular stomachs seem to be adapted to deal with food that other fish would find indigestible.

Sprats and pilchards

The sprat is as important a link in the marine food chain as it is an item of human diet. It is a cold-water clupeid sharing much of its range with the herring. Usually caught at less than six inches long, it has a sharp keel of scales between the ventral and anal fins. It is taken near the coastline in summer at depths of between thirty and 150 feet and in winter down to about 450 feet. Like the herring, it feeds on plankton. Sprats spawn mainly in the south-eastern North Sea and Skaggerak, although local populations inhabit large fjords in Denmark and the Baltic. They lay 6,000 to 10,000 floating eggs, which are very vulnerable to wind and cold; catches each season reflect the weather between January and July of the previous year. Sprats are marketed fresh, canned, or cooked in oil as 'brisling'. Older fish are marinated and often sold as 'anchovies'.

Less tolerant of low temperatures, the pilchard (known as a sardine in its smaller stages) is the basis of extensive fisheries in and around the Mediterranean, while its closest relatives supply

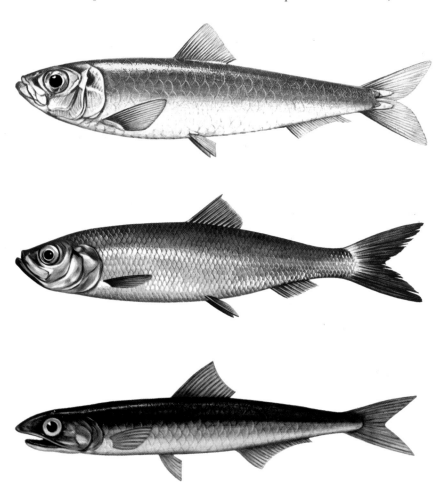

Left: three commercially important members of the Clupeidae, or herring family (not to scale). The pilchard (top), Sardinia pilchardus, *known as the sardine when young; the herring itself (middle),* Clupea harengus, *may be sold as whitebait when young; the anchovy (bottom),* Engraulis encrasicolus, *the most important commercial catch along the coast of South America.*
Right: the dense shoals formed by members of the herring family make them an easy prey for the nets of commercial fishing boats. However, they are notoriously fickle in their choice of breeding grounds, suddenly abandoning a particular area for no apparent reason

both food and fish meal in North America, Chile, South Africa, Japan and Australia. Pilchards have radial stripes on the gill covers and reach a maximum length of about ten inches. They move in enormous shoals of individuals of the same size and, like many herrings, gather into a writhing ball at the approach of danger – a manoeuvre singularly convenient for boats with encircling seine nets. They are also attracted to lights by night and congregate around baits of fish eggs. Pilchards spawn in the open sea, laying between 50,000 and 60,000 floating eggs off southern England from April to November, in the Bay of Biscay from December to February, or off Portugal from February to April. There is no clearly defined spawning season in the Mediterranean. After spawning, they move towards the coasts, north in summer, south in winter.

Anchovies

The anchovy is one of the least important clupeids in Europe, but it is essential to the economy of coastal South America. The fish reaches a maximum length of eight inches, and its lower jaw is set well back from the upper. It is one of the most numerous fish in the world. In small shoals, the sizes are mixed, with the smallest swimming near the surface to allow light to filter through the shoal. Large shoals are composed of fish of equal size. Unlike the herring, which snaps at selected members of the plankton, anchovies swim with their mouths open, taking everything. To ensure even distribution of food throughout the shoal, individuals take it in turn to circle backwards from the direction of travel, making a teardrop shape as they rejoin the rear. If the plankton is very dense, the shoal fans out to form an oval with its long axis at right-angles to the direction of travel. European anchovies haunt the Bay of Biscay and the Mediterranean, moving through the English Channel to spawn. Since their old grounds in the Ijsselmeer were reclaimed, they have taken to spawning in the Elbe estuary.

On the other side of the world in the rich waters of the Humboldt current off South America, anchovies (as four- to six-inch 'anchovetas') occur in their greatest concentrations. In the past they have been the food for millions of sea birds which in turn produce 'guano'. Thousands of tons of this excellent fertilizer were once collected and the birds were protected by law. In the early 1950s possible new applications for anchovetas were explored. Birds have to digest twenty tons of fish for every ton of guano produced, but the same amount of anchoveta can be ground to make four tons of meal. Combined with soya-bean meal, this can be marketed as feed for livestock. Between 1955 and 1964 the populations of Peru's ports quadrupled, and seven million tons of anchovetas were taken in a year, before legislation was introduced to limit the size of catches. The sea birds suffered, partially from a lack of food, but mainly, it is thought, from the accumulation of industrial poisons in the tissues of the fish. Anchovetas, like their fickle cousins the herrings, are also prone to abrupt changes of their migration routes – with disastrous consequences for both birds and fishermen.

Below: like other fish of the herring family, anchovies swim in large shoals. They feed on the minute floating life of the plankton, which they strain from the water by means of small projections across their gill openings known as gill rakers. Anchovies may reach a length of about eight inches

Viperfish and hatchetfish

Of the varied and numerous deep-sea fishes, the viperfish and hatchetfish are two of the more unusual and well studied forms. Although they are relatives of the salmon and herring, neither bear any outward resemblance to these fishes. Classed in the suborder Stomiatoidea, the closest relatives of the viper and hatchetfishes include the dragonfish, bristlemouths, snaggletooths and loosejaws.

The three species of viperfish, all of the genus *Chauliodus,* live in all seas of the world, at depths of 1,500 to 8,000 feet. They grow to a length of between six and ten inches although their long, eel-like bodies and heavy heads give them the appearance of larger fish. The fins are relatively small and transparent. Like the majority of deep-sea fishes, viperfish have light organs, or photophores, on their bodies, running in a double row along the lower flanks and back to the tail. In the darkness of the deep sea, the light produced chemically from these organs enables the fish to see prey and perhaps to avoid predators. There are also hundreds of photophores studding the roof of the mouth and inside of the eye sockets. The second ray of the dorsal fin is greatly extended and thread-like, with a light organ at its tip. This thread is dangled in front of the mouth and the luminous tip acts as a lure to small fish and crustaceans, which are enticed into the open and illuminated mouth.

The name 'viperfish' refers to the snake-like fangs which are long and curve back into the mouth. The two teeth at the front of the lower jaw are especially long and when the mouth is closed, these two fangs slip up along the sides of the head, outside the upper jaw.

Viperfish often swallow prey much larger than themselves. Like snakes, they have very distensible stomachs and their jaws are only loosely attached to the skull. When prey is to be swallowed, the upper jaw is pulled upwards and backwards and the lower jaw is shot outwards and downwards. The heart (located at the front of the body, near to the lower jaw) and the delicate gills are pulled outwards, thus protecting them from harm and leaving a clear passage for the struggling prey. Food is scarce in the depths and it must be quickly eaten and digested so that no opportunity is missed for further consumption.

Hatchetfish live at depths of between 300 and 1,500 feet in all tropical and temperate seas. The fish vary between one and two inches in length, the largest of the fifteen species, *Argyropelecus gigas,* measuring only three-and-a-half inches. The mouth is large, turned upwards and lined with many small sharp teeth. Hatchetfish migrate to the surface waters at night to feed on the tiny animals of the plankton. In their wake come viperfish and bristlemouths to feed on them. This daily vertical migration covers hundreds of feet.

The eyes of hatchetfish are remarkable. They are enormous and directed forwards on the head. Each eye is tubular with a large lens at the top of the tube and the retina, or light-sensitive layer, at its base. There is also a second retina lining the tube to make use of the little light available.

Below left: head of a viperfish, Chauliodus sloanei, *showing the snake-like fangs from which it takes its name. Below: hatchetfish,* Argyropelecus hemigymnus. *The upturned mouth is adapted to a world where food comes floating down as debris from above. The large eyes make best use of the little light present*

Salmon and trout

Salmon and their relatives, the trouts and chars, belong to the family Salmonidae. All the members of this family, which is part of the order Clupeiformes, are fish of the Northern Hemisphere and live primarily in cool waters, some within the Arctic Circle. They are perhaps best known as the inhabitants of lakes and fast-flowing rivers and streams in Europe, North America and Asia. Here they may often be seen, hanging motionless on the current or fighting their way powerfully upstream, and here too they often fall to the rod and line of the game fisherman.

Although some species spend their whole lives in fresh water, many spend much or most of their lives in the sea, entering fresh water only to spawn. Biologists term such species 'anadromous'. All salmon, with the exception of certain species that have become trapped in fresh water by changes in the earth's surface, and various species of trout and char fall into this category. A remarkable feature of salmon migration is the fact that the mature fish find their way back to the exact reach of a river or stream where they themselves were born. Thus they have not only to choose between the thousands of rivers which they might enter, but also to negotiate their way to a particular spot where they hatched several years before.

Biologists believe that the fish use various methods to navigate on their extraordinary journeys. It is possible that they use the sun and moon as guides in a similar way to birds. Also, it seems that a salmon is able to distinguish the taste of different waters as it nears its goal. The whole process of migration seems to be under the control of the thyroid glands. In an experiment, a coho salmon was injected with thyroid hormone – this caused it to seek sea water. When the injections ceased, the fish sought fresh water.

Distribution

There are two main groups of salmon, the Atlantic salmon and the Pacific salmon. The Pacific salmon can be distinguished from the Atlantic species and the trout by having a greater number of skeletal rays in the anal fin. The single species of Atlantic salmon, *Salmo salar*, is found around the coasts of the Atlantic Ocean. It ranges from the European Arctic Ocean to Iceland, Greenland, Quebec and northern Portugal. A few populations of Atlantic salmon became cut off from the sea during the glacial periods – examples are the entirely fresh-water salmon of Norway and Finland. The Pacific salmons, all of which belong to the genus *Oncorhynchus*, are separated into six species. The masu, or cherry salmon, *Oncorhynchus masu*, is restricted to the Asian side of the Pacific Ocean; the chum, or dog salmon, *O. keta*, is found from the Mackenzie and Lena Rivers in the Arctic, south to Japan and the Rogue River in Oregon;

the pink, or humpback salmon, *O. gorbuscha*, ranges from the Arctic to Japan and the Klamath River in California; the sockeye, or red salmon, *O. nerka*, ranges from the northern Bering Sea to Japan and the Columbia River on the Canadian–US border; the coho, or silver salmon, *O. kisutch*, is found from the Bering Sea to as far south as Japan and Monterey Bay in California; and the king, spring or chinook salmon, *O. tshawytscha*, ranges from the Yukon River in Alaska to China and the Sacramento River in California.

The amazing journey

Although the migrations of the various species of salmon differ in detail, the general story is the same for all of them.

Adult salmon live in the surface waters of the open ocean, where they hunt their prey – mainly smaller fish, such as sand eels and herrings, and also crustaceans. After spending between one and five years in the ocean, the salmon are ready to undertake their great voyage. The time of the year when they migrate depends on the species and also on local variations in the fish's environment. As the salmon head for the coast from their ocean feeding grounds, they stop eating and their digestive organs dwindle in size. During their time in the ocean, the fish have been feeding frequently and have built up large reserves of fat in their bodies, upon which they live during the rest of their lives. A portion of this food store is not converted into energy, but is used to make the eggs or sperm. As the fish near the coast, they undergo other changes, too. The colour of their bodies changes – from a silvery bluish-green to a brownish or greenish hue with red or orange mottling in the case of the Atlantic salmon. The male salmon develops a long curved hook or 'kype' on its lower jaw; the upper jaw also lengthens, but not nearly as much. Rival male salmon use their hooks as weapons when fighting for possession of a mate.

The spawning grounds of some salmon are located not far from the sea, but others may have to make a journey of 2,000 miles upstream to reach their birthplace. It is one of the mysteries of salmon migration that salmon fall to the baits offered by fishermen during the course of this journey, since they do not generally feed in fresh water. It is possible that the fish are motivated by some sort of curiosity when they take the bait.

In the autumn, on reaching the correct stretch of the correct stream, the female salmon digs a nest-hole or 'redd' in the gravel bed by sweeping her tail fin and the hind part of her body from side to side. She lays between 8,000 and 26,000 eggs in the redd, and the male swims past and fertilizes them. The eggs are heavier than water and slightly sticky, so that they remain embedded in the gravel throughout the winter months. Both

Right: a stirring sight – salmon fight their way against the powerful current of a waterfall on their journey from the ocean to the fresh-water spawning grounds where they were born

the male and female salmon are exhausted after their long journey and the effort of reproduction. All Pacific salmon, and many Atlantic salmon, die shortly after spawning, having been reduced to bags of bones floating downstream. Some of the Atlantic species, however, mostly females, recover from their ordeal and do reach the ocean once more. They are known to fishermen as 'kelts'. Some of these fish – a mere four to six per cent – return to spawn in their chosen streams a second time, while a few – perhaps one in a thousand – return to spawn a third time.

The young salmon usually emerge from the eggs about three months after they were laid, although the incubation rate depends on temperature and may take as little as sixty or as many as 200 days. The newly-hatched salmon, or 'alevins', which are about an inch long, live on the food which they carry with them in their yolk-sacs for several weeks before wriggling through the gravel to the surface waters to hunt their first prey – insect larvae and small worms. The salmon 'fry', as they are now called, grow rather slowly until they become 'parr' at the end of the second year, when they measure six inches in length. Later, the young fish, now known as 'smolt', begin to move towards the sea. On their migration downriver, they lose the greyish-blue spots on their sides, their flanks become silvery and the back darkens. As they reach the mouth of the river, various changes occur within their bodies to fit them for a life in salt water. When the smolt reach the estuaries, they change their diet, eating copepods and other small crustaceans.

The migration pattern of salmon differs in the different species. The humpback salmon, for instance, migrates eastwards as soon as it has hatched, whereas the Atlantic salmon does not move to the ocean until the end of its first year at the earliest, as with those in the region of the Rhine. Individuals in some northern localities, such as Norway, remain in fresh water for up to seven years.

The salmon and man

Although greatly prized as a sporting fish, the Atlantic salmon is not an important commercial fish compared to the Pacific species. There are a few commercial salmon fisheries for the Atlantic species, off Iceland, Newfoundland and the Gulf of St Lawrence.

The Pacific salmon are not only a favourite catch of the angler, but also important commercial fish – nearly 2,000 million pounds are caught annually, almost half this amount being pink salmon, one third chum salmon, and all but five per cent of the rest sockeye. At sea, salmon are mainly fished during their migrations towards the coasts. Nets used include drift nets and fixed nets or traps; they are also caught on floating long lines – up to several miles long – which bear large hooks baited with herring.

All countries fishing salmon have established strictly-defined 'close seasons' during which fish may not be caught, so overfishing is not a major problem. Also, there is an agreement between Canada and the United States that ensures that twenty per cent of each species of Pacific salmon are allowed to continue on their journeys to the spawning grounds. The greatest threat to the salmon stocks comes from the damming or diversion of streams and rivers and from the increasing pollution of both the ocean and fresh waters.

Trouts and chars

The so-called 'sea trout' is merely a form of the brown trout, *Salmo trutta*, of Europe that migrates from fresh water to the ocean like the salmon. Other individuals among the brown trout may move down from rivers into the estuaries to feed. Trout may be difficult to distinguish from salmon, but they generally have plumper bodies and are markedly spotted. They are popular sporting fish, being taken on artificial flies and spinners. The rainbow trout, *Salmo gairdneri*, which was introduced into Europe from California about 1890, also has a form, known as the steelhead trout, that migrates to the ocean. The handsome cut-throat trout, *Salmo clarkii*, of North America is another anadromous species.

In the southern parts of their range the chars, close relatives of the salmon and trout, inhabit deep cold lakes and rivers, but in more northerly regions, they migrate to the sea.

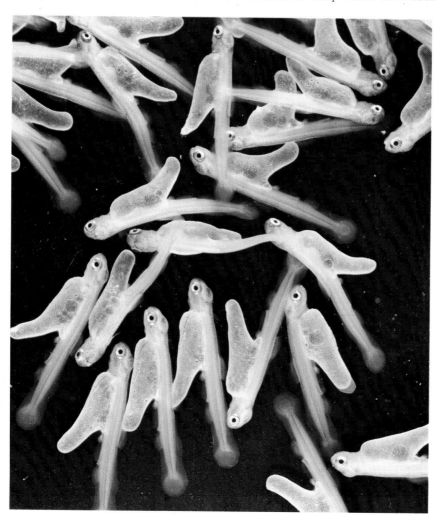

Below: young salmon, called alevins, four days after hatching. The yolk sacks attached to their bodies supply them with nourishment for the first few weeks

Eels

The sight of an eel wriggling through the damp grass of a river bank reminds many people more of a snake, but eels are fish; they are placed within the great group of bony fishes to which more familiar fish such as the salmon and herring belong. Typical fishes such as these have two sets of paired fins, just as other vertebrates have two pairs of limbs. These are the pectoral fins at the front end of the body, behind the gill openings, and the pelvic fins towards the rear. Most eels, however, are equipped with only the front pair. The moray eels lack even these. This modification of the normal fish form is an adaptation to the eels' way of life and method of swimming. Eels swim by undulations of the long dorsal fin running down their backs, which joins the anal fin and the much reduced tail fin and ventral fin.

Like most other fishes, eels breathe by extracting oxygen from the water with their gills, although freshwater eels can also breathe through their moist skins when travelling across damp ground. The gills are enclosed in gill pouches and open to the outside through a small slit on either side of the head. This is just in front of the pectoral fin, in those eels that have them.

In all eels, except for the freshwater eels, *Anguilla*, the smooth, muscular, snake-like body is covered by skin that is entirely without scales. Compared with other fish, eels have a much greater number of vertebrae, although the bones of the head, including those of the jaws, are reduced in number.

All true eels pass through a special larval stage known as the 'leptocephalus' (Latin for 'thin head', from their disproportionately small head). These tiny transparent creatures are very different from the adult eels into which they will grow, and they were once thought to be a com-

pletely different species from the adults. The larvae are very small; the leptocephalus of the common European freshwater eel, for example, hatches from the egg at about one-fifth of an inch long and grows to a length of about two and half inches. One exception to this was a larva measuring five feet in length that was recorded; this may have been the young of a giant eel that could have given rise to stories of huge sea serpents. Eels are classified by zoologists in the order Anguilliformes, sometimes known as the order Apoda (meaning 'without feet' and referring to their lack of hind fins). The order Anguilliformes is divided into a number of different families. Eels live in a wide range of environments, from lakes and streams far from the sea to the depths of the oceans. The different families may well have evolved from different groups.

Common eels

All eels are exclusively marine, except for a few, including all those in the family Anguillidae – the 'common' eels of North Africa, Europe, eastern North America, Asia and countries bordering the western Pacific Ocean. Common eels, of which there are a number of species, are probably nearest to other fishes, since they show the least modifications of the typical fish plan. For example, they have scales embedded in their skin, though these are tiny.

The life of the common eel follows a pattern which is the exact opposite of that of the salmon. While salmon spend their lives in the sea and enter fresh water only to spawn, the eels live in fresh or brackish waters and enter the sea to spawn. For this reason biologists term the common eel 'catadromous', in contrast to the salmon which is 'anadromous'. Like that of the salmon, the migration of the common eel takes the form of a long pilgrimmage to the place of its birth – in the case of the European and North American species this is the Sargasso Sea, an

Below: the common eel (Anguilla anguilla) is widely distributed in fresh water throughout Europe. This individual is a non-breeding 'yellow' eel. When mature, it will become a handsome silvery colour, and begin its long journey to the Sargasso Sea

area of relatively calm water, strewn with floating seaweed, near the middle of the North Atlantic. The adult eels do not return from this pilgrimmage.

The European eel, *Anguilla anguilla,* is a handsome fish which may attain a length of more than four feet. The adults live in estuaries, rivers, lakes and ponds. They are active mainly at night, feeding on fish and other small animals. The account which follows is primarily concerned with the life cycle of this species, although it gives an idea of the life history of other freshwater eels, such as the North American species, *Anguilla rostrata.*

The great voyage

The European eel has a remarkable life history. The tiny leptocephalus larvae hatch from the eggs during March and April in the Sargasso Sea at depths of from 300 to 1,000 feet, about 19,000 feet above the sea floor. They live in the surface waters, eating minute animals and plants of the floating plankton. At two months, they measure about one inch long; at eight months, they are one and three-quarter inches; at one and a half years, they have reached nearly three inches. This is when they are at their broadest, and most leaf-like. The body is crossed with numerous diagonal bands of muscle. As they grow the tiny leptocephali drift slowly with the Gulf Stream towards Europe. When they are three years of age they have shrunk slightly, so that they measure about two and half inches long. Now they begin to change into the young eels, or elvers. They are still transparent at this stage, and are often called 'glass eels'. After their three-year 2,500-mile journey across the Atlantic, they reach the European coast.

Then they move into the estuaries and up the rivers. This movement takes place at different times of the year, depending on how far the local-

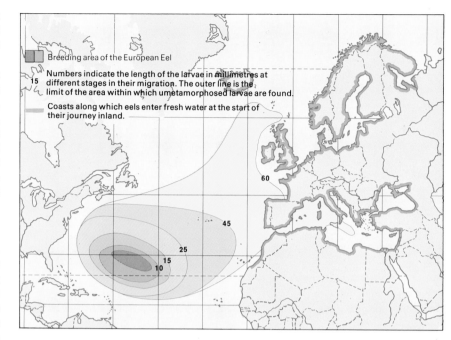

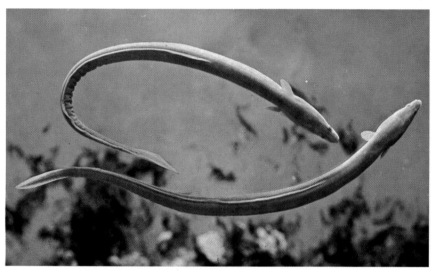

Top: this map shows the migration of the leptocephalus larvae of the common eel from the Sargasso Sea to the coasts of Europe. The figures indicate the sizes of the larvae in millimetres at various stages of their long journey across the Atlantic Ocean.
Above: young eels, or elvers – a later stage than the 'glass eels' (opposite).
Left: the conger eel differs from the common eel in its dorsal fin, which starts closer to the head, and in being entirely marine

ity is from the Sargasso. After a summer spent feeding, the elvers become darker. Some remain in the brackish waters of the estuaries, but others swim far upstream. The young eels begin to develop the pattern of tiny oval scales embedded in their skin.

By the first winter after they arrived at the coast, the young eels are about three inches long. They grow rapidly, for a year later they have attained seven inches.

During this period of feeding and growth, the elvers are known as 'yellow eels'. They have greyish-brown backs, and yellowish bellies and sides. Not all the young eels look exactly the same. There are two extremes – some with pointed snouts, which feed on small creatures such as worms, shrimps and insect larvae, and some with broader snouts, which eat larger prey, such as crabs, gobies and sticklebacks. This just seems to be an adaptive difference to different diets; there are many intermediate forms between the two extremes. The yellow

eels spend several years living in rivers, lakes or ponds.

Each year, as the weather grows colder, the eels swim to deeper water where the frost cannot penetrate. They spend the winter buried in the bottom mud.

When they are from four to twenty years old, the yellow eels undergo several changes. The age at which this happens depends on the sex, males undergoing it earlier than the females, which may not mature until twenty years old. The eyes become larger and more bulging, the head becomes more pointed, the belly changes from yellowish to a shiny, silvery-white colour. The eel gradually stops feeding and the gut atrophies. The body becomes firm and muscular. At this stage, the eels are known as 'silver eels' and can be as long as thirty-nine inches. The sex organs are still small and immature.

During September and October, the silver eels migrate downriver to the sea, sometimes crossing moist grass and travelling along ditches, and

Below: common eels pass through this 'glass eel' stage during their metamorphosis from the leptocephalus larvae into young eels. The backbone and internal organs are clearly visible through the fish's transparent body wall

eventually disappear into the deep waters of the Atlantic Ocean. From then on, the eel's life is largely a mystery, because of the great difficulty of following its movements once it passes from inland waters to the deep ocean.

The sex organs must have matured by the time the eels reach the Sargasso, but exactly when is not known. Sexually mature males have been found a few times in European coastal waters.

Before their great journey, the eels build up a large reserve of fats within their bodies. This must sustain them as they swim and is also needed to build up sperm or eggs. It is probable that they do not stop to feed on their journey; silver eels have lived without feeding for as long as four years in an aquarium.

It is not certain how long the eels take to reach the Sargasso. If they reach the spawning grounds in the spring following the autumn in which they set off, they must swim at a rate of approximately nineteen miles per day. But it is possible that they may spend an extra year on their great journey. One thing is certain – the eels that reach the Sargasso all die after spawning. The effort of the long journey and the breeding itself must prove too much for the eels. Eels prevented from moving out to sea have reached ages of from twenty-five to fifty years.

Another problem puzzling biologists is how the eels belonging to the two different species, European and American, know which way to migrate. The American larvae have to migrate west, and the European ones east. The American

species is very similar to the European; the main difference is in the number of vertebrae making up the backbone – more in the European than in the American species. Because no adult European eels have been seen returning to the Sargasso Sea to breed, some biologists have suggested that there may be no such thing as a European eel and that there is only one species, the American eel. This would produce all the eggs and young. The European eel might be merely a local variation due to differences in the temperature of the water where it hatched. It swims to Europe, for some reason, and dies without producing any young. The other kind – the American – swims to the east coast of North America, but does return to the Sargasso and reproduces. Fisheries biologists, however, tend to disbelieve this theory.

Conger eels

The congers (family Congridae) live in temperate and tropical waters of the Atlantic, Pacific and Indian Oceans. The common conger eel (*Conger conger*) is distributed widely around the Mediterranean, Atlantic, North Sea, Baltic and North American coasts. It is large (measuring up to nine feet long and weighing up to 160 pounds) and is a voracious predator, feeding on herring, cod, lobsters, crawfish and cuttlefish. The common conger is usually found over rocky coastal waters, at depths from the surface to 300 feet. It likes to insinuate its body into crevices between the rocks, lying in wait for unsuspecting prey. Like the freshwater eel, it spawns in deep

Below: the moray eel Gymnotora moringa, which lives along the coast of Florida. Below right: a moray eel from the Red Sea. Morays are fierce predators, seizing fish that swim too near their hiding-places among the rocks or the coral reefs

parts of the Atlantic Ocean, and has a similar transparent leptocephalus larva. The conger lays from three to eight million eggs. The eel dies after spawning. Unlike *Anguilla*, it is totally marine.

Moray eels and others

The morays (family Muraenidae) live in warm or tropical seas, especially among coral reefs. They have large, sharp teeth and very small gill openings, and neither pectoral nor pelvic fins. Some have poison fangs – in some species, the venom has proved fatal to man. They are fierce predators, lurking among the corals and sponges of reefs and seizing and devouring the reef fishes. The largest species of moray eels measure from six to ten feet, or longer. They are a wide range of colours, plain, mottled, or marked with bold patterns. Morays are sometimes called 'painted eels' because of their bright colours. The dragon moray of the Pacific, for example, is reddish-brown with white spots and bars and dark blotches.

Among the many different species of eel is the pugnose eel, which is placed in the family Simenchelidae. It leads a semi-parasitic life in deep waters, boring into the bodies of large fishes and feeding on their contents. It shows various adaptations to its strange way of life. For example, the skin contains a large number of mucus glands which produce a slimy secretion. This reduces the friction between the eel and its host's body wall, so that it can enter its victim more easily.

The snipe eels or thread-eels of the suborder Nemichthyoidea include deep-sea species with huge mouths, no paired fins and tiny eyes at the extreme front of the head. Many have long tails and threadlike jaws in a long beaklike snout. These deep-sea eels are rarely seen in an undamaged condition out of water, because their bodies are exceptionally fragile.

Just as the true eels are sometimes wrongly credited with affinities to snakes, many other sea fish may be wrongly identified as eels. Hagfish, lampreys, ling, hake and pipefish are described elsewhere in this chapter. Other fish, not members of the order Apoda either, are even called 'eels'. Prominent among them are the gulper eels of the order Lyomeri. These are deep-sea fish which may occasionally grow to a length of six feet. In spite of their enormous gaping mouths, they appear to feed exclusively on plankton. More familiar, because they are sometimes found buried in the sand between tide-marks, are the sand-eels. These fish are members of the Perciformes and, like the gulper eels, are not related to the true eels, although their slender eel-like bodies bear a striking resemblance to the latter in appearance.

Below: this moray eel belongs to the genus Muraena. *It has been recorded a few times from British coastal waters, but is widespread in the Mediterranean. Morays live in warm seas, mainly in the tropics and subtropics. Below right: a moray belonging to the genus* Gymnotora *from the island of Palau in the Pacific Ocean*

Flying fish

A familiar sight to passengers aboard ocean liners is small fish leaping out of the water, often to a height of fifteen feet, and gliding gracefully through the air, with wing-like fins outstretched. The flights, at speeds in excess of thirty m.p.h., cover distances of several hundred feet. These so-called flying fish live in all tropical and warm temperate waters of the world. Their flights are usually solitary, but sometimes a whole school of these fish take to the air at once. Such spectacular displays have a serious purpose for, lurking beneath the waves, are bonito, albacore and dolphin fish, voracious predators which feed on flying fish. However, in their efforts to evade the enemy below, flying fish are often seized in the air by frigate birds, fairy terns and gulls.

The flying fish belong to the order of bony fish called the Beloniformes, named after the chief representative, the needlefish or garfish *Belone*. Other members of the order are the half-beaks and the sauries or skippers. All have one feature in common. The lower jaw is longer than the upper jaw at some stage during their lives. Adult garfish have long beak-like jaws of almost equal length. The half-beaks, as their name implies, have unequal jaws, the lower one being greatly elongated. These fish frequent coastal and brackish waters. They often swim at the surface, feeding on insects. The beak looks like a piece of driftwood and a red spot at its tip has led biologists to think that it may act as a lure to insects which are then snapped up.

Flying fish are members of the family Exocoetidae. They do not have the characteristic beak of their relatives, but the young of at least one species have an elongated lower jaw, betraying their affinities to the garfish and half-beak families. The species is the four-inch sharpchin, *Fodiator acutus*, of the Indo-Pacific, generally considered to be the most primitive member of the group.

All members of the Beloniformes have the ability to make spasmodic leaps out of the water and skitter over the surface at great speed. The half-beaks especially can make aerial excursions and some can fly for distances of fifty yards or so. But flying fish have perfected this mode of travel and their bodies have become adapted accordingly.

Varying from about four inches to eighteen inches in length, the fifty or so species of flying fish are sometimes called the 'little bluebirds of the sea'. This popular name refers to their flying habits and to the colour of their bodies which is a metallic blue or bluish-green on the back, fading to a silvery white on the underside. The pectoral fins are placed high on the sides of the body and are greatly enlarged, in some species reaching as far as the base of the tail. Although they cannot flap their 'wings' like birds, the broad pectoral fins support the fish in the air in a similar way to the wings of a glider. The pelvic fins may also be enlarged and are set well back on the underside of the body for balance. The tail or caudal fin is sickle-shaped, the lower lobe being the longer of the two.

On the basis of the enlargement of the fins, flying fish are divided into two types – the two-winged and the four-winged types. In the former, only the pectoral fins are long and broad. The commonest flying fish of the Atlantic, *Exocoetus volitans*, has two wings. The four-winged species have both the pectoral and pelvic fins enlarged. The Californian flying fish, *Cypselurus californicus*, is an example. This species is found off the coast of California, where its aerial displays are a noted tourist attraction and, at eighteen inches long, it is the giant of the family. It is fished commercially in these waters and its flesh is delicate and palatable.

The flight of a flying fish begins underwater. The fish swims upwards towards the surface, at a speed of about 40 m.p.h., its body at an angle of 15° to the horizontal. As the fish leaves the water, the lower lobe of the tail fin vibrates rapidly from side to side, at a rate of some fifty beats a second. This vigorous movement leaves a V-shaped wake as the fish zig-zags across the surface. The pectoral fins unfold, stretching out at right-angles to the body, and the fish becomes airborne. In the four-winged species, the pelvic fins are spread at

Below: a flying fish of the four-winged type. The 'wings' are in fact elaborate developments of the normal pectoral and pelvic fins

the last moment and the tail is raised clear of the water.

An average flight lasts between four and ten seconds, at a height of three feet and covering a distance of about fifty yards. At the end of the flight, the fish may dive head-first into the sea, or it may do a belly flop or even land on its back. Very often, a second flight is initiated by closing the pelvic fins, thus lowering the lower lobe of the tail back into the water. The motive force provided by the tail's sculling motion lifts the fish into the air again. The longest flight recorded lasted some forty-two seconds, covering over 1,000 yards and involved more than ten such successive take-offs. If the fish is flying into the wind, it may be carried to great heights. Some-

times, flying fish land on the decks of ships some thirty-six feet above the water.

For many years there was controversy as to whether the fins were flapped during take-off and flight. Because of the speed involved, observation with the naked eye is impossible. Fortunately, the invention of ultra high-speed photography by electronic flash in the late 1930s put an end to the debate. By this method, multiple exposures are made at intervals of a fraction of a second, enabling one to study the successive movements of an animal in motion. Such photographs proved that flying fish do not flap their fins but glide with their wings held rigid.

There are other kinds of fish that fly. The flying gurnards of the family Dactylopteridae, for example, have long pectoral fins and can glide for short distances. But their flights are spasmodic, of short duration and clumsy in comparison to the flying fishes and, unlike the flying fish, they spend much of their time feeding on the seabed.

Beside their flight, little is known about the biology of flying fish. They feed on the tiny animals of the plankton, such as copepods and shrimps, and also on small fishes. Details of their reproduction are little known. They make nests among seaweed by binding the weed together with sticky threads and the eggs are laid there. Those species that live in the Atlantic seem to have their breeding grounds amongst the sargassum weeds in mid-ocean. The young of most species have long barbels that grow from the lower jaw. The significance of these appendages is not known but they are not present in the adults.

Above: a two-winged flying fish, Exocoetus volitans, *of the Atlantic, a familiar sight on Atlantic crossings. Left: a flying fish airborne over the Red Sea. The purpose of these flights is to escape from predators.*

Codfish

The codfish family, or Gadidae, are among the most important food fish in the world and, as such, they are among the most familiar, especially on either side of the Atlantic Ocean. Commercial fishermen land more than ten million tons of codfish every year, almost a fifth of the world's total fishery yield. Besides the Atlantic cod (*Gadus morhua*) itself, called the codling when it is young, the family includes the haddock, pollack, coalfish, whiting, ling and hake. All of these fish, classed in the order Gadiformes, are valued as food and as sport for the sea angler.

Nearly all the members of the cod family are marine fishes of cold and temperate waters, mainly restricted to the Northern Hemisphere. Their fins have soft rays and the ventral pair are set in front of the pectorals, on or near the throat. All are voracious feeders using their many taste buds to find their prey. The Atlantic cod, for example, has taste buds scattered on its lips, on its threadlike barbel, on its fins and its body.

The Atlantic cod
The Atlantic cod is the most familiar and widespread of the family. It is a round-bodied, large-headed fish with a pronounced snout and a barbel on its chin. It has three large fins on its back, with two in line below the body, and a pair near the throat. It lives over almost all types of sea bed, except muddy ones, in water at a temperature of between 32 and 43°F. Its colour varies with its habitat. In the algal zones it has brown or red marbled patterns on its green-grey background colour; among the underwater 'meadows' of eel-grass these are green, and in deep water or over sand they become pale grey. Although one extraordinary six-foot long specimen has been trawled which weighed 211 pounds, most of the cod that are caught weigh from three to twenty-five pounds.

Atlantic cod live on the continental shelves at depths ranging from 60 to 250 feet. The main populations centre around the North Sea, Norway, Bear Island, Labrador, Iceland, Greenland and Newfoundland. There is a closely-related species in the Pacific, as yet unexploited by man. Some Atlantic cod never leave their home waters, but large numbers migrate several hundred miles from feeding to spawning areas. Around England, for instance, the resident cod may be taken over deep, rocky ground all the year round, but inshore cod-fishing awaits the arrival in autumn and early winter of large numbers of migratory 'green' cod.

The Atlantic cod eats nearly anything that lives or moves and is small enough to take. It prefers herring, capelin (small, salmon-like shoaling fish) haddock and sand eels, but also eats squid, crabs, prawns, mussels and worms.

In open water, cod and many other gadids are caught in trawls. This method of fishing is so much used for taking cod that the pocket at the tapered end of the net is known as the 'cod-end'. Over rough ground, long lines bearing hundreds of hooks are set. These usually take slightly larger fish. Inshore gill nets and fixed traps also catch fair numbers. Cod flesh is very easily dried and salted, and many cod make their way to the

Below: the cod is a member of the family Gadidae. The fish has a pronounced snout and a barbel on its chin. It has three large fins on its back, two on the underside and a pair near the throat. The colour of the fish varies with its habitat

markets of the tropics in this form. In more northerly latitudes, people usually buy cod after they have been frozen and filleted.

Such intensive fishing is made possible only by the cod's prolific breeding. According to size, one female may lay from half a million to nine million eggs, usually in water at a temperature of from 4 to 6°C. These rise to the surface and drift with the plankton, hatching when two to four weeks old. The young move to the bottom after three to five months. Those of oceanic cod swim deep, while those of coastal types take to shallow water. They mature when they are four to five years old, or about two to three feet long.

The haddock

The haddock is a smaller fish than the cod, and is distinguished from it by its more streamlined shape and a large black spot, known as Saint Peter's thumbmark, above the pectoral fins. It inhabits deeper water and ranges from the Arctic, down both sides of the Atlantic, into the English Channel, but becomes scarce farther south. There have, however, been quite large catches of haddock as far south as the south coast of England, and the population appears to be shifting. There are signs of acute overfishing in the North Sea. Although haddock reach forty-four inches and thirty-six pounds weight, they are usually taken when between two and four pounds, and a good catch on rod and line weighs between five and ten pounds. Haddock live close to the bottom at depths of 40 to 600 feet, feeding on crustaceans, brittle stars, worms and shellfish, and occasionally hunting small fish. They are seldom caught from the shore, except where it drops away very sharply to deep water, but deep, sheltered bays can hold huge concentrated shoals. During the winter, they move to spawning grounds in the northern North Sea, seeking areas of high salinity to lay eggs between March and June.

Pollack and coalfish, the midwater predators

among the cod family, are the subjects of much confusion, for they look superficially alike and rejoice in a multitude of local names. The pollack, or lythe, is distinguished from its congenor, the coalfish, or saithe, by looking at the lateral line. On the pollack this looks like a raised seam, bending downwards behind the shoulder. On the coalfish, it is straight. Moreover, the pollack's lower jaw is protuberant.

Above: the pollack closely resembles its relative, the coalfish. However, the pollack's lateral line is not straight, as in the coalfish, and its lower jaw protrudes slightly. Left: the ling has a long thin body which gives it an eel-like appearance. The fish has a single barbel on its chin and an impressive array of sharp teeth. Below: the hake is a slender fish which has a wider mouth and is more silvery than the ling. It is a deep-water fish with an excellent flavour

Left: The three-bearded rockling has two barbels on the upper lip and one on the chin. The first dorsal fin is modified into a sensory organ

Pollack and coalfish

The pollack is a big-eyed, streamlined, dark fish, growing to over twenty pounds. It is usually deep grey to green on the back, grading to silver on the sides, although gold and copper coloured specimens occur in southern coastal waters. It inhabits the western Atlantic from Norway to Spain; some pollack are also found in the Mediterranean. It feeds from near the surface to a depth of 600 feet, moving down in strong light, and upwards at dawn and dusk. Pollack are exclusively predatory, and may be taken by drifting, trolling (fishing with a moving line) or spinning with live fish or artificial lures. The rubber eel and spoon type of lures prove particularly effective. Pollack live in different places according to the season. After their spawning journey from March to May, they live over rock, especially pinnacle rocks and large reefs. They disperse as the season goes on, and by autumn are scattered over many different sorts of seabed.

The coalfish has a more northerly distribution than the pollack, reaching the coasts of America where, to confuse the terminology still further, it is known as pollock. There is a sharp distinction between the behaviour and habitat of young and old coalfish. The youngsters of up to five pounds, known as billet, move in large shoals and will hunt in shallow, coastal waters. Older fish, reaching over three feet and around thirty pounds, live in water not less than 100 feet deep,

seldom feeding on the bottom. Billet eat crabs, shrimps and starfish. The adults take mainly fish, following shoals of sprats and herrings, and harrying them from below with such speed that they often leap clear of the water, the resultant commotion attracting hordes of gulls.

Less spectacular, but forming part of an important fishery, the whiting is a deep-bodied, silver to green fish with an elongated first anal fin and a black spot at the base of the pectorals. It reaches a length of about two feet in the northern part of its range, but is usually taken at around a foot. It is very common, frequents shallower water than most of its relatives, and lives over clean seabeds of sand or mud, feeding in low midwater. It spawns from January to September and young whiting, like the young of haddock and cod, often shelter among the tentacles of jellyfish, particularly *Cyanea*, deriving some protection from it and probably eating its eggs. They do not seem immune to the jellyfish's stings, so this proves a hazardous shelter. Whiting feed on any small prey, and provide consistent sport from piers in winter and boats in summer, often when other fishing is slack. Pout and poor-cod have a similar distribution and are often caught at the same time as whiting.

Ling and hake

Several members of the cod family – the ling, hake, and rockling – do not have the typical cod fin pattern. They have elongated second dorsal

Above: the pout or bib is a deep-bodied gadid with a conspicuous barbel on the chin. It is one of the British gadids with the most southerly distribution and is found in the western Mediterranean and off Spain. The fish is used only as fishmeal

and anal fins which, combined with their long, thin bodies, can give the fish, particularly the ling, an eel-like appearance.

There are three species of ling, ranging from the Arctic to the Mediterranean in deep water, usually from 300 to 2,000 feet. Their colour varies from grey to bronze and they grow to seven feet long and weigh a hundred pounds. Ling have a single long barbel on the chin. They live over rocky seabeds and around wrecks, where they hunt other fish, especially dab, haddock and mackerel as well as prawns and octopus. They are armed with an impressive array of very sharp teeth, and should be handled with care. Ling lay an extraordinary number of eggs; one 100-pound female ling was found to contain over 160 million of them.

The hake is wider-mouthed and more silvery than the ling, and feeds by night. It has become a progressively rarer catch since the advent of sophisticated commercial fishing gear. It lives at 300 – 2,400 feet, and lives by hunting all fish, as well as its own fry. Many fish practise cannibalism, but few do so to the same extent as the hake, which may make up a fifth of its diet with its own kind. Hake seldom exceed twenty-five pounds. The torsk is the only fish in this group to have its tail fused with the upper and lower fins. It occurs within a narrow belt on the borders of the Arctic, living over rough seabeds and feeding on bottom-living fish and crustaceans. Perhaps the least significant of the cod group are the rocklings, small ling-like fish that inhabit rocky coastal waters throughout the cod range. They are distinguished by a variable number of barbels on the head and can be used as bait.

Below: cod and many other gadids are caught in trawls. This method of fishing is so much associated with cod that the pocket at the tapered end of the net is called the 'cod-end'

Seahorses and pipefish

The seahorses are among the most bizarre, yet elegant, of all sea creatures. The horse-like head has a long, tubular snout and is mounted on an upright body, about four inches in length. This tiny frame is encased in a suit of bony armour and terminates in a long prehensile tail, like that of a monkey. Despite their strange appearance, the various species of seahorse are true bony fishes, like the cod and the bass. They are part of the order Gasterosteiformes which also includes the trumpetfish and the cornetfish.

The pipefishes are more conventional in appearance, but they are closely related to the seahorses and share the same family, Sygnathidae, within the Gasterosteiformes. They also display a similarity in their breeding habits. As their name suggests, pipefishes have slender, elongated bodies, giving them an eel-like look. However, the dorsal fin is shorter than that of an eel and is situated on the middle of the back. The pipefish's body is covered by bony plates, like the seahorse, and the snout is extended into a flexible tube with the mouth at the tip.

Seahorses and pipefish are shallow-water dwellers, living amongst the kelp or the eel- and turtle-grass near the shore. Several species of pipefish are found around the British coast. They include the five-inch-long worm pipefish and the great pipefish, which reaches a length of eighteen inches. Seahorses prefer warmer, more southerly

waters. The common seahorse, *Hippocampus guttulatus*, for example, lives off the shores of south-western Europe and in the Mediterranean Sea. The North American seahorse ranges down the eastern seaboard of the United States, from Cape Cod to Florida. There are twenty species in all, half of which live in the Indo-Australian region. Others live off the Atlantic coasts of Europe, Africa and North America, with two species on the Pacific coast of America.

Pipefish are masters of camouflage as they can blend so effectively with their surroundings. With bodies vertical and motionless in the water,

often with the head downwards, pipefish are indistinguishable from the blades of seaweed among which they hide. Seahorses can be equally well hidden. They are often coloured green or brown to match the weeds, and knobs and spines grow out from their bony skeletons, breaking up their general outlines and making them more difficult to see. They anchor themselves by wrapping their flexible tails around the weeds and floating upright in the water, wafting gently in the current. The Australian seahorse is a piece of living camouflage. Long leaf-like appendages grow from its body, making it look like a frond of brown seaweed.

Seahorses swim in a vertical position, rapidly beating the small pectoral fins on their cheeks and the single sail-like dorsal fin set on their backs. The supporting bony rays inside the fins oscillate like metronomes at a rate of seventy beats per second, propelling the little animal along. Pipefish swim in a similar manner, but they can move more quickly by throwing their long bodies into S-shaped curves like the sinuous motions of an eel.

Pipefish and their relatives feed on small fish, crustaceans and the eggs of sea animals. The tube-like snout acts like a pipette and the victims are sucked into the mouth by strong inhalent breaths. The snout also makes a fine probing instrument and is poked into crevices and into the sand to find food.

Probably the most remarkable thing about sea-

Above left: the eyes of a seahorse are mounted on turrets and can move independently of each other.
Left: pipefish blend so well with their surroundings that they are virtually indistinguishable from the seaweed among which they hide

horses and pipefish is their breeding habits. The usual sexual roles are reversed. It is the male which broods the eggs, in a pouch on his belly, and takes care of the young until they are grown-up.

In the case of the seahorse, mating follows an elaborate courtship dance in which the female takes the active part. Clicking sounds are made throughout the ritual as the seahorses toss their heads and rattle the bony plates of their bodies. Then, the female transfers her eggs to the pouch on the belly of her mate. Hundreds of eggs can be accommodated in the pouch and the male of one species goes around collecting eggs from many females in the area.

The eggs are brooded for about three or four weeks, at the end of which they hatch out as miniature adults. The pouch of the male seahorse is comparable to a womb. The walls of the pouch form a placenta-like membrane which grows between the eggs, providing them with nourishment and a plentiful supply of oxygen. This 'placenta' is shed after the birth of the young. While giving birth, the male goes through a series of convulsive movements, discharging the young, a few at a time through a tiny hole at the top of the pouch. The baby seahorses are about half an inch long at birth. The first thing that they do after birth is to swim to the surface and gulp air to fill their swimbladders. They grow rapidly and within two months they are over two inches in length.

The male pipefish does not go through these birth pangs. The walls of its pouch simply fold back and the young are released. They may return to their father's pouch to seek shelter if they are attacked. Aristotle's description of the birth of pipefish is very dramatic. He tells of the belly of *Belone* (the Greek name for the pipefish) bursting asunder and the ova being released through the vicious gash, which heals over the course of time.

Left: a seahorse wafting gently in the current, anchored to a weed by its tail. The colours of seahorses vary widely but are mostly light to medium brown, scattered with small white spots and often there are ornamental fleshy strands

Barracudas

The members of the family Sphyraenidae, the barracudas, are long, streamlined predators, mainly confined to tropical and subtropical seas. In appearance barracuda somewhat resemble the pike of rivers and lakes in Europe and North America, but the two are not closely related. The barracuda family belong to the order Mugiliformes, which they share with certain other less celebrated fishes. The chief reason for the barracuda's fame is its reputation as a maneater which, among sea fishes, is rivalled only by that of maneating sharks.

However, like sharks, not all of the twenty or so species of barracuda are equally dangerous. They include the barracouta or spet of the Mediterranean and eastern Atlantic which runs to a length of five feet or more, and the sennet of the north-western Atlantic which rarely exceeds eighteen inches. But the mightiest member of the family is the great barracuda, picuda or becuna (*Sphyraena barracuda*), which attains a size in excess of eight feet. It is to the great barracuda that the responsibility falls for nearly all the recorded attacks on human beings.

The great barracuda is aptly named, for it is an immense fish, larger than some sharks. It roams the waters of tropical and sub-tropical seas the world over. Strangely enough, however, it is more dangerous to man in some parts of the world than in others. Around Hawaii, for instance, it appears to be comparatively docile. It hunts both singly and in shoals. Young adults swim in company, but larger individuals separate themselves from the pack and become lone wolves.

There are a large number of reports to indicate that barracuda possess a fair measure of cunning. When hunting in shoals, they have often been seen to herd the smaller species of fish, that are their principal prey, into a confined space. The barracuda then prevent their escape while they feed at their leisure. Many people have watched barracuda lying around the edges of fish shoals. From time to time a single barracuda will dart into the middle of the shoal and emerge with a victim in its jaws to resume its place on guard.

The larger, solitary specimens may be observed lurking around coral reefs, hanging almost motionless in the water, until a potential meal ventures within range; whereupon they dart forward with lightning speed – a pattern of behaviour similar to that of pike in freshwater.

It is the lone-wolf barracuda that pose the greatest threat to man. Like all such reputations, that of the barracuda may have been subject to some exaggeration. Statistically, sharks are probably more to be feared than barracuda. But a number of attacks on bathers, formerly attributed to sharks, have subsequently been put down to barracuda. Moreover, barracuda hunt by sight. Their keen eyesight enables them to detect prey from far away and they are particularly attracted, like other predatory fish, by the glint

of metal that resembles a small fish. Consequently, they are often lured by the presence of a skin diver wearing breathing apparatus. Often, however, they do no more than follow the diver around, observing him with curiosity. But to be stalked in such fashion by an eight-foot long barracuda is, of itself, an unnerving experience.

When it strikes, the barracuda attacks quickly and takes a single mouthful in its sharp teeth. It seldom repeats the attack and consequently it is not likely to be fatal. However, swimmers standing in as little as twelve inches of water have been unlucky enough to have all the flesh torn from their lower leg.

Whereas its feeding habits are well known, the breeding habits of the barracuda are more of a closed book. We can only conjecture that spawning takes place in deep water.

Barracuda are edible, but fishermen in most parts of the world treat them with respect. Catching barracuda is a dangerous way to make a living. However, such a large and powerful fish provides excellent sport for the angler.

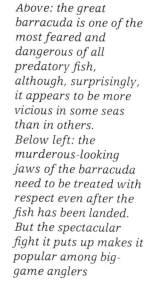

Above: the great barracuda is one of the most feared and dangerous of all predatory fish, although, surprisingly, it appears to be more vicious in some seas than in others.
Below left: the murderous-looking jaws of the barracuda need to be treated with respect even after the fish has been landed. But the spectacular fight it puts up makes it popular among big-game anglers

Sea basses and groupers

'Sea bass' and 'grouper' are names given to several members of the family Serranidae. Other species in this group are the wreckfish, jewfish, soapfish and blue-spotted argus. The whole family belongs to the order Perciformes. Among the familiar freshwater fish in this order are the perches and the North American sunfishes. The latter include two species that are called black basses and there are a few freshwater species in the Serranidae, but the two families are distinct.

All the Serranidae exhibit spiny rays in the dorsal pelvic and anal fins which are one of the principal distinguishing characteristics of the Perciformes. The spines of the dorsal fin are erected when the fish is threatened and they may inflict an injury if it is not handled with care.

The Serranidae are a large family of which the majority of members are found in the tropics. They are rapacious predators, feeding on marine invertebrates and other fish. The largest groupers are reputed to have swallowed skin divers in one gulp—a feat made possible by the cavernous mouths which are another feature of the family—although there is little concrete evidence to support this claim.

Many of the Serranidae are valuable food fish and they are also highly esteemed by sportsmen. The European sea bass and the North American striped bass are favourites with rod-and-line anglers, while the large groupers are a popular quarry of underwater spearfishermen in tropical seas.

Poor man's salmon

The European sea bass, *Morone labrax*, is a handsome, muscular fish, attaining a weight of about twenty pounds. It is common along the Atlantic coastline of Europe and in the Mediterranean. It is sometimes called the 'poor man's salmon' because it bears a superficial resemblance to the salmon, not only in appearance, but also as food and as a sporting quarry for anglers. Like the salmon, the bass enters fresh water and large numbers of small fish known as 'school bass' are sometimes encountered quite far inland. However, the migrations of bass are much less extensive than those of the salmon.

It is in summer that the bass move close inshore. They show a particular liking for rough water, in the vicinity of heavy surf or strong

Below: groupers are a popular quarry among sportsmen in tropical seas. They grow to a weight of 800 pounds and perhaps large enough to swallow a diver in one gulp

tidal currents. Here they pursue the huge shoals of herring and mackerel fry, collectively known as whitebait. Adult mackerel engage in the same pursuit and large bass are not averse to gulping down a whole mackerel when the opportunity presents itself. Most bass hunt in shoals, but older specimens may be solitary.

Bass are believed to spawn a few eggs at a time in estuaries and bays. Bass are slow developers and because of their slow reproductive cycle the fish stocks can easily be harmed. It may take a bass as long as six years to reach sexual maturity and a ten-pound specimen may be twenty years old. Consequently large bass have become rare fish in some areas owing to pollution or over-fishing.

The North American striped bass, *Roccus saxatilis,* is a close relative of the European species and they share many features of their appearance and behaviour. However, as the name suggests, the North American species has distinctive horizontal stripes along the back

and flanks. The striped bass is a native of the Atlantic coastline of North America, but during the nineteenth century it was transported over-land to the Pacific where it has spread and flourished.

Groupers

The groupers are predominantly fish of warm seas. Their English name originated in what they are called in Portugal, *garupa,* and not in any tendency to swim in groups. Groupers range in size from the diminutive golden striped grouper, *Grammistes sexlineatus,* which is about five inches long, to the giant Queensland grouper, *Epinephelus lanceolatus,* which may be twelve feet long and weigh half a ton. Like bass, they are voracious carnivores, but groupers are generally more stealthy in their feeding habits and they are often encountered lurking among the formations of tropical coral reefs. They are inquisitive fish and will approach divers under-water, quite unafraid.

Right: a Mediterranean grouper, Epinephelus guaza, *sometimes called the dusky perch, sports its coat of blotches, matching the seaweed-covered rocks. Below: the common bass, or sea perch, lives in the Atlantic. It grows to a length of about three feet and its pink flesh is covered by silvery-grey scales. Its diet consists of crustaceans, such as shrimps and crabs, and small fish*

Many groupers are masters of disguise. One of the supreme exponents of the art is *Epinephelus striatus*, the Nassau grouper, which can change its appearance between several different patterns and colour combinations within seconds. Its 'wardrobe' includes spots, brilliant stripes and blotches, in addition to uniform coloration. So variable is the coloration of this fish, in fact, it is impossible to say which variation represents its normal colour. However, it has been observed that all Nassau groupers turn pale with dark stripes when they are threatened. Another serranid which can change colour rapidly is the blue-spotted argus, *Cephalopholis argus*, which is widely distributed across the Indian and Pacific Oceans. This beautiful fish is also valued as food.

A member of the Serranidae which pays infrequent visits to British waters is the wreckfish, *Polyprion amricanum*, so named because it favours the neighbourhood of sub-merged wrecks and also lurks near wreckage floating on the surface. This is a large fish, growing to a length of six feet and noted for its ferocity. It has been seen to attack and kill other fish larger than itself.

'Jewfish' is a name given to several different members of the Serranidae in different parts of the world. Among them are the Californian jewfish, *Stereolepis gigas*, which has been recorded at 800 pounds, and the jewfish of the Caribbean, *Epinephelus itajara*, which attains 600 pounds. The name 'jewfish' has been given to these species because they are regarded as 'clean' under Levitical law. Other interestingly named fish in the family are the soapfishes, so called because they exude a slime which the fish beats into a lather when it is alarmed.

Sex-changers

A feature of many members of the Serranidae is 'intersexism'. This means that in the course of its lifetime a single fish displays characteristics of both sexes. Although it is quite common among invertebrate animals, intersexism is a rare phenomenon in fish. It is believed to occur in most species of grouper although the trait has not been studied in all of them.

Research reveals that the grouper reaches maturity within the space of two to five years, depending on species. At this stage it is a female. However, after a few years the fish has become a male. In fact, male sex organs had been present, in an undeveloped form, throughout its life. Likewise the vestiges of female sex organs are present after the fish has become a male. In the interim period the grouper passes through a phase of hermaphroditism, when the organs of both sexes are present, but neither are functional. Such fish are not normally capable of self-fertilization, although one serranid, the belted sandfish (*Serranellus subligarius*), is believed to have this ability. This six-inch-long fish is common among reefs in the shallow waters off the Florida coastline.

Sea breams

The various species of sea bream, or porgy, are members of the order Perciformes, like the basses and groupers. However, the breams are mainly smaller fish and not such formidable predators as the latter. Closer relations of the sea breams are the members of the mullet family (Mullidae) which includes such species as the red mullet of European waters and the American spotted goatfish.

The sea breams are not at all closely related to the breams of fresh water, although both are deep-bodied, shoaling fishes. The sea breams are found in both tropical and temperate seas, but few species venture into colder waters. The red sea bream, *Pagellus centrodontus,* is the most common species in British waters, followed by the black bream, *Spondyliosoma cantharus.* Three rarer species are the pandora, gilt-head and Spanish bream. An occasional visitor from warmer seas is a rapacious predator known as the dentex, *Dentex dentex.*

The different species show an extraordinary diversity of feeding habits, and each species has teeth and jaws suited best to its diet. Some graze on algae and minute organisms from rocks, by scraping with chisel-shaped front teeth, others browse on shellfish by crushing them between massive molars, and a few are completely predatory, using long, sharp canines to catch small fish and squid. Certain features are, however, common to the whole bream family (Sparidae). Bream have a single fin in the middle of the back with strong, spiny rays supporting the front of it and softer ones at the rear. The pelvic fin always has one spiny support and five soft ones, while the anal fin has three spiny rays and a variable number of soft ones. They are distinguished from the bass family by lacking both sharp, serrated edges on the front of the gill cover and spines on the rear of it.

Although not commonly regarded as a sporting or commercial fish in northern European waters, many bream are fished in the warmer waters where they are found. The centre of bream distribution appears to be South Africa – of thirty-four species found there, twenty-one are found nowhere else. The largest of the family, the musselcracker, *Cymatoceps nasutus,* named for its gigantic rear teeth, is caught for food and sport. It lives in shallow water and reaches over one-hundred pounds in weight. A similar bream, *Sparodon durbanensis,* in the same region regularly reaches forty pounds. Less welcome to the South African fishermen is the go-home fish, a species of small bream that takes bait only when every other fish appears to have stopped feeding – thus, when they start to be caught, one may as well go home.

In America, where bream are known as porgies, there are some fourteen species on the west coast of which two, the scup and the sheepshead, have some value. In contrast, the eastern Pacific is almost devoid of bream and *Monotaxis grandoculis,* the only type to be used regularly as food, is suspected of carrying the deadly ciguatera poison. The exact nature of this poison is a mystery, but it is suspected that damage to coral reefs liberates an unidentified blue-green alga, which is eaten by the bream and

Left: sea breams are typically shoaling fish and in warmer seas form part of the rich fauna of coral reefs. Below: the red sea bream Pagellus centrodontus, *the commonest European bream. The species varies from red to grey in colour over the head, body and fin. A large black spot can be seen at the beginning of the lateral line. The fish has blunt crushing teeth in the sides of the jaw*

Above: black bream or 'old wife' are found in British waters. Note the blue-grey body with vertical light stripes on the flanks. One male is threatening another which is intruding upon its nesting territory

then concentrates in the fish's tissues. Australia and Japan, too, catch some species of bream for food – in Australia, the bump-headed porgy, and a very similar species in Japan.

Moving north, the last large concentration of bream is in the Mediterranean. Here, tightly-packed, disciplined shoals of slim saupe patrol the shallow waters. Their brilliantly yellow-striped sides flash as they wheel and turn in their search for algae on rocks. Shoals of their young often inhabit water less than three feet deep, where they are continually dragged back and forth by wave action. Another medium-sized bream, the foot-long bogue, often swims on the fringes of saupe shoals. Both these fish are eaten, but of all the Mediterranean bream, the dentex is the most prized. Bluish in colour when young, assuming a dull red hue later, dentex is a power-ful predator, three feet or more long, with between four and six long, sharp fangs set in the

front of its wide-gaping mouth. It hunts fish, squid and octopus over rocky ground between thirty and six-hundred feet.

In British waters, only the black bream, or old wife, and the red sea bream are pursued by both sport and commercial fishermen. The old wife is very deep-bodied, blue-grey or black, with vertical light stripes on the flanks. It reaches a maximum length of around two feet. Rocks and wrecks, or sandy banks of weed, are its favourite haunts, and it is characterized by laying its eggs in a scrape in the sand on the sea bed. The red sea bream is of similar size and is caught over the same ground, but the body appears more elongated and is red to grey in colour, with a pro-nounced dark spot just above the gill cover, in specimens over a foot in length. The larger red bream frequent deeper water, however, and are common only at depths of between four-hundred to fifteen-hundred feet.

Butterfly fish

Among the most beautiful natural landscapes is that of the coral reef, but even more beautiful than the outcrops of coral themselves are the fish which make the reef their home. These display an astonishing variety of extravagant shapes and colours, and prominent among them are the butterfly fishes and angelfishes of the family Chaetodontidae.

The name Chaetodontidae refers to the bristle-like teeth which are a feature of these fishes which feed on tiny prey. The names 'butterfly fish' and 'angelfish' are also given to certain freshwater fish which are not members of the Chaetodontidae. The freshwater angelfish resembles its marine namesake in shape and, like the latter, is a popular choice for the home aquarium.

Marine butterfly fish and angelfish live in the warmer areas of the Atlantic, Pacific and Indian Oceans and are exclusively tropical in distribution. The splendour of their markings is reflected in the names of some species, such as the imperial angelfish, *Pomacanthus imperator,* of the Indo-Pacific and the queen angelfish, *Holacanthus ciliaris,* of the Caribbean and reefs off Florida.

The Chaetodontidae are mostly small fish, not usually exceeding a few inches in length, although a few are as much as two feet long. In front of the dorsal and anal fins there are a series of spines and, in addition, marine angelfishes have a long sharp spine at the lower edge of the gill cover which distinguishes them from other members of the Chaetodontidae. The body is

extremely deep and the fins well developed. The brilliant coloration of the sides is continued onto the fins, so the fish is easily visible when viewed from the side, even at a distance.

The markings on butterfly fish and angelfish are not simply a luxury, although their exact purpose is not known for certain. The coloration of most fish is designed to merge with their surroundings, either to conceal them from predators or, if they are predators themselves, to conceal them from their prey. The diet of the butterfly fish and angelfish means that they have no need to conceal themselves from prey, but without camouflage they appear to be extremely vulnerable themselves. In some marine animals

Above: the imperial angelfish, a reef-dweller of the Indo-Pacific Ocean.
Left: Holacanthus tricolor, *an angelfish found in the Gulf of Mexico. The spine which distinguishes angelfish from butterfly fish is visible at the base of the gill cover*

conspicuous patterns and colours are a sign that they are inedible or noxious in some way. So prospective predators are warned off, to the mutual advantage of both parties. Butterfly fish and angelfish sometimes contain poisons and so this may in part explain their coloration. Another possible explanation is that their coloration advertises their presence to other members of their own species. They are not shoaling fish and are generally seen singly or in pairs. Individuals appear to claim a particular area of the reef as their territory and their bold colours which stand out among the coral may serve to warn others against tresspassing.

It would be surprising that these fish could afford to make themselves so conspicuous if they were in fact defenceless. They might fall easy prey to the many large predators of the reef. However, the formation of a coral reef is such that it provides many nooks and crannies, too small for a large predator to enter, into which the fish can escape at the approach of danger. The fact that their bodies are extremely compressed laterally makes it easier for them to squeeze through a narrow opening where they will be out of harm's way. They also have a habit of turning face-on to danger, presenting the smallest possible area of their bodies to the eyes of a predator.

The size of the snouts in members of the Chaetodontidae is very variable. These are always protruding, but they range from the modest appendage of species like the clown butterfly fish, *Chaetodon ornatissimus*, to the extremely long snouts of the forceps fish of the genus *Forcipiger*. These differences reflect differences in feeding behaviour. Many of those with shorter snouts bite off individual polyps from the coral mass. The longer snouts make fine probing instruments with which the fish can seek out burrowing animals within the coral formations.

Butterfly fish and angelfish are attentive parents which clear a nest for their eggs on a flat surface and watch over them while they hatch. The fry seek refuge among rocks and weeds at first. At this stage they do not resemble their parents in shape and their bodies are long and slim. It takes three or four months for them to assume the characteristic shape of the adult. The young of some species do not display the same coloration as the adult while they are immature and they may look like a completely different species.

Four species of butterfly fish, illustrating the variable shape of the snout. Below: Chaetodon rostratus. Below right: Chaetodon striatus or the striped butterfly fish. Bottom: Chaetodon ornatissimus or the clown butterfly fish. Bottom right: Chaetodon bennetii

Damselfish

In the warm clear waters of tropical seas, many of the small, brilliantly-coloured fish that abound amongst the coral reefs belong to the damselfish or *demoiselle* family, the Pomacentridae. The popular names of these fish reflect their beauty. Dusky damsel, blue *Chromis*, cocoa damsel, Beau Gregory and yellow-tailed damsel are just a few members of the family. As members of the Perciformes, the delicate damsels have such unlikely relatives as the grouper and the tuna.

Damselfish are found in all tropical seas, at shallow depths, in and around coral reefs. They live among the rocks and weeds, darting for shelter at the least sign of danger. The garibaldi, *Hypsypops rubicundus*, also lives in semi-tropical waters, off southern California among the giant kelp weeds offshore. These underwater forests offer shelter like that of the reef.

Most damselfish measure less than six inches in length. The garibaldi is the largest of the family, growing to a length of twelve inches. Damselfish have a perch-like body and are flattened from side to side, a common feature of reef-dwelling fishes. The diet varies with the species. Some eat plant material, some feed on shrimps and small fish, while others are omnivorous, eating plant and animal matter. Sometimes, groups of damselfish rise to the surface of the sea at night to feed on the tiny animals of the plankton.

Mighty midgets

Despite their small size and pleasing appearance, all damsels are pugnacious creatures and fiercely aggressive, especially during the breeding season. (For this reason, some fish are unsuitable for the home aquarium.) In some species adults live alone or in pairs and are highly intolerant of any trespasser on their territory in the reef. Their aggressiveness is directed not only against members of their own species, but also against larger reef fish, such as wrasses. When annoyed, the damsels utter curious clicking sounds, produced by rubbing together the small teeth that line the throat or pharynx. They also assume aggressive postures when, for example, the spiny dorsal fin is raised and the pectoral fins are outspread at right angles to the body, giving them the appearance of a much larger fish. At the same time, the overall colour of the body may change and the mouth may be opened wide for a few seconds. If this stationary display does not intimidate the intruder, the damsel darts forward nipping furiously and butting the enemy. The males are particularly aggressive during the breeding season, since it is they that fashion a nest and guard the eggs until they hatch, a week or so after being laid. Even the female parent is driven away with gusto if she ventures too close.

The sergeant-major, *Abudefduf saxatilis*, is a species of damselfish that lives in the reefs around Florida and the West Indies and off the west coast

of Mexico. It is the most common of reef fish in these areas and, being very curious, often accompanies divers, who have named it 'the nuisance' or 'cock-eyed pilot'. It acquires its military nickname for the black stripes across its back. The body colour varies greatly. It may be blue, black, pale yellow, orange or green. Members of the Pomacentridae are, in general, difficult to classify, since one species may have several colour variants and there may be different colour phases during the life of an individual. The young of the garibaldi, for example, are bright green or orange with bright blue spots. The spots are lost as the fish gets older and the adult assumes an overall brilliant yellow or gold colour.

The Beau Gregory, or *pescado azul*, also has a very varied coloration. Sometimes, it is a deep blue with pale blue spots on its upper flanks, ending in a bright yellow tail. Then, it is called the jewelfish. But other variants include dull brown, or overall bright yellow. The bicolour damsel has an interesting vertical demarcation of colour. The front half of the body is brown and the posterior half is orange, fading to a white tail. The cocoa damsel has a horizontal division with a black back and a yellow belly.

Above: a pair of clownfish, Amphyprion bicinctus, *safe among the poisonous tentacles of a sea anemone. The fish acquaint themselves with their host by performing a special ceremony*

Anemone fishes

Some of the most fascinating and well studied of damselfish are the clown or anemone fishes, of the genera *Amphiprion* and *Premnas*. These fish, often in pairs, live in close association with large sea anemones on reefs, hiding amongst the anemones' venomous tentacles, which are capable of paralyzing and stinging small animals to death in a matter of seconds. Clownfish are small, about one to three inches long, and have distinctive markings on their bodies. *Amphiprion percula*, which usually associates with the giant anemone called *Stoichactis*, is a brilliant orange-red, with white bands encircling its body, behind the head, around the middle and at the base of the tail.

Clownfish are immune to the stinging cells of their anemone hosts and have even been found inside their hosts' stomachs, quite unharmed. The clowns' secret seems to lie in the mucus that covers their bodies. The mucus has an active constituent that somehow inhibits the discharge of the anemone's stinging cells. The clowns may lay their eggs among the tentacles, a safe nursery because the mucus surrounding the eggs contains the same constituent.

Some species of clownfish associate only with a specific type of anemone whilst other species are less selective about their host. Having chosen a potential host, by visual recognition, the fish swims closer to the anemone, making slow, vertical undulations of its body. The anemone probably recognises these characteristic vibrations in the water. When the fish physically contacts the anemone, the tentacles cling momentarily to the fish's body. With a violent jerk, the fish frees itself and continues to swim close to the waving tentacles. After more encounters, the clinging reaction of the tentacles begins to flag and eventually ceases. This habituation or acclimatization process has been observed to take about one hour under laboratory conditions.

The advantages of the partnership to the anemone are many. The fish eats the waste materials of the host, removes parasitic growths and debris from its skin, and acts as a decoy, luring other fish within reach of its tentacles. The clownfish obviously receives excellent protection from its host. If it is isolated from the anemone, in aquarium experiments, it is not long before it is snapped up by a larger fish.

Courtship among damselfish could be described as brief and stormy. The male chooses a site for the egg-laying, on a rock surface. He may prepare the site by clearing away any weed or debris. Then he selects a female and swims around her, circling for two to three minutes. Leading her back to the nest, the male rubs his underside against the rock several times. (The males of the *Chromis* species leap up and down in the water prior to this rubbing display.) If the female reacts appropriately, the two swim in a quivering manner towards the nest, bodies close together, sometimes touching. The eggs are laid in clusters in a circular pattern and are surrounded by sticky mucus. The male then promptly chases the female away and assumes his parental role of guarding the eggs, occasionally fanning them and nipping debris away with his mouth.

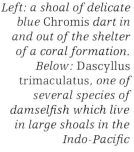

Left: a shoal of delicate blue Chromis *dart in and out of the shelter of a coral formation. Below:* Dascyllus trimaculatus, *one of several species of damselfish which live in large shoals in the Indo-Pacific*

Wrasses

The wrasses are another family which make up an important part of the colourful community of the coral reef. But, although the centre of their distribution is in the tropics, wrasses are also found in temperate areas of the world's oceans.

There are several hundred species in the wrasse family, or Labridae, living in the Atlantic, Indo-pacific and Mediterranean. In general they are small fish, although a few tropical species may reach a length of several feet. Their bodies are covered in large scales and they have a single dorsal fin, at the front of which there are several sharp spines. Wrasses usually have thick lips and strong teeth. There are bony plates in the throat which are used to crush and grind the shells of invertebrates which are one of their principal foods. Wrasses are territorial fish and specimens kept in aquaria have shown that they can be extremely pugnacious towards their own kind.

Many wrasses are noted for their brilliant colours, even in temperate waters. Certain species are remarkable in that the coloration differs markedly between male and female. One of these is the cuckoo wrasse, *Labrus mixtus.* The markings of adult males are a striking composition of orange, laced with bright blue stripes. The female cuckoo wrasse, on the other hand, is orange with three black blotches on her back near the tail.

The cuckoo wrasse ranges down the shores of western Europe from Scandinavia to the Mediterranean. It is a species in which the elaborate courtship ritual has been closely studied. The male digs a shallow nest in the sand with the aid of his tail. He then entices a female to the nest by means of a display involving butting and nibbling until she consents to accompany him. During these advances the male turns white over his head and part of his back. When hatched, the fry are planktonic.

Wherever they live, wrasse are fish of reefs and seaweed-covered rocks, rarely venturing far into open water. Some of the smaller species are found in rock pools that have been cut off by the retreating tide. Because they frequently need to manoeuvre in confined spaces among the rocks

Below: Crenilabrus ocellatus, *a wrasse of the Mediterranean, showing the long dorsal fin, large scales and intricate coloration, typical of wrasses*

and reefs of their home, the wrasses have evolved an unusual method of swimming. Fish usually swim by strokes of their tail, but wrasses use their tails only when an extra burst of speed is required. The rest of the time wrasse propel themselves by undulations of the dorsal and anal fins, and paddling movements of their pectoral fins.

Fish have no eyelids and do not sleep in the normal sense of the word. However, they do exhibit behaviour which is analogous to sleep, undergoing regular periods of inactivity. This behaviour is particularly pronounced in the wrasses. During the day they are often to be found in one particular spot, apparently resting and they return there for the night, sometimes even lying on their sides. This behaviour may often be witnessed in an aquarium. Equally remarkable is the behaviour of certain species of wrasse which bury themsleves completely in the sand at night. Other species form a sort of mucous cocoon in which to rest, in a similar way to their relatives, the parrot fishes.

Among the smallest species of wrasse are those

Right: Coris gaimardi, *a member of the genus which includes some most colourful wrasses. Below: a cleaner wrasse at work in the gills of a squirrelfish*

of the genus *Labroides,* the cleaner wrasses. The cleaner wrasses are so called because they act as cleaners for other fish, removing parasites and dead skin from their bodies. The haunts of these little fish are a sort of centre where their 'clients' come to receive treatment. Many of the clients are large predatory fish, such as groupers, which would normally have no hesitation in eating a wrasse. But they permit the cleaners to enter their gill cavities and even their mouths without harming them. Cleaner wrasse have characteristic markings, including a dark stripe down their flanks, which makes them easily distinguishable. This coloration evidently grants the wrasse immunity from predators. When a prospective client approaches, the cleaner wrasse performs a special wriggling dance which persuades the larger fish to remain still while it receives treatment. At times there may be a queue of fish waiting to avail themselves of the cleaner's services.

The advantage of this symbiotic relationship for the wrasse is that it receives a plentiful supply of food in the form of the parasites which it removes from its clients' skins. The advantage for the clients is that they are cleaned of organisms which might otherwise damage their health. The importance of the cleaner wrasse to the other inhabitants of the reef is evidenced by the fact that, when the wrasses are removed experimentally, it is not long before the other fish have left the area too.

The markings of the cleaner wrasse have been copied by the 'false-cleaner' blenny, *Aspidontus taeniatus.* It resembles the wrasse so closely that other fish mistake it for the genuine article. It even imitates the wrasse's introductory dance. However, instead of cleaning the other fish, it seizes the opportunity to tear off a shred of their skin.

Surgeonfish

The family Acanthuridae are another widespread group of tropical fish in the order Perciformes. The common name for the 200 or so species in the family is 'surgeonfish'. These are small to medium-sized fish, some species attaining a length of two feet. Their deep, laterally compressed bodies are almost oval in shape. They may be highly coloured, but usually their markings are somewhat less brilliant than those of their fellow reef-dwellers, the butterfly fishes, tending more towards pastel shades.

Like butterfly fish, surgeons have protruding snouts, but their diet is almost entirely vegetarian and their mouths are adapted to cropping plants and algae off the coral. They also have the characteristic long intestine of herbivores. Shoals of surgeonfish may often be seen feeding around coral reefs. Research has shown that the different species tend to feed in different parts of a reef.

Their diet is one reason why surgeonfishes have no need to be fast swimmers. Another reason is that they are moderately safe from predators because they are equipped with a unique defensive weapon. This is a small spine on either side of the body near the base of the tail stalk. It is from this scalpel-like spine that the surgeonfishes take their name (one species, *Acanthurus hepatus*, is called the doctorfish). The spine is extremely sharp and capable of inflicting a deep wound, serious enough to deter all but the most deter-

mined predator. When not in use the spine can be retracted into a groove.

Most surgeonfish have only one pair of spines, but those of the genus *Naso* have two or even three pairs. One member of this group is the bumphead surgeon, *Naso tuberosus*, of Australian waters. This species takes its name from another feature – a pronounced bump on its forehead, which gives it an almost grotesque appearance.

Near relatives of the surgeonfish are the moorish idols of the genus *Zanclus*, but in appearance these are more like the butterfly fishes. However, they have larger mouths and a pair of distinctive horn-like protrusions over the eyes. Their sides are pale yellow with two broad dark vertical stripes. The dorsal fin is long and, in younger specimens exaggerated by an extended spine which may be twice as long as the body.

Below: one of the most brilliantly coloured surgeonfish, Acanthurus leucosternon. *The spine is invisible in its groove near the base of the tail stalk.*
Bottom: a shoal of surgeonfish, Acanthurus triostegus, *over the Great Barrier Reef. Surgeons graze in shoals, much like land-living herbivores. They are peaceable, the spine being used only in defence*

Swordfish

The Scombroidea, a sub-order of the order Perciformes, includes some of the fastest-moving animals in the ocean. Among them are the mackerels and tunas, and their relative, the swordfish of the family Xiphiidae.

The swordfish or broadbill is a fish of the open seas. Together with its close relatives, the spearfish or marlin and the sailfish, it is highly regarded as a game fish, challenging the fisherman with its great strength, tenacity and speed, both in and out of the water. All these fish are also prized as food.

Swordfish, *Xiphias gladius,* live in tropical and warm temperate seas, including the Mediterranean. They are particularly abundant between the latitudes of 30° and 45° North of the equator. Occasionally, they venture into colder waters and have been seen off the south and south-western coasts of Britain, especially in late summer.

The swordfish is so called because of the beak-like projection of the upper jaw, which is broad and flat, hence its other popular name of 'broadbill'. The bill may account for one-third of the total length of the body which can attain twenty feet, but on average varies between six and twelve feet. Like the tunny, swordfish follow the schools of herring, sardine and mackerel on their migrations. Swimming through a school of such fish, the swordfish swings its bill to and fro, stunning and killing the fish which are then eaten at leisure. Sometimes by accident bills have become embedded in the side of a ship.

Like all its relatives, the swordfish is beautifully streamlined. The torpedo-shaped body is smooth and scaleless. The sickle-shaped dorsal fin is high and cuts through the water like a sabre. Killer whales used to be called 'sword fish' because of the shape of their dorsal fins and have earned the true swordfish undeserved notoriety. The pectoral fins are long and set low on the sides of the body. While swimming, they are folded tightly against the flanks, so as not to impair speed. There are no pelvic fins and the second dorsal and anal fins are placed well back near the base of the tail, a characteristic of fast-swimming, surface fishes. The tail is crescent-shaped and its powerful muscles provide the propulsive force. The overall colour of the body is dark purplish-blue on the back, fading to a silvery-grey on the belly. The sword is also dark on top and pale beneath. Some biologists have suggested that the sword is an extreme case of streamlining of the body, like the long, tapering nose of a jet aircraft.

Undoubtedly, the swordfish is among the fastest of oceanic fish, rivalling the mako and porbeagle sharks, the tunny and sailfish for speed. The swordfish is estimated to attain a speed of 60 m.p.h. in short bursts, but this figure has yet to be verified. There are various anatomical and physiological adaptations connected with fast-swimming. The backbone is particularly rigid due to interlocking 'processes' between the individual vertebrae, thus giving the tail muscles a solid structure against which to act. The blood of swordfish has been found to be several degrees higher in temperature than the surrounding seawater, as is the case in certain other fast-swimming fish. It is estimated that with every 10°C increase in body temperature, the muscular activity is increased threefold. Thus, swordfish are warm-blooded, at least for temporary periods including bursts of strenuous activity. Another important adaptation for a fast-moving existence is the increased surface area of the gills. Cross-connections of tissue between the gill filaments allow for a greater amount of oxygen to be absorbed into the blood, thus enabling the fish to swim faster and for longer periods, without exhausting its muscle power.

Below: a fine pair of swordfish taken from the Strait of Messina. A ship's timber in the British Museum contains a swordfish's bill which penetrated to a depth of 22 inches

Mackerel and tuna

Streamlined, powerful fish of the warm and temperate seas, the members of the Scombridae or mackerel family offer a unique combination of sporting potential and commercial importance. Pound for pound they are among the most persistent and energetic fighters to be taken on rod and line, while the fishing industry harvests some two million tons of scombrids annually, from the diminutive Atlantic mackerel to the huge tunny. Most members of the family have sleek, torpedo-shaped bodies, narrowing to a slender tail-stalk, and decorated with from four to nine small separate fins between the tail fin and the second dorsal and anal fins. Much of their swimming strength is derived from the size and anatomy of the tail fin. This is large in relation to the body and is divided into two distinct lobes. The fin rays extend over the last vertebra, giving the whole structure considerable rigidity to transfer the energy of the fish's muscles to the tail. Keels on either side precede the tail fin. The tunnies have three of these keels, with the largest in the middle. Mackerel have only the two smaller ones.

All scombrids have small scales, although many species sport a 'corselet' of larger scales in an irregular band from the head to the first dorsal fin. They are shoaling, pelagic fish with a high metabolic rate; their body temperature is often several degrees above that of the surrounding water. Their flesh is rich and oily but should always be eaten fresh, since it rots quickly, forming poisons in apparently palatable flesh.

The Atlantic mackerel

Seasonally common to the point of abundance in European waters, the Atlantic mackerel offers summer sport to anglers, as well as supporting a large industry. It ranges from Norway to the Canaries in the east and from Chesapeake Bay to the Gulf of Maine in the west. Similar species occur on both sides of the Pacific. Although the horse mackerel, or scad, shares much of this range and is superficially similar, it is not closely related, belonging to the family Carangidae.

The Atlantic mackerel reaches a maximum length of around twenty inches and a weight of over four-and-a-half pounds. Its slim, elongated body is silver below; above it is green with patterns of darker scribble marks, which are sometimes replaced by dots or light ripples. Like most scombrids it forms large, migratory shoals near the surface, following the warm water with the seasons. In late autumn the mackerel take to the bottom, lying densely packed in the troughs and trenches of the sea bed. Few of them feed until January, when they spread out and swim to the surface to begin their breeding movements. At this time they sieve plankton from the water by means of their fine gill rakers.

Popular belief had it that mackerel were blind at the beginning of the year, but underwater observation has shown that this is unlikely, for they can select and eat particular items in the plankton. Between April and June they reach

Below right: the Atlantic mackerel. Their migrations bring the huge shoals close inshore in summer.
Below: the common mackerel, Scomber scombrus, *of the North Atlantic.*
Bottom: the mackerel Pneumatophorus japonicus *of the western Pacific and Indian Oceans*

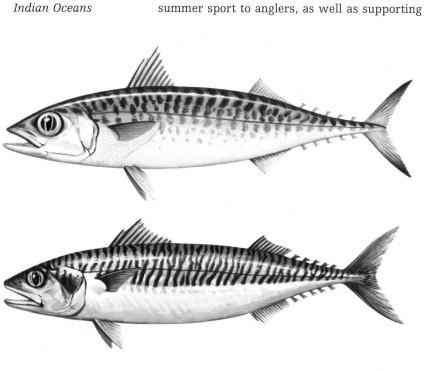

their destination in coastal waters at 52–57° Fahrenheit (11–14° Centigrade), and off Britain breed around the south coast of England and Ireland. The female lays about a quarter of a million floating eggs, which hatch in about six days. The young fish stay near the coast until autumn, and mature when three years old.

When spawning is over, the mackerel split up into smaller shoals and begin the voracious, indiscriminate feeding that allows them to be easily caught by the sea angler, from the casual holidaymaker trailing feathered hooks from a pleasure boat to the serious angler seeking bait or lively sport on light tackle. Mackerel follow small herrings, sprats and sand eels, using both sight and smell; many commercial fishermen pour decaying fish and blood into the water to attract them. Atlantic mackerel will, however, snap at anything that moves. Coloured feathered hooks are favourite lures, but bright silver spinners or, better still, a moving strip of mackerel, will attract them. In emergencies, a piece of silver paper wrapped around the hook shank is quite an effective lure.

Since their flesh is extremely oily and they are themselves prey to many larger fish, mackerel make excellent bait, either filleted for small species, or as the three-fish 'bunch of bananas' that lures sharks. Commercially, mackerel fall to fixed 'keddle' nets inshore and drift nets set in the upper waters. Shoals of mackerel are also particularly easy to catch by encircling them with seine nets. As a general rule, they may be netted at sea from March to June, and by hooks and lines from July to October. However, occasional stragglers are taken at almost all times of year on baits intended for other species.

The bluefin tuna

Dwarfing their mackerel cousins, the tunas range all over the warmer waters of the world. There are many species, distinguished by the numbers of fin rays and gill rakers which they possess, by their tail finlets, and by their internal anatomy. The giant among them is the bluefin, or tunny, capable of tipping the scales at 1,400 pounds at a length of fourteen feet, although more usually taken when six to eight feet long. It is a perfectly streamlined fish with the dorsal fins set close together and a short pectoral fin. The tail is not sharply-lobed and is crescent-shaped when viewed from the side. The fish is blue-black on the upper parts and silvery-white below. The fins are dark, with the exception of the tail finlets,

Below (top to bottom): frigate mackerel, Auxis thazard; *false albacore,* Euthynnus alletteratus; *oceanic bonito,* Katsuwonus pelamis; *bluefin tuna,* Thunnus thynnus

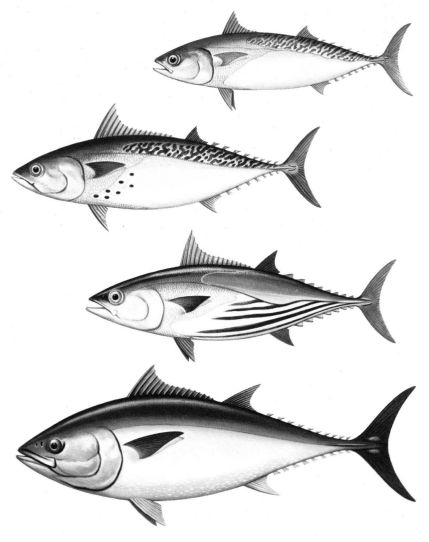

the anal fins, and occasionally the pelvic fins, which may be yellow. Such is the energy with which this handsome fish resists capture on rod and line that millions of words must have been written about tunny fishing. Closer inspection, however, reveals that comparatively little is known about the biology of the bluefin. It has been suggested that the Atlantic population is continuous in its distribution, corresponding to the circular current system across that ocean. For instance, two fish tagged off Florida during the autumn of 1951 were caught off Norway, 4,500 miles away, after only 120 days. Others tagged off Martha's Vineyard, Massachusetts, in summer 1954 were taken in the Bay of Biscay five years later. On the other hand, the populations on each side of the Atlantic seem to have anatomical differences and different breeding seasons.

Whatever their worldwide movements, tunny do not venture into water colder than 50–54°F (10–12°C). Shoals of tunny consist of fish of approximately the same size; also the size of the shoal is related to the size of the fish – the larger the fish, the fewer in the shoal. Very large tunny are often solitary. In summer bluefins swim close to the surface – so close that both commercial and sport fishermen employ high lookout masts and, in America, even scouting helicopters. In winter the tunny stay between 100 and 600 feet down. Like all scombrids, they swim with their mouths slightly open, using their forward motion to force water across the gills. Their oxygen requirements are very high because of their intense muscular activity; tunny have been observed to reach fifty m.p.h. and are probably capable of higher speeds. To sustain such speeds, bluefins have to have voracious appetites. Tunny continually sieve the water across their gill rakers to extract animal plankton and the larvae of pilchard, herring, and anchovy. If a group of

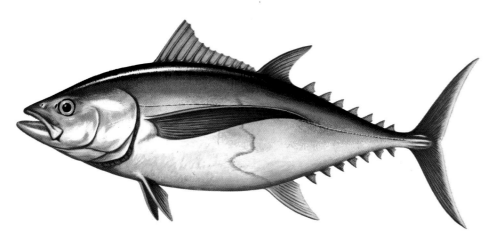

Above right: the longfin tuna, or albacore, is distinguished by its extremely long pectoral fins. Albacore breed in both Atlantic and Pacific oceans. They migrate northwards after spawning in May and June, staying in water of a certain temperature and salinity.

Right: tuna trapped in a net. They are so fast-moving that they are rarely photographed in the open sea

tunny encounters a shoal of mackerel, garfish, herring or flying fishes, they attack with great ferocity, lashing out in all directions, charging the prey, and leaping completely clear of the water, killing and stunning in all directions. In deeper water they eat redfish, ling, and some squid and cuttlefish.

The European spawning grounds of the tunny are in the Mediterranean and in the Atlantic off south-west Spain in Europe, while the American spawning areas are off Florida and the Bahamas. The European fish lay an unknown number of small eggs in June. These float near the surface for two days before hatching into quarter-of-an-inch-long larvae. The growth rate is extraordinary: by three months, the tunny weigh a pound; by a year, ten pounds; by two years, twenty-one pounds; and by four years, fifty-six pounds. They mature when three to four years old. The fish from Martha's Vineyard, mentioned above, were tagged at around two years of age when they weighed eighteen pounds, and were recaught at seven years old, when they were found to weigh about 150 pounds.

The albacore

Several other species of bluefin exist, although lack of data precludes any attempts at a definitive classification. Many that are now considered separate species may be merely variations within a worldwide population. The most familiar, due to its intensive commercial exploitation, is the albacore or long-fin tuna, *Thunnus alalunga.* This species can be instantly identified by its immensely elongated pectoral fins, which reach back past the second dorsal and anal fins. Albacore roam all the world's oceans where the water is above 59°F (15°C). Tagging and observation seem to indicate that the North and South Pacific populations are homogeneous and continuous,

Below: seething water indicates the frenzied attempts of a shoal of tuna to escape from a net off Sicily. If a single fish finds a hole in the net or manages to jump over the top, the entire catch may follow within seconds

with those fish that spawn nearer the equator feeding in more temperate water. The Atlantic population spawns near the Mediterranean from May to June, arriving in the region between Cape Finisterre and Ireland during July, a month after the tunny. Their diet is similar to that of the tunny, but they seldom grow to more than four feet long or a weight of sixty-five pounds. Their white meat, however, makes them very attractive commercially, particularly for canning, and Europe lands some 35,000 tons a year.

The yellowfin tuna

The yellowfin types of tuna are similarly widely distributed, although they frequent warmer waters than the bluefin types. They are most common in the Pacific where the largest species, the yellowfin, *Thunnus albacares,* attains eight feet in length and 450 pounds in weight, sometimes gaining as much as sixty pounds in a year. Yellowfin are abundant in the Pacific, but rarer in the Atlantic. The so-called 'Allison' tuna of sea anglers is not a separate species, but a long-finned growth phase of the ordinary yellowfin. Far less obvious, the bigeye yellowfin, *T. obesus,* is more of a deep-water species, distinguished by its larger eyes, longer pectoral fins, and striations on the edges of the liver. There are several species of spotted tuna, but their dark meat discourages fishermen and little is known about them.

The striped tunas

The striped tunas make up the final category of the tuna types. These include the skipjack, *Katsuwonus pelamis,* up to four feet long and eighty pounds in weight, with longitudinal stripes on the abdomen. It lives only four years, and moves in dense shoals. The bonitos, with stripes on the back, are more familiar in Europe. The Atlantic bonito or pelamid, *Sarda sarda,* is a common catch in the North Sea. Distinguished by seven to twenty oblique stripes on the back, it reaches only two or three feet in length. It is caught by fishermen in the Black Sea and off Morocco as it passes on its spawning migration.

Tuna fisheries are almost as old as history. Since fishing began, men have concealed hooks behind flashing lures to tempt them; in modern times, commercial boats trail multiple lures from outriggers for larger catches, while sportsmen spend small fortunes on specialized craft and detection apparatus in order to find the catch of a lifetime. On the other hand, many people still harpoon tuna or shoot them with spear guns.

One of the most spectacular methods of catching tuna is single or double-handed live-baiting. Livebait is used to attract tuna to within range of a series of baited hooks on immensely strong line, fixed to one or two bamboo poles. As soon as a fish takes the bait, the man (or men) gives a sudden powerful heave, and before the fish can show any fight, it has been pulled clear of the water in a neat arc, to land flapping in the shallow fish hold of a Breton or Californian fishing boat. Always effective with shoaling fish, purse-seining takes tons of tuna in the open ocean, while a special combination of seine net and fixed trap takes its place in shallow water, especially in the Philippines and the Mediterranean. A very long 'leader' net is laid in the path of migrating tuna. The net diverts them shorewards to an elaborate trap, or 'heart'. A gate is shut on the panic-stricken fish, divers ensure that the bottom of the net is sealed, then the trap is constricted until the fish can be killed with clubs, knives or spears by men in small boats.

Left (top and bottom): a bluefin tuna is hauled aboard a fishing boat. The bluefin, or tunny, is the largest of the tunas. It falls prey to fishermen at points where its seasonal migration routes take it close inshore

Blennies

'Blennies' is the collective name given to the members of the suborder Blennioidea, although many species are not individually known as blennies. They are the last fishes in the order Perciformes – the large and varied group which is headed by the sea basses and groupers – to be described in this book. Like the order Perciformes as a whole, the blennies are an extremely widespread group found in tropical and temperate seas the world over.

Blennies are typically small fish of shallow inshore waters and they may often be encountered in rock pools at low tide. The shanny, *Blennius pholis*, of the family Blennidae, is the commonest shore fish in the British Isles. Like other members of this family, it has no scales and is elongated in shape. A single continuous dorsal fin runs the whole way down its back and the pelvic fins are attached under the throat, a feature typical of the blennies. It grows to about six inches long.

Because it lives between tidemarks, the blenny often has to contend with being stranded at low tide. It can live for short periods out of the water and has adapted to this ever-changing environment to such an extent that specimens kept in aquaria actually try to wriggle out of the water at the time of low tide. When stranded blennies are given some protection from gulls and other predators by their camouflage. Their mottled coloration merges with rocks and seaweed and some, like the shanny, can change colour to match the background.

Blennies are omnivorous and feed on algae and small invertebrates. When not feeding they tend to take cover under rocks, or in empty shells or even old tin cans. A rigid 'pecking order' is found among blennies, chiefly determined by individual size. Smaller specimens are chased away when they venture too close to their elders and a large individual may expel a smaller one from its hiding place. Blennies lay their eggs in such places and until they hatch they are guarded by the male who moves his tail to keep up a supply of oxygen to them. However, the viviparous blenny, *Zoarces viviparus*, of the family Zoarcidae does not lay eggs. Instead, it gives birth to living young.

Other members of the Zoarcidae are the eel pouts. The klipfishes of the tropics are close relatives of the Blennidae, but are distinguished by the possession of scales. The wolf fishes (Anarhichadidae) are much larger fish of northern waters, some growing to eight feet in length. The gunnels (Pholidae) are fish of the north Pacific and Atlantic, some of which are called butterfish on account of their very slippery skin.

Above right: the butterfly blenny has a large black spot on the side of its sail-like dorsal fin.
Right: shannies with other inhabitants of a rock pool. The larger fish is expelling the smaller one from its hiding place. The shanny is unusual in having no crests on its head like other blennies

Flatfish

There are approximately 600 species of flatfish, distributed around the ocean in all but the coldest waters. All are bottom-dwellers, rarely venturing far from the sea bed. Some species are flatter than others (the turbot, for example, is a comparatively thick-bodied flatfish), but it is impossible to mistake any of them for any other kind of fish and zoologists group them all into a single order, the Pleuronectiformes. The purpose of their curiously flattened body is twofold. First, it serves to conceal them from predators, their low profile making them hard to distinguish on the flat sea bed. Second, in the case of the active predatory flatfishes, the low profile gives prey minimal warning of their approach.

As a further aid to concealment some species, such as the plaice and the sole, possess the ability to change colour, blending almost perfectly with the sea bed on which they are lying. This effect is achieved by the expansion of the appropriate pigment in branching cells within the skin of the fish's back. These branching cells are controlled by nerves which respond to impulses from the eyes. As in other fish, the underside of the flatfish is white, so that the fish is as inconspicuous as possible when viewed against the light from the surface.

Eye migration

In some ways flatfishes resemble the skates and rays, which share their flattened body shape. But a momentary comparison of fish from the two groups reveals several marked dissimilarities. For example, the mouth of a skate or ray is on the underside of the body, while that of a flatfish is located at the front. However, the most radical difference lies in the fact that flatfish are asymmetrical in appearance. This is a reflection of the remarkable way in which they have acquired their flattened bodies.

When they hatch from their floating eggs, young flatfish resemble other fish. Their bodies are deep and narrow and they have one eye on either side, one set of gills on either side, and fins distributed in the conventional manner. Their bodies are not at this stage flattened vertically at all, and indeed they never really become so. Instead, one eye starts to migrate over the head, eventually assuming a position on the opposite side of the body, alongside the other eye. At the same time, other external alterations take place and the flatfish abandons its free-swimming existence to spend the rest of its life lying on its side on the sea bed.

In the majority of flatfish, the side to which the eye migrates depends on the family; if both eyes lie on the right side of the head, the fish belongs to the plaice, sole or halibut groups; if both eyes are on the left, it is in the turbot group. The flounders are particularly confusing in this respect, for in some species the position of the eye seems to depend on the area in which the fish lives, or it is merely random. Flounders are grouped with the plaice group because they hatch from eggs lacking the oil globule secreted by the other two groups.

Flatfish range in size from a few inches to twelve feet, and in colour from the drab, camouflagged sole to the brilliant blue-ringed peacock flounder of American waters. They inhabit both the shallowest waters and the depths, where the grotesque Hawaiian *Pelecanthichthys crumenalis*, an elongate, ten-inch flatfish with its lower jaw extending far beyond the upper, lives at depths of many thousands of feet. The majority of flatfish, however, are small fish inhabiting coastal shelves. A small number of species make a major contribution to the world's food resources. Plaice, flounder, turbot, sole, and the immense halibut, for example, are all readily fished and highly regarded as food.

Left: a dab, one of the flatfishes whose right side is uppermost and which have both eyes on that side, like the plaice. Note the asymmetrical distribution of the fins and the lateral line which runs down the top of the body and not the flanks as in other fish.
Below: the head of a plaice. The distortion of its features is due to the way in which its body has become flattened

Right-sided flatfish

The most familiar of the flatfish are those belonging to the plaice group, with the eyes on the right side of the head. This group includes the plaice, the flounder, the dabs and the halibut. The plaice is by far the most important commercially; 170,000 tons are caught yearly by fishermen in European waters, and it is a prize quarry of anglers of all ages. Averaging about eighteen inches long, very occasionally reaching three feet, it is coloured in varying shades of grey-brown on the upper surface, with distinct red or orange blotches, while the lower side is whitish. It is often confused with the flounder, with which it sometimes interbreeds, but there are several distinguishing characteristics. The plaice lacks the rows of bony warts at the bases of the dorsal and anal fins found on the flounder; only four to seven bony knobs run back from its eyes, while in the flounder many more extend right down its back along the lateral line. The tail fin of a plaice is rounded, and the tail stalk is nearly all finned, while the flounder has a square-cut tail and an apparently longer stalk with less fin margin on it. The red blotches on the back, characteristic of the plaice, are, however, often found on the flounder, too.

Plaice range from Iceland to the western Mediterranean, on sandy, muddy, or gravel seabeds from just below the shoreline down to 600 feet. They are particularly active at night, when large specimens often venture close inshore. They are often found in great numbers over shellfish beds. Plaice are able to make short work of quite tough shells. The teeth in the jaws are chisel-like, while those in the throat are large and blunt. Shellfish are crushed in the throat, while the extended bodies of worms and the 'feet' of some shellfish are efficiently snipped by a swift lunge of the head and a snap of the forward teeth. Plaice migrate to specific spawning grounds in winter where each female lays from 50,000 to half a million floating eggs, according to her size. The young assume the characteristic flatfish shape at two months old, drift to the bottom, and are carried by tides and currents to their inshore nursery grounds. They grow slowly, reaching sexual maturity at three to four years old and seven to ten inches long in the males, six years old and a foot long in the females. A two-foot plaice is twenty or more years old. Since plaice are easily fished and grow at such a slow rate, they have easily become locally over-fished, and without further fishery regulations may soon become scarce in inshore waters.

The dab is the most common flatfish in the North-east Atlantic. It lacks any bony warts, and its lateral line is curved deeply over the pectoral fin. It lives over sandy ground in shallower water than the plaice, and is the main-stay of their sport for many beach-anglers. The dab eats nearly anything small enough, and in some areas is a serious competitor of the more valuable plaice. It takes small sea-urchins, hermit crabs, worms and molluscs, together with the occasional sand-eel and goby. Dabs seldom exceed a foot in length. The lemon dab, often called the lemon sole, is a slightly larger fish of coarser, gravel or rocky, ground. Red-brown to yellowish, marbled with dark markings, it has a small head and lacks the anal spine – a movable, sharp thorn in front of the anal fin – possessed by most of its right-sided relatives. Gravel beds and rough sand down to 300 feet are its habitat.

The flounder is the flatfish most tolerant of low-salinity water. It is found on sand and mud from the tidal zone down to 120 feet in winter, often

Above left: the turbot is a flatfish of sandy or muddy seabeds that is unevenly distributed around the coasts of Britain, being found mainly off the south and west coasts of Ireland, in the Channel and the North Sea. Above: a good catch of halibut in Icelandic waters. Like the plaice, the halibut is an important food fish. It is found mainly in the Arctic and sub-Arctic; its southern limit is the English Channel concentrating in estuaries and even entering completely fresh water in summer. The flounder spends most of the day buried under a shallow layer of sand, moving at dusk to feed on worms, shrimps, and small crabs. It seldom attempts to eat shellfish with tougher bodies. Flounders grow to a little over eighteen inches long, and tend to be unpopular catches in many areas because they seem particularly susceptible to a skin parasite that creates ugly blisters on the upper surface.

A giant among flatfish

In contrast, the halibut, a monster among flatfish, is a valuable sporting and commercial catch on both sides of the Atlantic and in the northern Pacific. The Atlantic species is the largest flatfish, with a maximum recorded size of twelve feet long and 700 pounds weight. Specimens over six feet long, however, are very rarely caught nowadays. The halibut is thick-bodied and less flattened than most of its relatives. Its massive jaw, reaching well past the eyes, is an indication of its feeding habits. A voracious predator, it eats cod, haddock, herring and many other fish in its summer depths of around 250 feet, restricting itself mainly to the deep-sea prawn *Pandanus borealis* in its winter depths of down to 6,000 feet. Less confined to the bottom than other flatfish, the halibut hunts in the middle waters and over all kinds of seabeds, except muddy ones. It is usually taken on long lines: The flesh is strongly flavoured, and at its best in winter. Since halibut do not mature until they are from seven to eigh-

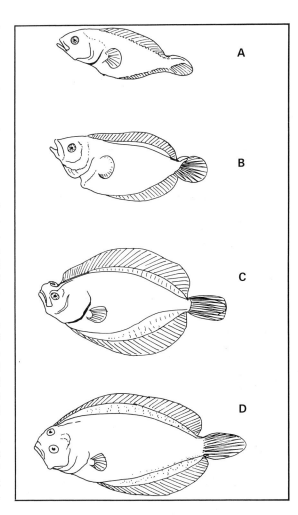

Left: after hatching from floating eggs, a young flatfish (A) swims in the surface waters. At this stage it is like a normal fish, with an eye on each side of the head. After a while, the fish becomes more flattened and the mouth twists round (B). The fish sinks to the seabed. Meanwhile, one eye moves round to the opposite side of the head (C). Finally, the transformation is complete (D), and both eyes now lie close together on the upper surface of the head. Below: a flounder cruises through the water just above the seabed. Flatfish swim by undulating the long dorsal and anal fins that fringe the edges of the body

Right: a plaice on a gravel sea bed, illustrating the remarkable powers of camouflage possessed by many flatfishes. The upper surface of the fish changes colour to match the background in response to impulses from the eyes. Below right: a sole swimming at speed. The elongated oval shape of the sole gives it its name

teen years old and grow very slowly, they have been the subject of extensive study and protection, especially off America and Norway.

The soles are a widespread group, favouring warmer waters, although the majority of them are too small to be fished commercially. Oval and elongated, they have a semicircular mouth situated on the lower front edge of the body. Most familiar in European waters are the common, or Dover, sole and the sand, or French, sole. Both are varying shades of dark brown in colour, and grow up to about eighteen inches long. They live at depths of from thirty to two hundred feet on sand or mud. The sand sole is distinguished by a large nostril surrounded by a rosette-shaped layer of skin on the blind side. Soles appear to hunt by scent and touch, moving by night with the head raised, sometimes patting the bottom. The fish will often sense a morsel, retreat, inspect it, and finally eat it. The main diet consists of thin-shelled molluscs, crustaceans, bristle-worms, and a few small fish. By day, the sole lies buried in the bottom. Much esteemed as a food fish, the sole's flesh is at its best two to three days after the fish's death.

Left-sided flatfish

The turbots have their eyes on the left side of their bodies and are distinguished by the shapes of their mouths and bodies. The turbot, considered by many the most delicious of the edible flatfish, is a wide, almost circular, predatory fish reaching a maximum of fifty-five pounds, but more usually taken at twenty-five to thirty-two pounds. Its skin is scaleless on the eyed side, but bony knobs are scattered all over the surface. It ranges from the Mediterranean to as far north as Bergen on the Norwegian coast, on sandy, rocky, or mixed seabeds at sixty to two hundred feet. It feeds on small, bottom-dwelling fish, including other

flatfish, and, to a lesser extent, on shrimps, crabs and molluscs. A favourite feeding ground is in the lee of large humps and banks of gravel. Lying just below the crest, the turbot allows the current to sweep its food to where its highly-camouflaged body gives it the advantage of surprise over its unfortunate prey.

The brill is another member of the turbot group and very similar in appearance to the turbot. Other members of the group, less important commercially, include the topknots, megrim and scaldfish.

Scorpionfish

'Scorpionfish' is the common name for fishes of the family Scorpaenidae. They are a predominantly tropical family, related to the sculpins or bullheads of northern waters with whom they share the order Scleroparei. The members of this order have a skeletal peculiarity in the form of a bony ridge or 'stay' which runs across the cheek from eye to gill. The scorpionfishes are also distinctive in more obvious ways. Many of them are strikingly coloured and numerous spines and other appendages radiate out from the body. Whether they are considered beautiful or grotesque is very much a matter of taste, but their appearance is certainly remarkable. In addition, like real scorpions, they are often extremely venomous.

It is no coincidence that such distinctive fishes are also poisonous. Scorpionfishes are slow-moving and would be very vulnerable to predators, were it not for their venom. However, predators might seize them first and discover their noxious properties later, if they were not so easily distinguishable from other prey. As it is, most predators give them a wide berth, which is to the advantage of both parties.

Among the best known scorpionfishes are those of the genus *Pterois*. The lionfish, *Pterois volitans*, is also known as the turkeyfish, dragonfish, firefish, zebrafish or butterfly cod. The eyes are set high up on the large head. The mouth is wide and turned down at the corners, giving the fish a distinctly bad-tempered expression. The body and fins are always boldly striped but the coloration varies between red and blue, and brown and yellow. The pectoral fins of the lionfish are extremely long and divided into separate fronds which spread out like a fan around the fish's body. The high dorsal fin is also divided up and incorporates thirteen separate spines. At the base of these spines, which are very sharp, there are poison glands and there is also a poisonous spine in each of the pectoral fins and three in the anal fin.

Scorpionfishes use their venom only for defence. They seize their prey, which consists of small fish and invertebrates, in their mouths. They live mainly on or near the sea bed and are generally sluggish in behaviour, not actively pursuing their prey. Many species are ovoviviparous, a single female perhaps giving birth to more than 10,000 live young. A few, such as the California scorpionfish (*Scorpaena guttata*), are egg-layers. The eggs are contained in a pair of pear-shaped lumps of jelly which float at the surface of the sea. The young sink down to the bottom when they hatch.

Most members of the Scorpaenidae are excellent food fish, but some people are deterred from eating them by their unappetising appearance. However, several species are fished commercially. One of them is the redfish, *Sebastes marinus*, sometimes called the Norway haddock (although this name should really be reserved for a dif-

Above: Pterois radiata, *a relative of the lionfish which lives in the Red Sea. The spines are poisonous and the bold colours are a warning to predators to keep their distance.*
Left: Scorpaena plumieri, *one of the more grotesque scorpionfishes, found off Florida. Like many others it is capable of changing its colour*

ferent, though closely related, species, *Sebastes viviparus*). The redfish is a North Atlantic species, more fish-like and more free-swimming than other scorpionfishes, and is often taken in trawls. Its red skin is removed before the fish is offered to the public and most people who have eaten it would not recognize a redfish if they saw one in the sea.

The least active of all the scorpionfishes are the stonefishes of the genus *Synanceja*. Their mottled coloration makes them almost invisible among the weed and rocks of the sea bed. Small fish which do not notice them are snapped up as they swim by. In general the shallow-water scorpionfishes are more venomous than those that frequent deeper water. The stonefishes, which are sometimes found in water a few inches deep, are the most venomous fish in the world. Victims may suffer six hours of agonizing pain, culminating in death. Unfortunately, because they enter such shallow water and because they are so hard to see, it is easy to step on one when paddling. Stonefishes are found around most shores of the Indian Ocean.

A stonefish's venom is contained in a pair of sacs near the tip of each spine. The spines are grooved and, when they have pierced a victim's skin, poison flows along the grooves into the open wound. Although the venom is exceptionally potent, it is thought that the sacs cannot be replenished once it has been used.

Unlike the lionfish whose spines are permanently extended, the stonefish erects its spines only when danger threatens. Moreover, while the lionfish may point its spines towards an intruder or even lunge at him with them, the stonefish remains perfectly still. Such lethargic behaviour has disadvantages, however, since among the few enemies of the stonefish are large sea snails.

Below: the lionfish or turkeyfish, Pterois volitans. *It normally lies on the sea bed in wait for its prey, but it may drive small fish into a corner with its outspread fins*

Anglerfish

To the casual observer, the anglerfish and its relatives may look like survivals from the age of prehistoric monsters. But zoologists number them among the most highly developed of all fishes. Their grotesque appearance, which seems primitive in the eyes of the layman, is really the embodiment of some ingenious and specialized adaptations to their unique way of life.

The members of this order, the Lophiiformes, include more than 350 species, many of which are deep-sea fish. These creatures account for the majority of all fish found in the deeper waters of the bathypelagic zone, around 6,000 feet down. But more familiar, because it lives in the shallower waters over the European continental shelf, is the common European anglerfish, *Lophius piscatorius.* This fish is a bottom-dweller whose body is flattened and almost circular in shape.

The angler takes its name from the rod-like protrusion that projects from the top of its head. On the end of this 'fishing rod' there hangs a fleshy flap of skin which the fish waves above its enormous gaping mouth. The purpose of this apparatus—which is in fact an elaborate development of the foremost ray of the dorsal fin—is to entice smaller fish within range of the angler's jaws, in the belief that the lure constitutes some kind of food. Once the unwary victim has been coaxed within reach, the outwardly lethargic anglerfish opens its mouth and, with lightning speed, seizes the prey between its sharp teeth.

This sophisticated technique is complemented by the angler's remarkable camouflage. Its mottled coloration and skirt of weed-like appendages which grow around its body render the fish virtually indistinguishable from the rough sea floor which it haunts.

Whereas the anglerfish can attain a considerable size—sixty or seventy pounds, and a length of four feet—its close relative, the American goosefish (*Lophius americanus*), runs to five feet

Above right: Linophyrne arborifer, one of the many species of anglerfish which inhabit the perpetual darkness of the deep sea. The luminescent organ on the snout probably serves to attract a mate, as well as prey. Below: the common anglerfish. This species is common around the shores of western Europe. Its angling apparatus is clearly visible

and over a hundred pounds. Other members of this order, the Lophiiformes, do not exceed a few inches. These fish include the frogfishes of the coral seas whose rods are short and stumpy, the batfishes whose rods are retracted into a tube when not in use, and the sargassum or weedfish.

The deep-sea anglerfishes are other members of the order Lophiiformes. They live in the darkness of the oceanic abyss. Many of them carry a luminous lure on the end of their fishing rods, enticing deep-sea prawns and smaller fish towards the huge toothy mouth. *Lasiognathus saccostoma* has a very long fishing line, and *Linophryne arborifer*—sometimes called the tubby—sports a peculiar weed-like growth from its lower jaw, as well as the normal fishing equipment.

Another remarkable feature of these deep-sea anglerfishes is the fact that the male spends most of its life attached by its mouth to the female, on whom it is then entirely parasitic. All the male's organs degenerate, except those concerned with reproduction.

Unlike these more exotic anglerfishes, the shallow-water species are a not uncommon catch for sea anglers—comparative newcomers to an art in which the anglerfish itself has been expert for many millions of years.

Reptiles
marine turtles, iguanas and snakes

venture far below the surface, to which they must return periodically to breathe. The different groups have adopted different methods of swimming. Sea snakes swim like eels by undulations of the body and their tails are laterally flattened for the purpose, like those of true eels. Turtles, on the other hand, do not have the long tail or flexible body needed to swim like other marine animals. In fact their body, encased in its rigid carapace, is perhaps the least flexible of any found in a vertebrate animal. Instead, marine turtles possess modified feet which they use as paddles to propel themselves.

Reptiles once played a much larger part in the life of the sea than they do today. We know from fossil remains that marine reptiles were far more plentiful during the Mesozoic Era of the earth's history, between 100 and 200 million years ago. During this period, when the dinosaur ruled the land, the seas were roamed by many now-extinct reptiles, including plesiosaurs, mosasaurs and ichthyosaurs. Plesiosaurs were probably fish-eaters which used their long necks to follow the evasive movements of their darting prey. Mosasaurs were giant marine lizards, some growing to fifty feet in length. Ichthyosaurs were the most fish-like of all marine reptiles. With their pointed snouts and streamlined bodies, they bore a striking resemblance to dolphins.

Ichthyosaurs were truly aquatic reptiles in the sense that they did not return to land even to breed, giving birth to their young in the sea. All modern marine reptiles breed on land, although marine turtles and sea snakes spend the rest of their lives at sea. The marine iguana of the Galapagos is basically a land reptile which enters the sea to feed. However, its aquatic habits are so unusual that they have attracted a great deal of interest from naturalists.

The iguana is a relative newcomer to the ranks of marine reptiles. Turtles have lived in the sea for many millions of years. They witnessed the heyday of the great marine reptiles and survived their demise 100 million years ago.

Above: the marine iguana is a relative newcomer among marine reptiles. Most of its life is spent out of the water.
Left: the turtle is the oldest marine reptile and spends almost its entire life at sea, only coming ashore to breed

Marine reptiles are few in number compared to the other vertebrate animals of the sea. The two main groups of reptiles now living in the sea are the turtles and the sea snakes. Both are chiefly confined to the tropics. Unlike the invertebrates and fish described in previous chapters, marine reptiles are descendants of land animals and have had to undergo adaptations to fit them for life in the sea.

The way in which features developed for terrestial life have been remodified for use in the sea is a subject of absorbing interest for students of evolution. In this respect, marine reptiles are like the mammals which had to overcome similar problems in the course of their evolution, although reptiles are cold-blooded and lack the thick layer of fur or blubber which marine mammals use to conserve their body heat in the sea.

Marine reptiles have lungs and do not generally

Marine turtles

Marine turtles are the largest reptiles now living in the sea. There are only five extant species, all of which are natives of tropical and subtropical waters. The study of fossil remains has satisfied palaeontologists that the shell of a turtle, which is called the 'carapace', is virtually the same in modern species as it was in primitive forms that existed many millions of years ago. How such a shell developed and when the earliest turtles appeared on earth are questions whose answers are lost in prehistory. Like all the animals variously called turtles, tortoises and terrapins, marine turtles have evolved only slowly, lumbering through the ages with very little change over the course of millions of years.

The earliest fossil remains have been discovered in sedimentary rocks of the Upper Cretaceous period, dating from about eighty million years ago. This was the time when the largest known tortoise, *Archelon*, flourished. But scientists believe that even more primitive forms existed in the Triassic period, 200 million years ago.

Marine turtles are animals of considerable economic, as well as scientific, interest. Sadly this has led to their slaughter on a large scale.

Adaptation to marine life

Like freshwater turtles, marine species are more streamlined in shape than their terrestial relatives. Their carapaces are also much flatter, more lightweight and less tightly sealed. But an even more significant difference is seen in the feet. Aquatic turtles spend a great part of their time in the water and their feet have gradually adapted to the needs of swimming instead of walking on land. This transformation is most strikingly marked in the marine species, whose claws have atrophied and whose limbs have turned into flippers.

The surviving marine turtles are divided into two families. The Cheloniidae comprise four hard-shelled species – the loggerhead *Caretta caretta*, the hawksbill *Eretmochelys imbricata*, the green turtle *Chelonia mydas* and the Kemp's Ridley turtle *Lepidochelys kempi*. According to some authors there are two species of *Lepidochelys*, but others recognize only two sub-

Left: after having laid her last batch of eggs, a female leathery turtle crawls back to the sea. This species is easily recognized by the longitudinal ridges along the carapace, or shell Below: the green turtle Chelonia mydas *is widely distributed in tropical seas. Superbly adapted to life in the water, marine turtles normally leave the ocean only to lay their eggs on selected beaches, although green turtles sometimes bask in the sun on small islands or on rocks*

species. The Dermochelyidae have only one living representative, the leatherback turtle *Dermochelys coriacea*, which is the largest of all turtles.

Strange as it may seem, considering their size and relative abundance, little is known of the biology and behaviour of these marine turtles. The lack of information stems largely from the fact that they spend almost their entire life in the water, often below the surface. Furthermore, zoologists have only recently begun to take a real interest in them.

Drama on the beach

Reproduction is the only phase of the sea turtle's life cycle which has been observed in detail, for this dramatic activity takes place on land. When the time draws near for egg-laying, the females swim to certain tropical beaches. The sites are always the same, year after year. Most probably this breeding behaviour is a kind of genetic 'imprinting', the information concerning place and timing being transmitted from generation to generation within a species, even within a given population.

On certain shores the local people profit from these ancestral behaviour patterns by killing the females, not when they first set foot on land, but after they have laid their eggs. Each female lays approximately 400 eggs, but at intervals and in different places. Dispersing the eggs in this manner is undoubtedly a safety measure designed to avert the possible catastrophe of losing most or all of the eggs to land predators. While the females are laying their eggs, the males assemble on the same beaches, waiting until their partners return to the water before copulating with them. This curious habit, rare among other vertebrates, arises partly from the fact that the spermatozoa of turtles are extraordinarily potent, remaining alive in the genital tracts of the females for many months and sometimes being active for several years after copulation occurs. It is therefore possible that a newly laid egg will be fertilized by a spermatozoon received on a previous mating. But even stronger reasons for this unusual form of mating behaviour are the needs to conserve energy and to guarantee security. Consequently males and females couple once only and in a particular spot where the sexual act and egg-laying can take place simultaneously.

So far no real light has been shed on other aspects of sea turtles' behaviour – especially the means by which they find their way through the vast uncharted ocean, from the regions where they normally live, back to the beaches where they lay their eggs. How do they select the routes and what methods do they use for navigating so unerringly to their chosen destinations?

It has been suggested that marine turtles find their way through the oceans by observing the positions of the sun and the stars, although so far there has been no absolute proof of this. The theory has also been put forward that the

reptiles make use of their sense of smell, in the same manner as salmon, to identify the waters through which they travel, but this again is no more than hypothesis.

Danger of extinction

The relationship between man and the various species of sea turtles is a sad example of the disastrous consequences of greed and ignorance which in so many parallel cases has led to the massacre, sometimes extermination, of a zoological group. For centuries the inhabitants

*Far left: a female
green turtle lays up
to 400 eggs over a
period of several
weeks, in hollows
which she scrapes out
of the sand. She then
returns to the sea
and leaves the eggs to
hatch by themselves.
Far left below: an
egg-laying green
turtle is almost buried
by the sand which she
has scraped away.
Left: baby turtles
scuttle down the beach
to the sea almost as
soon as they hatch.
Many are devoured by
predators; those that
reach the sea keep
close to the shore for
several months before
striking out into the
open ocean.
Below: green turtles
migrate thousands of
miles to their
breeding beaches*

of regions where turtles gather for breeding have eaten the flesh and eggs of the reptiles, but have taken only as much as they need so as not to jeopardize future supplies. No such common-sense has motivated the activities of the industrial concerns which have more recently discovered the huge profits to be made in canning turtle soup (obtained from the cartilaginous substance filling the interstices of the plastron). It did not take long for this trade to destroy the age-old equilibrium of the turtle population. The demand has become so great that entire communities of turtles have been massacred in the breeding season, bringing about an alarming decline in numbers. Today, unless this insane traffic is halted or controlled, there is a real danger of sea turtles disappearing for ever.

Hatching of the eggs takes only a brief time and occurs almost simultaneously in every colony. Consequently hordes of newly hatched turtles may be seen heading blindly for the sea. This is the most critical stage in their life. Completely defenceless, the tiny reptiles inevitably attract a number of land predators, including sea birds, and sometimes only a very small proportion reaches its destination.

The green turtle

The green turtle is probably the best known of the marine species, both because of its abundance and from the fact that it is the principal source of turtle soup. The majority of green turtles live in comparatively shallow tropical waters, generally in the open sea, where the rocky

bottom is well covered with algae which also provides places of refuge.

Essentially herbivorous, the green turtle feeds chiefly on the marine plants eel-grass and turtle-grass, but occasionally supplements its diet with molluscs and crustaceans. Zoologists sometimes distinguish two subspecies, one an inhabitant of the Pacific, the other of the Atlantic, which are additionally differentiated by colour.

The breeding season varies considerably according to where the different communities live. Those that lay their eggs away from tropical

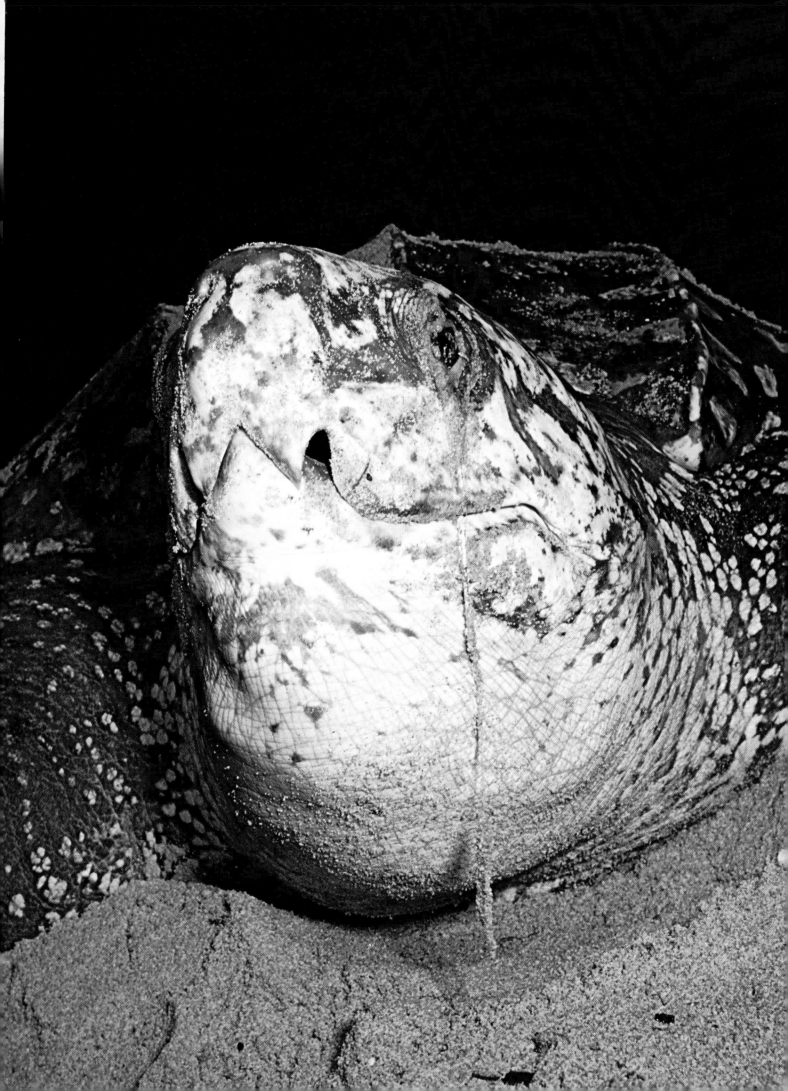

latitudes tend to concentrate all their sexual activity into the three hottest summer months. On the other hand, the green turtles of the tropics lay their eggs all the year round. Incidentally they are among the rare reptiles which do not reproduce regularly each year. In Borneo, for example, the female lays eggs once every third year, in Central America in alternate years.

As is the case with other sea turtles, the journey from the water's edge to the nesting site is long and arduous. The enormous animal drags herself heavily up the beach, leaving a deep furrow behind her. From time to time she comes to a halt, the sounds of her noisy breathing being rather like a series of heavy sighs. This breathlessness is understandable, for a really tremendous effort is required for these animals, out of their natural element, to fill their lungs with air. Furthermore, because the air is so dry, the ocular glands of the turtles exude a thick, translucent liquid, popularly, but mistakenly, supposed to be tears of grief!

Having selected a convenient nesting site, each female excavates a hole with her hind flippers, into which she deposits the eggs (looking like ping-pong balls). She then covers them with sand and carefully flattens the surface. Now unburdened, and taking advantage of the descending slope of the beach, she makes her way rapidly back to the ocean. But she will repeat the process more than once, in fact between two and seven times, at approximately two-week intervals, until she has laid about 400 eggs. The incubation period ranges from forty to seventy-two days, according to the latitude. How many eggs will hatch is largely a matter of luck, for the various nests may be ransacked by rodents and dogs as well as by man.

Copulation takes place after all the eggs have been laid, usually in the open sea, far from the shore. It is quite common to see two males accompanying each female. When the incubation period is over the babies break the shells of the eggs with the aid of a horny egg-tooth on the tip of the upper jaw, and burrow out of the sand. By some miracle of timing, they all hatch more or less simultaneously, which means they emerge from the sand in large groups. Their forelimbs are already well developed and they lose no time in scuttling as fast as they can towards the sea. Those that manage to evade predators and reach the ocean do not swim out very far at this early stage of life, but feed principally on invertebrates caught near the coast. They are seldom seen in company with adults which normally feed far from the shore. The only place where they have been observed in large numbers is on the west coast of Florida, where they gather in the spring. Here they remain until the autumn. But before striking out for more distant waters they change their diet, concentrating mainly on aquatic plants. Then they begin their migration, disappearing without trace in the open seas and not revisiting land until they return as adults to breed.

The hawksbill

The hawksbill is easily identified by its attractive shell, made up of multicoloured, translucent plates. This carapace forms the basis of the lucrative tortoiseshell industry of the Orient, notably in Ceylon, Indonesia and Japan.

This species inhabits tropical seas but unlike the green turtle is generally to be found in bays, river estuaries and any areas of shallow water with scattered plant cover. Although its distribution may sometimes coincide with that of the green turtle and the loggerhead, it is not usually present in such numbers. Of medium size (the shell of an adult does not measure more than three feet in length), this turtle is omnivorous, though there is a preference for substances of animal origin. The diet consists mainly of crustaceans, molluscs and algae.

Experts sometimes distinguish two subspecies, again with one race in the Pacific and the other in the Atlantic. The former breeds from November until February, the latter from April to August. Eggs are laid in two or three stages, at intervals of less than three weeks, until about 500 have been deposited by each female. At birth the individual shields of the carapace overlap one another but as the baby turtle grows these gradually lock into the normal position.

The loggerhead

Considerably larger than the green turtle is the loggerhead, which differs from other marine turtles by reason of an elongated carapace with characteristically marked external plates. This species frequents shallow bays, sometimes appearing in river estuaries, but is seldom observed on the high seas.

Basically carnivorous, the loggerhead feeds

Above: the Kemp's Ridley turtle Lepidochelys kempi *is the smallest of the sea turtles. Once abundant in the Pacific, Indian and Atlantic Oceans, it is today an endangered species.*
Left: a female leathery turtle Dermochelys coriacea *scoops a nest-hole out of the sand. The 'tears' flowing from her eyes help to counteract the dryness of the air*

Left: the loggerhead turtle Caretta caretta *is usually found in shallow coastal waters, sometimes visiting estuaries, and is rarely seen in the open ocean*

in the main on fishes, molluscs, crustaceans and sponges. But analyses of stomach contents have revealed the presence of a certain amount of plant matter, notably eel-grass and turtle-grass.

The range of distribution of the loggerhead extends from the northern to the southern limits of the tropics, and here too there are two distinct subspecies in the Pacific and Atlantic Oceans. The Pacific race breeds along the entire length of the Californian coastline, the Atlantic subspecies off the shores of Florida and Georgia. The females lay their eggs (from 120 to 150) in May, June and July, although the first batches, according to reports of local fishermen, usually appear at the time of the first spring tide in June. As a protection against the tides, the eggs are laid beyond the high-tide mark. The incubation period is between thirty and seventy-five days.

The Kemp's Ridley turtle

Until comparatively recently zoologists regarded the populations of the Kemp's Ridley turtles inhabiting the Atlantic and the Pacific/Indian Oceans as two distinct species, the Kemp's Ridley and the olive Ridley. Today, however, they are usually classified as subspecies of *Lepidochelys kempi.* Unlike green turtles, they have five pairs of lateral shields on the carapace.

The Kemp's Ridley turtles are the smallest of the sea turtles, for the carapace of the adults does not exceed twenty-eight inches in length. Among Florida fishermen it is popularly believed that they are crosses between green turtles and hawksbills, but this seems unlikely in view of the fact that they are distinguished from these two species by their marginal plates.

These turtles generally inhabit shallow waters. Their diet is basically vegetarian, supplemented

occasionally by molluscs and crustaceans.

The populations found in the Caribbean reproduce between December and February, those of the eastern Pacific from August until November, those from the waters around Ceylon from September to January, and those found off Burma either in March or April.

The leathery turtle

The leathery turtle or leatherback is the only representative of the family Dermochelyidae. Although the distribution range of the species extends to the warm waters of many oceans, individuals normally tend to confine themselves to a particular region. Just the same, leatherbacks sometimes make long journeys through the high seas to appear off the shores of the British Isles, Spain, South Africa and Argentina.

Of all turtles, including freshwater species, they are the best suited to aquatic life. Largest of the whole order, the adults may weigh more than 1,200 pounds and measure up to seven-and-a-half feet long. In general appearance they look much like other turtles but their forefeet are transformed into enormously powerful flippers. The carapace too has undergone modification, having become elongated and smooth, possibly to facilitate passage through the water. It consists of small, juxtaposed bony shields of various shapes, which lie under the skin, and it is marked by seven longitudinal ridges. This type of armour-plating is thus different in structure from the shells of other species.

Little is known about the feeding habits of these huge turtles. But analysis of the stomach contents of several individuals has revealed a virtually omnivorous diet, including fishes, crustaceans, algae and young octopuses.

Marine iguanas

When Charles Darwin visited the Galapagos Islands in 1835, as a young naturalist on board HMS *Beagle,* he found it was the home of a number of unusual species of animal. Because of their isolation from the mainland, the animals of the Galapagos had been able to evolve in various unique ways, and Darwin's observations of these animals gave him the key to his theory of evolution.

The first arrivals

We can only speculate about how the first land reptiles arrived in the Galapagos. The islands are situated in the Pacific Ocean, 600 miles west of the shores of Ecuador. Geological evidence suggests that the group was never connected to the mainland of South America and the archipelago is possibly volcanic in origin. The most likely explanation for the presence of the land reptiles is that they arrived by chance, on rafts of floating vegetation carried by the Galapagos on the cool Peru Current. Among the species which colonized the islands – perhaps in this way – were lizards, snakes, tortoises and iguanas.

One of the iguanas evolved into a unique species – the marine iguana (*Amblyrhynchus cristatus*), which has taken advantage of what was presumably once an unexploited food source – seaweed. This it crops from the rocks either when they are exposed at low tide – though this is a very restricted zone as the tidal rise and fall is only six feet – or by swimming out and diving as much as thirty-five feet to the sea-bed. Here it can stay for at least thirty minutes; Darwin noted that one survived after being forcibly held under-water for an hour. This experiment has, fortunately, not been repeated!

The iguana swims by moving its flattened tail from side to side. The legs are held limp by the creature's sides. The feet have long toes with strong claws, giving an extremely strong grip which is needed when the iguana has to hang onto rocks or come ashore through raging surf.

Despite their popular name, marine iguanas rarely venture far from land, and never from island to island. This geographic separation of the iguana populations is essential for the process of speciation – the development of new animal

Left: a colony of marine iguanas on land. At the start of the day marine iguanas bask in the sun in order to build up enough reserves of body heat to enable them to stay in the cool water

species through evolution. Such a separation is probably even now bringing about the splitting up of one species into several, for there are marked differences in colour and pattern of markings between the populations on different islands of the Galapagos.

There are also great differences in size between the iguanas of a single island. Sometimes there are as many as several thousand small individuals (about two-and-a-half to three feet long) in one place, while only a few miles away there may be far fewer but larger individuals, measuring five foot three inches or more in length. These differences are probably due to local feeding conditions in different parts of the island.

Iguanas, like all other reptiles, are cold-blooded. Thus, having to spend much time in relatively cool water poses some problems. At the start of its day an iguana will bask in the sun on the black lava until its body temperature rises. It then goes into the water to feed, remaining there until the cold forces it to come ashore to warm up again. Much has been written about how these animals prefer to be on land. Observers have noticed that if they caught one and threw it into the sea it always came ashore, apparently because it did not like being in the water. However, the correct explanation is that the animals which are hot are easier to catch because they are found basking in the open. These individuals lose body heat when they enter cold water and so they have no wish to stay in the sea. On the other hand, the same iguanas when their body temperature is low suffer no loss through being immersed; consequently such individuals are more content to swim away.

Seaweed-eaters

The iguanas' diet of seaweed contains large quantities of salt, and this is excreted by a pair of glands situated between the eye and nostril on each side of the head. From time to time, a jet of salty water is shot out forcibly through the nostrils into the air.

Female iguanas lay two or three large, soft white eggs in a burrow dug in the sand. These are hatched by the heat of the sun, the young emerging after some two months. Although fully-grown iguanas have few enemies, the small ones are much sought after by herons, hawks, snakes and other predators, and must therefore be far more secretive than the adults, which can bask in the sun without danger when not feeding.

Of the two or three thousand species of lizard in the world today (about 700 of which are classified as iguanas) the Galapagos marine iguana is the only marine species. Because of this fact it has enjoyed a certain fame, disproportionate to its numbers. It is obviously far from being totally marine, but we should bear in mind that its evolution is not yet complete.

Left: a pair of iguanas under water. They can stay there for as long as 30 minutes. Both this and their diet of seaweed make them unique

Sea snakes

Many species of snake are excellent swimmers (the common grass snake is a good example), but certain species have adopted an almost totally marine existence. These snakes number among the most dangerous animals in the sea, in some ways more dangerous than maneating sharks. Their venom is more deadly, even, than that of their land-based cousins, the cobras and mambas of south-east Asia.

Sea snakes are found in warm tropical seas, in the Indian and western Pacific Oceans, ranging from the Persian Gulf in the west to the waters off Japan in the east. They occur mainly in shallow inshore waters where they may often be seen basking in the sun on the surface, which, as reptiles, is their only way of maintaining their body temperature. However, one species has extended its realm into the open ocean and is now found from the eastern shores of Africa to the western seaboard of the Americas. This is the yellow-bellied sea snake, *Pelamis platurus*. Although there are no sea snakes in the Atlantic at present, it seems possible that *Pelamis platurus* or another species may one day find its way into the Caribbean.

Sea serpents

The sea snakes belong to the family called Hydrophidiiae which contains about fifty species. A typical sea snake measures about three or four feet in length, but some may grow to nearer ten. The gigantic serpents of legend, which threw their serpentine coils around the ships of the early seafarers, dragging them to their doom, have yet to be substantiated by scientific evidence.

The ancestors of modern sea snakes were land animals that lived in forests and grasslands. Over the course of time these snakes took to the sea and their bodies adapted to an aquatic existence. No major anatomical changes were necessary to effect this transformation. The body of a snake is eel-like, and like the true eels the sea snake has also become flattened at the sides, as an aid to swimming (one species, *Laticauda colubrina*, is actually called the flat-tailed sea snake). The tail is rudder-shaped and the snake propels itself by powerful sculling strokes on a serpentine course through the water.

Another feature that distinguishes sea snakes from their counterparts on land is the exaggerated difference between the proportions of the head and those of the remainder of the body. Compared to the head, the hind part of the body is usually very thick, often two or three times larger in diameter than the head and neck. One genus in particular is called *Microcephalophis*, which means 'small-headed'. The sea snakes of this genus have a head which is so tiny as to be grotesque, when compared to the size of the abdomen, five times thicker than the fore part of the body. The function of this heavy hind body seems to be to act as a fulcrum. Thus when the snake shoots its head forward to strike at its prey it has a longer reach. If the whole body was more or less uniform in weight, the rear part would be propelled backwards through the water as

Right: sea snakes differ from other snakes in that their heads and necks tend to be smaller and slimmer in proportion to the rest of their body. Their nostrils are set high up on the head so they can breath without raising their heads out of the water

much as the forepart moved forward when the snake lunged.

As air-breathing reptiles, sea snakes must return to the surface periodically to breathe. Their nostrils are set on top of the snout so the animals need only break the water to get oxygen. Valves close off the nostrils when the snakes submerge. Like most snakes, there is only one lung, but it is extremely long, often three quarters of the length of the body. At the base of the lung, there is a small sac for storing air and the whole lung acts as a hydrostatic organ, effecting the buoyancy of the body. The epiglottis, the cartilaginous flap covering the opening to the windpipe, can be inserted into the nasal passage to form a tube leading from the nostrils to the lung. Thus, when the snake is feeding, no water passes down the windpipe to enter the lung. Depending on the species, water temperature and activity, sea snakes vary in their ability to remain submerged. Some snakes have been observed to stay underwater for two hours or more, whilst others remain down for only a few minutes.

The large scales on the belly, which aid land snakes in crawling over rough terrain, are reduced or absent in sea snakes. This feature is used to divide the family into two subfamilies, namely the Laticaudinae and the Hydrophinae. The former are the most primitive members of the sea snake group. They have large scales on their bellies, enabling them to creep about over tidal flats or rocks which they frequent to lay their eggs or to prey on the eggs or young of shore birds. *Laticauda* is a member of this sub-

Right: the flat-tailed sea snake (Laticauda colubrina) *occasionally ventures on land to supplement its diet with the eggs of sea birds. Its tail is flattened as an aid to swimming. Females attain a length of 56 inches, almost twice that of the male*

family. It grows to a length of six feet and its body measures about three inches in diameter. Due to their habit of coming ashore, the natives of the Philippines and Polynesia hunt these snakes in great numbers, roasting their flesh on spits and seasoning it with rich sauces. In these islands, as in Japan and China, sea snake flesh is considered a great delicacy and well worth the risk taken to catch these venomous reptiles.

The second subfamily of sea snakes, the Hydrophinae, are truely marine, never coming onto dry land. Unlike their egg-laying relatives, members of the Hydrophinae are viviparous, giving birth to live young. A simple placenta-like membrane connects the developing young to the mother's oviduct. Water and oxygen are transferred across this membrane, but it has not yet been established whether food is also given from the mother's blood supply. Some sea snakes give birth to as many as nine young but others only produce one or two.

The belly scales of the Hydrophinae are very small, similar to the scales covering the rest of the body. They glide smoothly through the sea, offering little resistance to the water. The largest sea snakes belong to this subfamily. The blue-banded snakes, called *Hydrophis*, reach a length of eight feet, sometimes ten feet. One species of this genus, *Hydrophis semperi*, has become adapted to freshwater, living in the landlocked Lake Taal, in southern Luzon in the Philippines.

Deadly venom

Fish, especially eels, are the chief food of sea snakes. Since they are slow swimmers and cannot pursue their prey, the snakes rely on stealth, cornering their victims amongst crevices in the rocks. With lightning speed, they strike at the prey, stabbing with their sharp fangs which protrude from the upper jaw. A deadly venom is secreted from the salivary glands and flows down a groove on the outside of each fang into the wound in the victim's flesh. The venom causes instant paralysis and the prey is swallowed whole. Some sea snakes feed on prawns and others on fish eggs. The latter do not use their venom and assume the comical pose of burying their heads in the sand with their long bodies drifting upright, like an anchor chain. During this leisurely meal, of sucking eggs from the sand, the sea snake is completely unprotected. But it has few enemies. No species of fish in the Pacific or Indian Ocean will touch a sea snake. Even sharks, the scavengers of the sea, will not attack them. All seem to have learned, probably from bitter experience over millions of years of evolution, that to eat one of these serpents means certain death. Besides man, their sole predators seem to be sea eagles, who swoop down and seize them from the surface waters while the snakes are sun bathing.

Sight is probably the main sense involved in hunting, the eyes being placed well out on the sides of the head for maximum vision. The forked tongue, which is the organ of smell in land snakes, is small in sea snakes since the sense of smell is reduced in an aquatic environment.

The venom is produced in small quantities, for example only 55.4 milligrams of venom being extracted from the beaked sea snake *Enhydrina*, in comparison to 700 milligrams from the Egyptian cobra and 1,530 milligrams from a viper species. But the venom from the beaked sea snake has been shown, in laboratory tests, to be the most potent of all snake venoms. It is said that one drop of *Enhydrina's* venom will kill five men. It is the most feared sea snake of the tropics. Several deaths are reported each year, especially among Malayan fishermen, bitten whilst disentangling these snakes from their nets. The small-headed sea snakes come second on the list for snake toxicity.

Sea snake venom is unique in that there is no immediate pain or swelling in the bitten area. The reaction comes several hours later, when

the symptoms include weakness, stiff jaws and general muscle fatigue. The venom attacks the nerves and destroys myoglobin, the protein substance of muscles, which is excreted in the urine, turning it a reddish-brown colour. The victim may die in less than twelve hours, though it usually takes several days. Unfortunately, since so little is known about sea snakes, few antivenoms have been made. In Penang and parts of Australia, intensive research is going on to produce antivenoms. It has been found that antivenom for tiger snake bite is partially effective in neutralizing the poison of some sea snakes. However, much work remains to be done to protect people from this deadly scourge of tropical seas.

Above: yellow-bellied sea snakes (Pelamis platurus) *are the most wide-ranging species. They are found from the east coast of Africa to the west coast of America. They are sometimes seen hunting in groups near the surface*

Mammals

warm-blooded animals of the sea

Above: sealions spend part of their time out of the water, although they are better adapted to swimming than moving over land. Left: dolphins and porpoises are among the most aquatic mammals, spending their whole lives at sea

Although they are few in number compared to the myriads of marine invertebrates and fish, mammals are prominent in the life of the sea. One of them is the largest animal that has ever lived, while some rank among the most intelligent animals in the world.

Marine mammals exhibit typical mammalian features. They suckle their young, which are born alive, and they are warm blooded. Whales, which have lost the hair on their bodies during the course of evolution, are the most unlike other mammals. Otters, for example, are clearly not far removed from land mammals, but we cannot even guess the appearance of the terrestial animals from which whales are descended.

The whales and dolphins, together with the sea cows, are the most aquatic mammals, spending their entire lives in the sea. The sea otter and the seals come ashore periodically to rest or

breed. The animals in the first group use their fish-like tails for propulsion (although the two flukes of the tail project horizontally not vertically as in fish.) On the other hand, seals swim with their feet, while sea otters propel themselves by wriggling their whole body and tail like an eel.

However, marine mammals share certain features of their adaptation to marine life, even though they are descended from different ancestors. In most, the overall shape of the body is smooth and streamlined. The legs tend to be short – or nonexistent – and the feet are broad and flipper-like. The nostrils are sited high on the head and important physiological changes have taken place, such as a slowing of the heart-beat when they dive, enabling them to remain underwater for long periods.

A mammal's well developed vision is of limited use in the sea, where visibility is generally poor. However, scientists have shown that dolphins possess highly efficient systems of echo-location with which they can locate and identify their prey. They also use sounds to communicate with one another. Other whales, both baleen and toothed, make noises and it is possible that they have similar powers.

Because they are warm-blooded, marine mammals have developed special insulation which preserves their body heat, even in the coldest seas. This takes the form of a layer of fat, or blubber, in the whales, thick fur in the sea otter, and a combination of both in the seals.

It is the last-mentioned feature, in particular, which gives marine mammals enormous commercial value. Unfortunately, indiscriminate slaughter has brought some species to the brink of extinction, and beyond. Because they are less prolific than sea fish and other commercially important marine animals, they are less well able to recover from the effects of persecution. Paradoxically, marine mammals, which people find the most impressive and appealing animals in the sea, have also been the most ruthlessly exploited by man.

Baleen whales

The blue whale, attaining a length of a hundred feet and approaching a weight of 150 tons, is the largest animal alive today, and possibly ever to have lived. Even the huge dinosaurs that ruled the earth over seventy million years ago did not reach this size. The blue whale is surely the mighty Leviathan mentioned by Job in the Bible that 'maketh the deep to boil like a pot; he maketh the sea like a pot of ointment'.

Besides the blue, the right, grey, fin, sei and humpback whales are all members of the suborder Mysticeti, within the great order Cetacea, the whales. The Mysticeti are the baleen or whalebone whales, named after the hair-like bristles called the baleen, that hang down from the roof of the mouth like an internal moustache. The name Mysticeti is derived from the Latin word *mystax,* meaning moustache. The baleen is used as a filter, for straining the tiny animals of the plankton out of the water – the food of these giant mammals. There are three families of baleen whale – the rorquals of the family Balaenopteridae, the right whales of the family Balaenidae and the grey whales of the Eschrichtiidae family.

Rorquals are streamlined, torpedo-shaped whales that can attain a speed of twenty-five knots in short bursts. They have a dorsal fin set far back on the body, the head is flattened and a number of grooves run from the lower lip halfway along the underside of the body. Until recently rorquals have been depicted as having a capacious mouth and throat that gives them the appearance of chronic obesity. This representation is based on dead whales hauled ashore at whaling stations. In life, the floor of the mouth is flattened, so that these whales are even more streamlined than has previously been supposed.

The largest rorqual is the blue whale *Balaenoptera musculus.* It is a cosmopolitan species, migrating during the spring and summer from tropical waters to the edge of the pack ice in the northern and southern hemispheres. Pygmy blue whales have been reported from the southern Indian Ocean, but these are considered to be a race rather than a separate species.

Second in size to the blue is the fin whale *B. physalus,* which may attain a length of eighty feet. It has a larger dorsal fin than the blue whale, and its underside is pure white. It also has an asymmetric colour pattern, the lower right lip being white while the left side is pigmented. The baleen hairs are all blue-grey, except those on the right at the front of the mouth which are yellow-white. It has a similar distribution to the blue whale, though not frequenting tropical waters to the same extent.

The three smaller species of rorqual are the sei (pronounced sigh), Bryde's (pronounced brooder's) and the minke whale (often called the little piked or lesser rorqual). These species reach a length of about sixty, fifty and thirty feet respectively. The sei and Bryde's whales are distinguished from each other by the longer grooves running to the navel and the longitudinal ridges on the snout of Bryde's whale. The latter is restricted to tropical and subtropical waters, unlike the sei whale which is found in all the world's oceans. The cosmopolitan minke whales have white baleen and their flippers are decorated with a white band.

Somewhat different from the other rorquals is the humpback whale *Megaptera novaeangliae.* Growing to a length of about fifty feet, its body is stout and the characteristic streamlining of the rorqual is lost. The outstanding feature of the humpback is the extremely long flippers, which may be one-third the length of the body. Sensitive bristles grow out of knobs scattered on the snout and lower lip. The flippers have irregular edges, also covered with protuberances.

Persecution of the right whale

The right whales received their name because in the early days of whaling they were the right whales to catch. The Basques were the first people to hunt them systematically during the eleventh century. These whales swam slowly, cruising at about three knots, or up to ten knots when pursued. Another useful feature was that they floated when dead. Thus they could be captured and handled from small boats. Furthermore, their whalebone plates were extremely long. Before the invention of plastics, whalebone was very valuable and, at one time during the history of whaling, right whales were stripped of their whalebone and the carcasses cast free, without even having the blubber removed. As a consequence of their value and ease of capture, the right whales became very scarce and today are rarely seen.

The three species are the Biscayan or black right whale, the Greenland right whale or bowhead, and the pygmy right whale. All are characterised by huge heads (one-third the total body length), arched upper jaws and greatly enlarged lower lips to accommodate the long baleen, which, in the case of the Greenland right whale, may grow up to fourteen feet in length. The Biscayan right whale has an outgrowth of horny skin on the snout called the 'bonnet'. The pygmy right whale is the only one of the three to bear a dorsal fin, while none of them have the ventral grooves characteristic of the rorqual.

The grey whale *Eschrichtius gibbosus*, of the family Eschrichtiidae, was also massacred on a vast scale by whalers and became very rare. It has been estimated that in 1946–1947 there were a mere 250 grey whales left alive. Fortunately, under strict protection, their numbers have increased in recent years. Thousands of tourists now flock to the Pacific coasts of California and Mexico to watch the grey whales return from the Bering Sea to give birth to their calves in the warm, sheltered coastal waters. Although they are now confined to the north Pacific, fossil remains found in the Zuider Zee prove that grey whales were once abundant in the Atlantic, where they were hunted in medieval times.

Structurally, the grey whale lies between the rorqual and the right whale. Like the latter, it has no dorsal fin (there are a number of small humps running along the tail) but, like the rorqual, it has grooves on the underside of the body. However, there are only about two or three short grooves on the throat, as compared to the ninety or so grooves of the fin or blue whale.

Diving adaptations

Since whales are mammals, they must return to the surface of the water to breathe. They are wonderfully adapted to their aquatic way of life. The nostrils, or blowholes, are placed on top of the head, allowing the animal to breathe with a minimum of its body breaking the surface. Just before it dives, the whale takes a deep breath and powerful muscles around the blow-

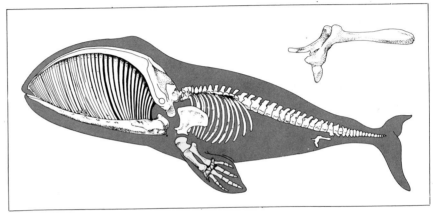

hole close it tightly so no water enters the lungs. And when a whale is feeding underwater, the windpipe leading to the lungs fits neatly into the blowhole pipe, thus forming a sealed tube, ensuring that the whole system is waterproof.

The lungs of a baleen whale are not large in comparison to the size of its body. But a whale breathes deeply, filling its lungs to capacity before a dive, and the blood is rapidly charged with oxygen. During a dive, the heartbeat slows down and many of the blood vessels become distended so that blood flows through them much more slowly. This decreases the rate at which oxygen is absorbed by the tissues. The blood circulates only to vital organs – the brain, heart, muscles and the rest of the nervous system; circulation to less vital parts of the body, such as the alimentary canal, is slowed down.

There is a further aid to diving. The muscles are a deep red due to the presence of myoglobin, a substance similar to the oxygen-carrier of the blood, haemoglobin. Myoglobin has a great affinity for oxygen, combining with it and storing it in the muscles. This is why a rorqual can hold its breathe for up to forty minutes during a dive, using the oxygen store in its muscles as its life support.

On surfacing, the whale blows, forcing the air out of its lungs with a rasping whistle. As the air rushes out a spout of vapour appears, hangs momentarily and disperses. People used to think this was a fountain of water. More recently,

Right: the skeleton of a right whale. The jaw bones are highly arched to accommodate the long blades of baleen which hang from the roof of the mouth. During their long evolution from cloven-hoofed mammals, whales have lost all trace of external hind limbs. All that remains to testify to their land origins are the hip bones (also shown enlarged), embedded deep in the muscles of the underside. In some whales the leg bones also remain, fused to the hip bones

Biscayan or North Atlantic right whale
(*Eubalaena glacialis*)

Bowhead or Greenland right whale
(*Balaena mysticetus*)

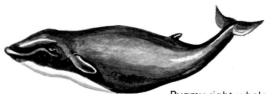

Pygmy right whale
(*Neobalaena marginata*)

Common rorqual or fin whale
(*Balaenoptera physalus*)

Rudolph's rorqual or sei whale
(*Balaenoptera borealis*)

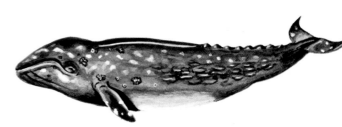

Californian or Pacific grey whale
(*Eschrichtius gibbosus*)

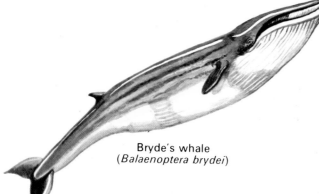

Bryde's whale
(*Balaenoptera brydei*)

Lesser rorqual or minke whale
(*Balaenoptera acutorostrata*)

Blue whale
(*Balaenoptera musculus*)

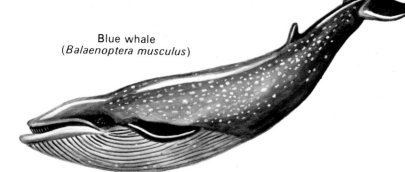

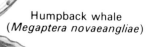

Humpback whale
(*Megaptera novaeangliae*)

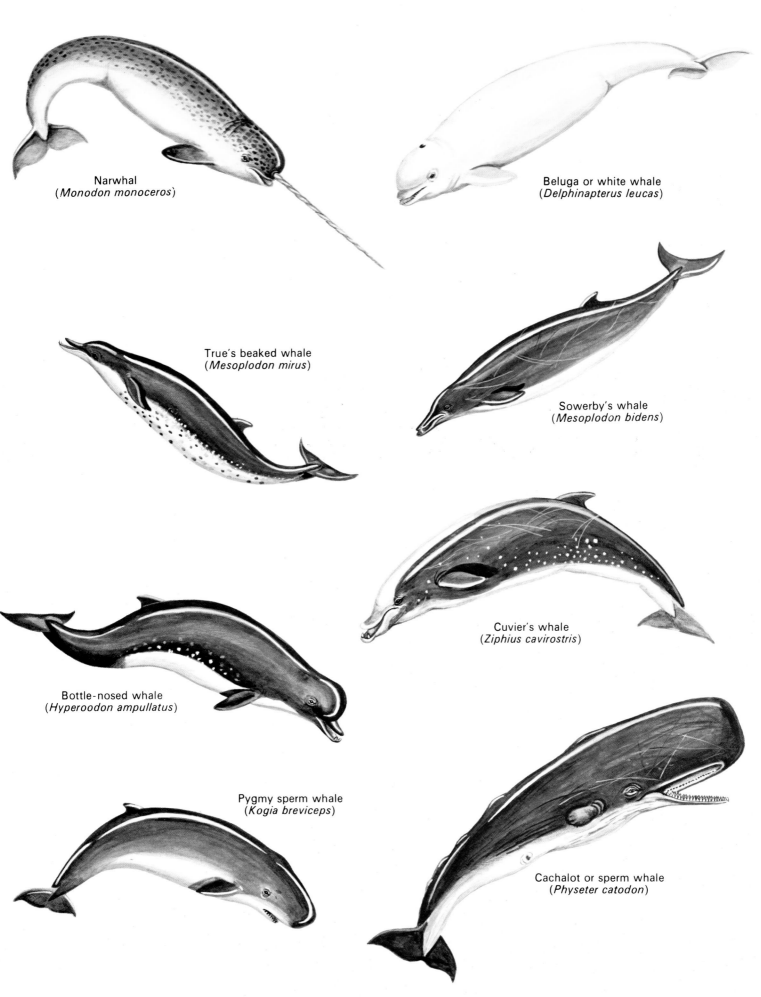

Narwhal
(*Monodon monoceros*)

Beluga or white whale
(*Delphinapterus leucas*)

True's beaked whale
(*Mesoplodon mirus*)

Sowerby's whale
(*Mesoplodon bidens*)

Cuvier's whale
(*Ziphius cavirostris*)

Bottle-nosed whale
(*Hyperoodon ampullatus*)

Pygmy sperm whale
(*Kogia breviceps*)

Cachalot or sperm whale
(*Physeter catodon*)

Above: upside-down view of the upper jaw of a baleen whale. Clearly visible are the masses of baleen hairs which grow down from the roof of the whale's mouth. These act like a sieve, filtering millions of tiny planktonic organisms from the water as it passes through the mouth

it has been regarded as a cloud of water vapour caused by the sudden cooling of the exhaled breath, as happens to our breathe on a cold day. But, in the warm air of the tropics, the blow is seen to consist, at least in part, of an oily foam. Along the length of the nasal passage, there are numerous sinuses filled with a foam, a mixture of water, air and oil. The oil is thought to absorb nitrogen contained in the air inhaled, and so safeguard the whale against the 'bends'. This is an illness which affects human divers who surface too quickly. Bubbles of nitrogen form in the blood, causing severe pain and even death. In the whale's blow, any excess nitrogen is expelled from the body.

The baleen whales are great travellers. Nearly all the species migrate annually between feeding grounds in the Arctic or Antarctic and the breeding grounds in warmer waters. The exceptions are the Greenland right whale of the Arctic and Bryde's whale which stays in warmer waters all year round.

Food for giants

Baleen whales do not dive to great depths, in the usual course of events, as they feed near the surface of the sea. Their food consists mainly of small planktonic animals. In the Antarctic seas baleen whales feed almost exclusively on *Euphausia superba,* a small shrimp-like crustacean, usually known by the Norwegian whalers' name of 'krill'. These animals live in the surface layers of the sea where they feed, in turn, on microscopic planktonic algae. In the summer

months, *Euphausia* swarms in untold millions, providing a rich feast for the whales. Other animals also feed on krill, including the crab-eating seal, squid, fish, penguins and other birds.

Outside the Antarctic, the baleen whales exploit other planktonic populations. Larger prey is also caught, particularly by the smaller rorquals such as the sei, minke and Bryde's whales, which take considerable numbers of squid or shoaling fish, such as herrings and sardines.

Food is strained out of the water by the baleen plates. These are arranged crossways on the roof of the mouth and are made of the same substance, keratin, as hair and nails. Like these, the plates grow continuously. Each plate is made up of fibres set in a horny sheath but those on the inside edge of the plate separate to make a coarse fringe that meshes with the fibres from neighbouring plates. The mesh of fibres from the hundreds of plates in the whale's mouth make the filter that traps the food. There are two basic ways of straining plankton. The right whales plough through the sea with their mouths open. Water flows into the mouth and is forced out through the baleen mesh, where the plankton is skimmed off. The rorquals on the other hand are gulpers. The grooves in the chin are pleats that allow the mouth to expand greatly, allowing a huge mass of water to be sucked in. The mouth is closed and the tongue is raised to force the water out through the sides of the mouth. Presumably the tongue is then used to scrape the food off the baleen and pass it to the back of the mouth where it can be swallowed, but no one has had the opportunity of watching a baleen whale feed. Neither is it known how the whales find their food. They must have some method of locating swarms of krill or shoals of fish but it is not known which sense is involved.

The senses of whales

Our knowledge of the senses of whales comes mainly from the anatomical study of their sense organs. Baleen whales have a rudimentary sense of smell. The olfactory membrane (the sensory tissue in the nose) and nerve are small and it is unlikely that they are of any use, especially since a whale is literally holding its nose when it dives. The eyes are adapted for underwater vision in the same way as in other aquatic animals but, again, they must be of limited use because at a depth of thirty feet the light intensity is reduced to one-tenth and the eyes of whales are so set that they cannot see ahead of them.

Hearing, on the other hand, is a well-developed sense and probably the one most relied upon. Several changes have occurred in the anatomy of a whale's ear so that it can function underwater. Perhaps the most important is that which allows it to tell the direction of a sound. The direction of sound is ascertained by the tiny differences in the time of arrival, or loudness, of sound waves in each ear. We cannot tell the direction of sound underwater because sound waves pass easily from water to bone, so the waves bypass the usual route around the head and down the ears, and travel direct to the inner ear. The whales have solved this problem by insulating the inner ear with a layer of dense bone and surrounding the whole system with a cushion of foam-filled sacs. The use which whales make of their hearing is not yet fully understood. It has been suggested that they may navigate or find food by means of sonar or echo-location, as do dolphins, and it is very likely that they communicate with each other by sound. The 'songs' of the humpback whale are now well known but, long before the invention of the hydrophone, whalers knew that whales made noises. The wooden hull of a boat is a good transducer for converting water-borne sound into air-borne sound. The songs are probably used for keeping in touch with other members of the species, possibly over distances of hundreds of miles.

The recording of the songs of whales may be a breakthrough in the study of the private lives of baleen whales as it is particularly difficult to study the habits of an animal that lives underwater and is too large to keep in a seaquarium.

Reproduction and migration

The sexual cycle of baleen whales is closely related to their cycle of migration. Mating takes place in the subtropical waters in the winter months, after which the whales migrate to polar waters where the huge concentrations of plankton that appear in the summer allow them to build up

Next page: a humpback whale clears the water. It is easily recognized by its long white flippers. Inset left: the head of a fin whale. The closed eye is visible near the corner of the mouth. Inset right: the back of a fin whale, showing the small dorsal fin. Below: two baleen whales spouting. The blow of whales has always been regarded as condensed water vapour blown out of the respiratory tract. But some of the blow is now thought to consist of an oily foam found in the nasal sinuses

large reserves of fat in the form of a blubber layer. They then return to warm waters in autumn where birth takes place and the calf is suckled. Weaning takes place early the following summer.

To accomplish this pattern of reproduction the baleen whales have to break several physiological records. The foetus grows very little during the summer feeding period, after its conception. A humpback foetus, for example, is only one foot long after four months whereas during the next eight months it grows to a full-term size of fourteen feet. It appears that the mother concentrates on laying down a food reserve during the summer, then moves into warmer waters to complete the gestation period. During this time she does not feed but the foetus can grow rapidly at the expense of her blubber and the warm water reduces the energy she has to expend on maintaining a constant body temperature.

Birth also takes place in warm water, so there is less of a strain on the newborn whale. The gestation time for a blue whale is about $9\frac{3}{4}$ months and the development of the fertilized egg into a 23-foot calf weighing two tons is the fastest growth rate in the animal kingdom. Surprisingly, the smaller rorquals have a longer gestation although they have a shorter period of lactation. The blue whale cow feeds her calf for seven months. It puts on weight at the rate of about 200 pounds per day and is weaned by the time it has accompanied its mother to polar waters. There is then abundant food to help it over the difficult period when it must learn to feed itself.

Whale folklore

In present days a seafarer is lucky to spot a baleen whale. Not only are they so much rarer than formerly, but they are likely to keep clear of noisy, motor-driven vessels. In bygone times the larger whales must have been a common sight and it is not surprising that they have found a place in folklore. 'The whale's way' was a poetic synonym for the sea in the Norse sagas and whales must have been very familiar to the Vikings. Indeed, the abundance of whales was one of the attractions of settling in Iceland, although the early Icelanders would only have made use of baleen whales that were stranded on the shore. According to the Icelandic legends, there were good and bad whales. The names of the latter were taboo at sea and could not be uttered for fear that the whales would destroy the ship and even devour the crew. On the other hand, fin whales were good and might even come to the rescue of ships being attacked by bad whales, or, according to Norwegian folklore, lead fishermen to herring shoals.

Right: a member of a British Antarctic Survey team makes friends with a minke whale. Note the shape of the blowhole. The friendliness of whales is not always reciprocated by man. Below: the sad end. The giant whalebone whales have been hunted since before the Middle Ages but the real impact on their numbers was made from the 18th century onwards

Toothed whales

The whales fall naturally into two groups: the baleen whales of the Sub-Order Mysticeti and the toothed whales of the Sub-Order Odontoceti which includes the dolphins and porpoises. The division between the whales and the dolphins and porpoises is rather arbitrary but 'whale' is reserved for the larger members. The dividing line between the two has been drawn by different authorities at twenty feet and thirty feet in length; but there are anomalies as the pigmy sperm whale *Kogia breviceps* does not exceed thirteen feet in length and the killer whale *Orcinus orca*, which may grow to more than thirty feet, is a member of the family Delphinidae, the true dolphins. In practice, however, the whales are those that are in fact called whales. Twenty-four species of toothed whale fall into this category, of which sixteen are little known. Our knowledge of them is based almost entirely on stranded specimens and some have been discovered only in the last two decades. Whether these species are really rare cannot be said for certain. The false killer whale *Pseudorca crassidens* was described from subfossil skeletons found in 1846 and was thought to be extinct, until a huge school of 100 whales appeared in the Bay of Kiel some years later.

As the names suggest, the toothed whales differ from the baleen whales in the possession of teeth instead of baleen plates. This, at once, establishes the major difference between the two sub-orders.

Left: the white whale has a domed forehead and no dorsal fin. Like many other whales, it has suffered greatly at the hand of man, its skin, which is unusually thick, being suitable for tanning. Above right: the largest of the toothed whales, the sperm whale, was the chief quarry of whalers during the eighteenth and early nineteenth centuries, and is again an important catch since the baleen whales have become overfished. Right: a sperm whale's head appears above the waves. The huge 'snout' is on the right, with the slender lower jaw on the left. The teeth in the latter may weigh up to two pounds each

The baleen whales subsist by straining small marine animals from the sea, whereas the toothed whales are hunters that pursue active prey such as squid and fish. Toothed whales are also more gregarious, commonly associating in large schools that may number some hundreds of animals. Except for the sperm whale, very little is known of the social organization within the schools. Indeed, apart from studies on the anatomy of stranded specimens and experiments on captive dolphins our knowledge of the biology of toothed whales is very limited.

The sperm whale

As the largest of the toothed whales, the sperm whale was the mainstay of the whaling industry for two centuries. Sperm-whaling started in 1712 when a New England whaler, Christopher Hussey, found himself among a sperm-whale school, killed one and towed it home. Thereafter sperm whaling boomed into the industry that has been described in detail by such authors as Melville, Bullen and others – the industry of open rowing boats pursuing whales through the South Seas to the cry of 'A dead whale or a stove boat!' and of the arduous task of cutting up the carcase as it lay alongside the mother ship. Sperm whaling went into eclipse when steam, and later oil, powered whaling ships bearing Svend Føyn's harpoon gun in the bows were able to catch the larger and more valuable baleen whales. Latterly, as the numbers of baleen whales have been reduced, sperm-whaling has revived.

Sperm whales, *Physeter catadon*, reach sixty feet and are giants of the toothed whales. There is a great difference in the size of the sexes, females growing to no more than forty feet. This sexual 'dimorphism' is related to the polygamous social life of the species, there being a sudden spurt of growth among males as they reach maturity. In appearance, the sperm whale is decidedly bizarre. The basic body plan is that of a dolphin except that the dorsal fin is replaced by a series of low humps. Of greater consequence is the form of the head. The melon or fatty 'forehead' of a dolphin is enlarged to an enormous barrel-shaped snout in the sperm whale. As in other toothed whales, the skull is asymmetrical and the single blowhole is on the side of the head, at the tip of the snout. The upper part of the snout is a hollow chamber called the 'case' and is filled with a clear liquid called 'spermaceti'. Old-time whalers used to ladle spermaceti out of the case. When cooled it set as a wax and was used for the finest candles and in cosmetics and medicines. Below the case lies the fibrous 'junk' which also contains spermaceti. The lower jaw is slender and underslung and bears teeth in the older males. The two rows of conical teeth fit into sockets in the upper jaw. Before they become worn they measure as much as eight inches. Engraving these teeth to make 'scrimshaw' was a favoured leisure occupation of the old-time whalers.

The range of the sperm whales extends over

Above right: the wide-ranging false killer whale is about the same size as the twenty-foot-long killer whale, but is black all over, and has a much shorter dorsal fin. Both species are members of the dolphin family.
Above far right: the killer whale or grampus is one of the fiercest predators on earth. It devours a wide range of prey, including squid, fish, sea birds, seals, dolphins and even whales far larger than itself. Despite this, killer whales have never been proved to attack man. They live and hunt in packs ranging from three to 50 animals.
Bottom right: killer whales are most common in Arctic and Antarctic waters. They sometimes rocket upwards through the pack ice, tipping basking seals off into the water, where they can then devour them

most of the world's oceans but the whales are most concentrated in tropical waters. They keep to deep waters but come quite close to oceanic islands. There are regular migrations, heading north and south from the tropics in summer. Migrations of bulls are much more extensive than those of cows.

Sperm whales are largely gregarious and can usually be seen travelling in parties. The largest and most closely packed schools are of adult cows and young animals, numbering up to twenty-five whales. In these schools there are pregnant and nursing cows with their calves and immature males and females. As young bulls begin to mature, they leave these 'harem' schools and join the loose, scattered herds of young bulls. Eventually, as they grow older, the bulls become solitary, except in the mating season when one or possibly more bulls joins a harem school for mating purposes. There appears to be a considerable amount of aggression between bulls contesting for this privilege. Fights have been witnessed in which jaws have been broken.

The mating season for sperm whales in the

southern hemisphere runs from August to December, but from January to July in the north. Both mating and birth take place while the schools are in tropical waters. The calf spends twelve to thirteen months with its mother before it is weaned. Because of the narrow, underslung lower jaw, suckling is awkward. The cow turns on her side and the calf grasps the nipple in the angle of the mouth. Mother sperm whales are solicitous parents and stay with their sick or wounded calves, often with other cows.

The food of sperm whales is squid, with occasional fish and octopus and, rarely, seals and sharks. Squid live at great depths, although many come to the surface at night. The sperm whale is, therefore, a champion diver. The record dive lasted for ninety minutes and a sperm whale carcase was recovered from a depth of 3,700 feet where it had become entangled in a submarine cable. Long dives must place a strain on the whale's metabolism and it 'pants' on returning to the surface, spouting roughly once for every minute spent under water. Most of the squid captured are no more than a few feet long but there are occasional battles with monsters. A sperm whale was caught off the Azores with a 34-foot squid in its stomach and the marks of suckers on the skin of sperm whales show that they grapple with even larger specimens.

Sperm whales are probably the only whales that are aggressive towards man. Readers of

'Moby Dick' will be familiar with the hazards of harpooning sperm whales from an open boat and the destruction that a harpooned whale wreaks is more than a result of it thrashing out blindly when wounded. There are numerous records of sperm whales attacking, and sinking, sailing ships for no apparent reason. The whale may, however, be under the impression that the ship is a threat to him. By contrast, the killer whale, of evil reputation, does not attack human beings. There are no definite records of killer whales killing people, although they have been responsible for drownings because of their habit of rubbing themselves against small boats.

Killer whales and blackfish

Killer whales are cosmopolitan, roaming the world's seas and frequently coming close inshore. Like the sperm whales, they exhibit sexual dimorphism, adult males being much larger, up to thirty feet long, and having a tall, six-foot dorsal fin. The fins of adult males make the identification of a school of killer whales simple but they can also be distinguished by an oval white patch behind the eye and a faint grey crescent behind the fin. Little is known about the movements of killer-whale schools but it seems that they are often attracted to an area by the presence of shoals of fish.

Analysis of stomach contents has shown that the main food of killer whales is fish, followed by squid, but it is as predators of large animals that killer whales are famous. They kill and eat seals, sealions and dolphins and are sometimes seen attacking large baleen whales. Adults

Above right: a school of white whales, or belugas. Many of the toothed whales live in schools containing from a few to several hundred individuals. Right: a pilot, or caa'ing, whale at the surface. Also called the blackfish, this whale is found in most of the world's oceans. Far right: a beached narwhal clearly shows the long tusk, indicating that it is probably an adult male. This tusk, once though to belong to the fabled unicorn, is actually one of the narwhal's two teeth; it may grow to over nine feet long. Its function is unknown, but may be connected with sexual display

often escape but calves are frequently killed. Relations between killer whales and seals are not simple. Sometimes the seals flee in panic and seek the safety of rocks, but there are many records of killer whales swimming past seals with neither animal noticing the other.

The pilot whale or blackfish *Globicephala melaena* is a twenty-foot whale that has been regularly hunted for centuries. It is black save for a white patch below the jaw and on the belly, and has long slender flippers. The scientific name refers to the rounded, protuberant forehead which contains the equivalent of the sperm whale's spermaceti, an oil used for fine lubricants. Open boat whalers hunted pilot whales for this oil, an enterprise which was worthwhile because pilot whales live in schools numbering hundreds. The large schools and a proneness to panic have been exploited since medieval times in a fishery called 'the caa' in Shetland and *grindadrap* in the Faeroe Islands.

Within recent years commercial whalers have taken increasingly to hunting small whales such as the killer whale and pilot whale and the bottlenosed whale, *Hyperoodon ampullatus* of the

Arctic. The southern bottlenose whale *H. planifrons* is similar but is not hunted. Both grow to about thirty-feet and their long narrow snouts show them to be members of the beaked whale family Ziphiidae. The northern bottlenosed whale migrates between arctic and tropical waters.

Toothless whales

A peculiarity of the beaked-whale family is that they are almost toothless. In the bottlenosed whales a single tooth erupts on each side of the lower jaw in old males alone. No teeth erupt in females. Similar arrangements of teeth are found in other beaked whales and teeth erupt only in the lower jaws of older sperm whales. It seems that teeth are not really necessary for catching slippery squid and fish and that they are secondary sexual characteristics used as status symbols like the antlers of deer.

Few of the beaked whales are at all common. Cuvier's beaked whale *Ziphius cavirostris* and Sowerby's whale *Mesoplodon bidens* are abundant but little is known of their habits. Others are known solely from a few skeletons. *Mesoplodon europaeus* is known from three specimens, one found floating in the English Channel and the others stranded in New Jersey. *M. Stejnegeri* is known from two specimens from the Pacific coast of North America and *Tasmacetus shepherdi* from one individual cast up in New Zealand and a lower jaw of unknown origin. How rare are these animals? They could be quite common like the false killer whale and their apparent rarity owing to a way of life that keeps them in deep water where they are seen by few skilled observers. In order to resolve this situation, it is important that all stranded cetaceans – whales and dolphins – should be reported to the correct authority. In Britain this is the British Museum (Natural History) at South Kensington or the coastguard.

Narwhal and beluga

One family of toothed whales is restricted to Arctic waters. The family Monodontidae consists of the narwhal *Monodon monoceros* and the white whale *Delphinapterus leucas.* Narwhals, which have been known to stray as far as British coasts, grow to thirteen feet, have rounded foreheads and lack dorsal fins. Their most peculiar feature is the single spiral tusk on the forehead. It grows to eight feet and is found usually in males alone. Adults of both sexes have a single pair of teeth in the upper jaw and the left-hand one grows through the upper lip in males. Very occasionally both teeth grow into tusks and a few females carry them. The function of the tusk is not known for certain, but it seems very likely that it is a secondary sexual characteristic like the teeth of other toothed whales. Narwhal tusks were greatly prized in historical times as unicorn horns. As such, they had the ability to detect and neutralize poisons.

Narwhals live in schools, of a few dozen that sometimes band into herds of hundreds. They

Above: the white whale may grow to a length of eighteen feet. The thick skin of a young white whale is grey; it does not become white (by progressive loss of the black pigment called 'melanin') until the animal is about four years old, often passing through an intermediate mottled brown and white phase. Like its close relative the narwhal, the white whale is an Arctic species, occasionally wandering southwards

feed on cuttlefish, squid and crustaceans and occasionally swim up rivers – one being found 700 miles up the Yukon River. In winter a school may get trapped in a pool in the frozen sea. The Eskimo name for such a pool is a *savssat*. The narwhals can keep the pool open for breathing purposes but their dependence on it makes them an easy target for the Eskimo's harpoons. Several hundred may be trapped in a *savssat* and the Eskimoes are thereby assured a winter's supply of meat and blubber. The hide of narwhals is used for thongs which remain supple in icy conditions. The hide with a thin layer of blubber still attached is a delicacy called *mattak*. It is eaten raw and contains as much Vitamin C as the fresh fruit and vegetables that are missing from the Eskimo diet.

The white whale – also called the beluga, but not to be confused with the sturgeon of the same name – can be distinguished from other whales by its pure white skin. Young white whales are grey when born but they grow paler with age and are white when four years old. Like the narwhal, white whales have a rounded forehead and no dorsal fin. They have the same Arctic distribution and are sometimes driven into

temperate seas by hard winters. Occasionally they swim up rivers. The food of the white whale is mixed and includes shrimps, cuttlefish, crabs and several kinds of fish. Unlike many toothed whales, white whales actually have a set of teeth, numbering between thirty-two and forty, although they swallow their food without chewing it.

White whales have been traditionally hunted by Eskimoes and other Arctic peoples, using harpoons and nets, and Europeans have joined in with the consequent reduction in numbers of the species. As early as 1688, the Hudson's Bay Company started catching white whales. The skin, like that of the narwhal but, unlike that of other whales, is thick enough for tanning.

The old English whalers called the white whale the 'sea canary' on account of the trilling sounds that are audible above the surface of the water. In Russia a noisy person is described as 'singing like a beluga'. It is now known that many whales make noises, including the sperm whale and the baleen whales, but in only a few dolphins has it been shown for certain that these sounds are for echo-location or communicating between individual whales.

Dolphins

It is not so simple as it may seem to decide precisely what is a dolphin, because the name is one that is popularly used for a number of small whale-like animals and has no strict scientific meaning. Use of the terms 'dolphin' and 'porpoise' differs in Britain and America. What the British know as the common dolphin is called the saddle-backed porpoise in America and the bottlenose dolphin is called the harbor porpoise. In America, the name 'porpoise' is restricted to small toothed whales of the family Phocaenidae, and 'dolphin' to the family Delphinidae. However, the largest members of the Delphinidae are called whales on both sides of the Atlantic. The name dolphin is also applied to the related river dolphins, in the family Platanistidae, and long-beaked dolphins, in the family Stenidae.

There are over thirty species of true dolphin, the common and bottlenosed being the best known. The bottlenosed dolphin, *Tursiops truncatus* is found in the North Atlantic Ocean and Mediterranean Sea, while *T. gilli* lives in the Pacific Ocean and *T. aduncus* is found in the Indian Ocean and the Red Sea. The bottlenosed dolphins are those most commonly seen in seaquaria. They are named after the beak formed by the long jaws that bear rows of pointed teeth. This beak is a feature of many dolphins, although some, such as Risso's dolphin *Grampus griseus*, lack one. The name 'grampus', which is also used as a common name for the killer whale, comes from the sixteenth century English word *graunde-pose*, meaning 'great fish'. Risso's dolphin is

Below: a spotted dolphin, one of the dolphins classified in the genus Stenella. *These dolphins are not very well known, as they generally live in deeper water far from the shoreline.* Stenella *dolphins are found throughout the warmer oceans of the world*

found in both hemispheres and one specimen achieved fame as Pelorus Jack. It frequented Pelorus Sound between Nelson and Wellington, New Zealand, and regularly followed ships as they passed through the Sound. It became so popular that a special Order-in-Council was made to protect it from unscrupulous hunters.

In the Southern Hemisphere there are about a dozen species of the genus *Cephalorhynchus*. None are well known but all are strikingly marked with black and white. Commerson's dolphin *C. commersoni* is perhaps the most striking of all dolphins, being white with black on the head, flippers, fin and tail. It is found around South America, as is the white-bellied dolphin *C. albiventris*. Heaviside's dolphin *C. heavisidei* is a frequent visitor to South African coasts. It was named after a Captain Haviside but the spelling of the name has become corrupted.

The colder waters of north and south are the home of dolphins placed in the genus *Lagenorhynchus*. Wilson's hour-glass dolphin (*L. wilsoni*) which lives at the edge of the Antarctic packice is named after its pattern of black and white markings, as is the cruciger dolphin *L. cruciger*. Little is known about these two species. The white-sided and white-beaked dolphins (*L. acutus* and *L. albirostris*) are common North Atlantic species.

The dolphins in the genus *Stenella* are also little known, perhaps because they tend to stay in deeper water away from coasts. Two Pacific species are called 'spinner dolphins' from their habit of spinning about their long axis as they leap clear of the water.

Finally, in the family Delphinidae, there are the two right whale dolphins *Lissodelphis peroni* and *L. borealis*, which live in the Pacific. They are so named because they lack a dorsal fin, like right whales. Also in the family Delphinidae is the Irrawaddy dolphin *Orcaella brevirostris* of Asian coastal waters. This dolphin, which is placed in the family Orcinae together with the ferocious killer whale (*Orcinus orca*) makes its way as far as 900 miles from the sea, up the Irrawaddy River in Burma.

The long-beaked dolphin family, Stenidae, comprises some seven species. Most are little known, but the Chinese white dolphin *Sousa sinensis*, a milky white animal, lives in the Yangtze River in China as well as in coastal waters, while *S. teuszii* lives in the estuaries of West Africa, in Senegal and the Cameroons, and the bufeo *S. fluviatilis* is found in the Amazon and Orinoco systems. Other members of the family are generally found in coastal waters.

The trend towards fresh water has been taken further by the river dolphins within the family Platanistidae. The South American boutu *Inia geoffrensis* is found in the Amazon and Orinoco, the white flag dolphin *Lipotes vexillifer* is confined to Tung Ting lake, 600 miles up the Yangtze River and the susu *Platanista gangetica* is found in the Indus, Ganges and Brahmaputra river systems of India. The susu is completely blind. The La Plata dolphin *Pontoporia blainvillei* is the only member of the family that enters salt water. It lives in the Plata estuary and migrates along the coasts in winter. All river dolphins have long beaks with large numbers of long teeth. The La Plata dolphin has nearly 250 teeth, more than any other mammal.

The porpoises of the family Phocaenidae are small cetaceans with no beak. The common porpoise *Phocaena phocaena* is six feet long and is found in coastal waters of the North Atlantic, sometimes ascending rivers. The other three *Phocaena* porpoises are found in the southern hemisphere. Dall's and True's porpoises *Phocaenoides dalli* and *P. truei* live in the North Pacific as does the finless black porpoise *Neomeris phocaenoides* which ascends the Yangtze River.

Of the many species of dolphins and porpoises, some are extremely abundant. In some parts, sightings are everyday occurences and the common dolphin, for instance, may live in schools of many thousands, but other species are extremely rare. An example is Hose's Sarawak dolphin, *Lagenodelphis hosei*, which is known from a single skeleton obtained in 1895. Despite the abundance of some species, little is known of their biology. Their private lives are enacted at sea, where it is impossible to watch them, except by chance encounter. Furthermore, it is by no means easy to identify even the commoner species in conditions of visibility at sea and, until recently, most of our knowledge of dolphins and porpoises has been obtained from the study of dead specimens. Since World War II, immense

Left: a dolphin must surface regularly to inhale air through its 'blowhole' or nostril (centre of picture), which is closed by a muscle when the animal is submerged. The passage leading to the blowhole forms part of the dolphin's echo-location system, which it uses to find its prey.
Right: dolphins are highly sociable animals. In the wild, dolphins of different species may play together. These two are in a 'seaquarium'. The larger one is a bottlenose dolphin, and the smaller one is a Pacific striped dolphin

Above: dolphins frequently leap high out of the water. They can swim at speeds of up to 25 m.p.h., being little affected by water resistance because of their smooth, flexible skin. Dolphins can dive as deep as 70 feet and stay underwater for at least 15 minutes

strides have been made through the keeping of dolphins in seaquaria. The bottlenose dolphin is the usual seaquarium species but the striped dolphin *Lagenorhynchus obliquidens* is a champion display jumper, and small killer whales have also been exhibited.

Studying dolphins

Seaquaria have enabled scientists to study the intimate details of dolphins' lives and to carry out experiments that show just how exquisitely adapted dolphins are for an aquatic existence. These studies have also shown how intelligent dolphins are. Although it is difficult to get relative measurements of different animals' intelligence, dolphins appear to be among the most intelligent creatures on earth, at least as intelligent as the apes. Anatomical studies show that the dolphin's brain is proportionately larger and more complex than that of man and, perhaps most important, the cerebral cortex, the seat of intelligent behaviour, has half as many more nerve cells. The dolphins' intelligence is evident from the speed with which captive dolphins learn tricks.

Dolphins and porpoises are animals of the sea's surface. They do not normally dive deep but live on fish and squid caught near the surface. To catch their prey, dolphins use their eyes, except in the case of the blind susu, or their marvellously accurate sonar or echo-location system. Just as a bat hunts by emitting a series of ultrasonic squeaks and listening for the echoes returning from flying insects, so dolphins catch fish or navigate through murky, estuarine water by listening to the echoes of a train of sounds produced in the air passage leading to the blow-

hole. These sounds are emitted at frequencies of up to 170 kilocycles per second, well beyond the range of human hearing, but they occur in short bursts that can be heard as clicks. Quite how the dolphin operates its sonar is not known for certain. Some scientists think that the oily 'melon' that lies in the bulbous forehead acts as a lens to focus the ultrasonic pulses, and that the echoes are picked up and conveyed to the ears by the jawbones. Other scientists believe that the ears work in the normal fashion, with modifications that enable them to work underwater. But however dolphin sonar works, it is clearly a very efficient apparatus. Captive dolphins can use their sonar to distinguish between fishes of different species or between different sized fish of the same species.

Although so efficient, sonar does not prevent dolphins from becoming stranded on beaches. Sometimes whole schools become cast up on the shore and attempts to rescue them come to nothing because as soon as one is towed off, it swims back to join its fellows, perhaps in response to their distress calls. Once aground, a dolphin has little chance of survival. The weight of its body pressing on its lungs hinders breathing, and the water may cover its blowhole and drown it before it can float free. Why whole schools should go aground is a mystery but the usual explanation is that dolphins are commonly stranded on gently sloping beaches because their sonar is beamed to the front and cannot easily detect slight inclines. Once grounded, the dolphin's efforts to extricate itself results in its sinking in the sand or mud.

Dolphin sonar is also, strangely, unable to save them from being trapped in fishing nets. On the Pacific seaboard of the United States, huge nets are used for catching tuna. In 1970–71 the colossal total of 388,000 spotted dolphins, 117,000 'spinner' dolphins and 15,000 common dolphins were trapped in the nets and drowned.

In pursuing fish and squid, dolphins make use of an extraordinary turn of speed. The bottlenose can swim at 20–25 miles per hour, perhaps more over short distances. At one time it was a mystery as to how this speed could be achieved. It appeared, from what was known of the hydrodynamics of ships, that the muscles of dolphins could not develop sufficient power to propel them so fast. The paradox was resolved by the discovery that their skin was flexible and that it could change shape to accommodate turbulence in the water passing over the skin. By ironing out such turbulence, a laminar flow is produced and the drag, or resistance to the body's movement, is greatly reduced. Since this discovery there have been attempts to apply this principle to the hulls of ships.

Observations in seaquaria have given us what little information we have about the breeding habits of dolphins. Bottlenosed dolphins become sexually mature when five to six years old. Mating and birth take place in the spring and summer, the gestation period being eleven to 12 months.

Births have been witnessed in seaquaria, the calf being born tail-first, as is usual with marine mammals. As soon as it has been expelled, the three foot long, twenty-five pound calf swims to the surface to fill its lungs. Until it has done this, it lacks buoyancy and its mother may have to help it up. During the birth the mother may be guarded from attack by other cows and while the calf is still young she will be accompanied by a cow who acts as an 'aunt' and shares in caring for the calf. When the calf is two weeks old it will leave its mother's side for a short while. It is not weaned until it is six months or older. Suckling takes place underwater. The mother's nipples lie in grooves on the abdomen and the calf sizes one between tongue and palate while the cow actively pumps milk into its mouth by squeezing the milk glands with special muscles. As the calf has to surface to breathe every half minute, suckling has to be a rapid process and, when the calf is very young, it takes place every half hour.

Conclusions drawn from studies of captive animals always have to be viewed with caution because there is no guarantee that the animals will be behaving normally. Captive dolphins, for instance, may be mixed at random. Dolphin schools in the wild are made up of a loose assembly of animals with no particular leader but there is a hierarchy, particularly among the males. It appears that the individuals within a school recognize each other and keep in contact by using calls.

The co-ordination of behaviour can best be seen when a school of dolphins plays together. They perform acrobatics with extreme agility, apparently just for the fun of it. They leap out of the water, sometimes landing with a 'belly flop'; they swim on their backs, and twist, roll and smack their tails on the surface. The whole school joins in and they may make co-ordinated jumps or swim in perfect line abreast. But the most impressive co-ordination between dolphins occurs when one is injured. The dolphins gather round their unfortunate comrade and help him remain at the surface so that he can breathe. Such behaviour has often been reported over the centuries and there have been claims that dolphins have helped drowning men in the same way. At first zoologists were sceptical but rescue behaviour has now been seen in seaquaria and from research ships and has been recorded in bottlenose, common and Pacific white-sided dolphins.

Left: a school of dolphins leaps clear out of the water. Dolphins often play together, performing beautifully co-ordinated acrobatics apparently just for sheer enjoyment

Communal life in a school, with co-ordinated play and rescue behaviour, requires communication between individuals and the study of communication is the most intriguing aspect of dolphin research. That they are intelligent is evident from the speed with which they learn new tricks to delight the crowds that throng the seaquaria, but what we would like to know is just how intelligent they are. Intelligence is not easy to study or to measure but there is a chance that dolphins have almost reached our level of mental development.

Language and learning

An experiment involving a pair of bottlenose dolphins has shown the possibility of a dolphin language. The dolphins were first trained to operate two levers with their snouts. They had to push the left-hand lever when a light flashed intermittently and push the right-hand lever when the light shone steadily. If they performed correctly, they were rewarded with a fish. Then the game was made harder. The female had to wait until her mate had pressed his lever before pressing hers. It took no time to teach them to do this – a good sign of intelligence in itself – but the next step was to separate the dolphins so that only the female could see the light. This did not interfere with their performance, provided that they were within earshot of each other. A soundproof barrier caused the experiment to fail. The only conclusion that can be drawn is that when the light came on, the female dolphin told the male whether it was steady or flashing. He pushed his lever as appropriate and then told her that it was now time to push her lever and to get the reward.

The language of dolphins is still unknown. It is vocal, like ours, but probably very subtle and complex because dolphins live in a world of sounds whereas our main sense is sight. Not content with the idea of dolphins talking to each other, some scientists have claimed that dolphins can learn human speech. It has been claimed that dolphins can imitate the commands of their human keepers but this has been disputed and it does not mean that the dolphin has any more idea of what it is saying than does a parrot.

These experiments have justified ancient stories of dolphins' special relationship with man, as a friend who will aid a man in distress or help round up fish. Unfortunately, there is now a fear that man, or at least some men, are acting in the self-centred way that man has always treated his animal companions. Instead of developing the relationship with dolphins, there has been a tendency to exploit the intelligence and friendliness of dolphins, to their detriment.

Danger from Man

Dolphins and porpoises have for long been a traditional food. Porpoise was a dish for medieval English kings. Dolphins are caught by means of nets and harpoons or are driven ashore, and many are drowned accidentally in fishing nets. In some parts of the world dolphins and porpoises are becoming scarce but only recently have there been attempts to give dolphins the protection enjoyed by the larger whales.

There are also fears that dolphins are suffering because of the ease with which they can be trained. While most people might feel that it is reasonable to keep dolphins in seaquaria to study their habits or to provide entertainment – and the dolphins appear to be enjoying the performance as much as the spectators – some seaquaria are substandard and result in a high mortality. Much less justifiable are some of the uses to which free-swimming, trained dolphins have been put. They make good assistants for divers, carrying tools and equipment between the diver and the surface craft or retrieving practice torpedos but the dolphins are also being trained for warlike purposes such as seeking out enemy divers and mines, as, for instance, in the United States 30 million-dollar 'Sea Mammal Program'. The enemy is likely to counter by destroying the dolphins so there is a clear ethical question as to what extent we can exploit animals, particularly when they are so intelligent.

Below: dolphins live in groups called 'schools'. Because they are so difficult to study in the sea, little is known about dolphins' social behaviour in the wild

Sea otter

Much prized for its fur, the sea otter *Enhydra, lutris,* was nearly wiped out in the nineteenth century but, under careful protection, its numbers are now increasing. The sea otter is different from other otters. It is the only wholly marine species, although the common otter of Europe frequently lives along seashores. The sea otter lives on the coasts of the North Pacific, from the Kurile Islands south to Lower California. It rarely goes far out to sea and does not often come ashore. A sea otter rests by floating on its back; it uses strands of kelp for an anchor when it sleeps. Only where there is no kelp do sea otters habitually come ashore, but even then they rarely stray farther than five yards from the water's edge.

Natural insulation

The sea otter is the largest of all the mammals placed in the family Mustelidae, which also includes other otters, badgers, weasels and skunks, but it is the smallest of all sea mammals. The largest sea otters weigh up to 100 pounds with a total length of five feet but, on average, males weigh about sixty pounds and females forty-five pounds. They have numerous adapta-tions to their almost totally aquatic life; one of the chief ones is their thick coat of fur which keeps them warm and dry, even in ice-cold water. The coat consists of two layers – a sparse cover-ing of long, coarse guard hairs and a dense layer of soft underfur, the hairs of which are about an inch long. Bundles of about seventy underfur hairs, together with one guard hair, sprout from each follicle. There is only one hair per follicle in human skin. It is the great density of hair that makes sea otter fur both so efficient as a protec-tive coat and so valuable. The underfur traps a layer of air which insulates the body from the cold water and gives it buoyancy. If the air layer is lost, the sea otter soon dies; unlike other marine mammals, such as seals and whales, that are more fully adapted to an aquatic life, the sea otter does not have a thick layer of fat insulating it from the cold water. As a consequence, it spends much of its time grooming its fur. First the otter washes its fur by rubbing it underwater with the forepaws, then it dries it by squeezing it with the forepaws or tongue. Air is sometimes replaced by the animal blowing into the fur.

Sea otters swim by vertical undulations of the flattened tail and by beating the hindlegs, which have been transformed into webbed flippers. Unlike that of any other mammal, the fifth toe is

Below: the sea otter keeps itself warm in the cold water by trapping a layer of air, which it warms, among the hairs of its thick fur coat. Sea otters cannot fast like seals and whales because they are unable to store a thick layer of blubber beneath their skin. They must eat great amounts of food and digest it rapidly to provide enough energy to keep warm

the longest and this makes the flippers more efficient when the sea otter is swimming on its back. The forefeet, by contrast, are rounded like mittens and bear retractile claws. Sea otters swim at the surface, unlike other sea mammals, and are rather slow, cruising at five and a half miles per hour; but they can reach fifteen miles per hour. When chased sea otters do not break any records at diving. The usual duration is one to one and a half minutes when feeding, with the longest known dive of just over four minutes made by a sea otter trying to escape from a pursuing boat. The greatest depth recorded is 164 feet.

Using a tool

The food of the sea otter is mainly fish and shell-fish, along with some starfish, sea urchins, worms, crustaceans and other animals. The otter gathers these from the seabed with its forepaws, using its delicate sense of touch and sometimes its eyesight. The teeth are also employed for collecting small animals, while abalones are removed from rocks by being pounded with a stone – a rare example of an animal using a tool. Fish are brought to the surface and killed with a single bite, then torn into pieces and chewed up. The molar teeth are unusual in that they are rounded and have no cutting edges. This is a design for crushing shelled animals such as crabs, sea urchins and molluscs, but sea otters also break open shellfish by pounding them on a stone. A stone – often the same one used to dislodge the prey, as described above – is brought to the surface and placed on the sea otter's chest as it lies on its back. The shell is smashed open by being thumped against the stone which acts as an anvil. Sometimes two shellfish are banged together. This is another instance where the sea otter joins the exclusive ranks of the tool-users.

The sea otter's diet varies from place to place. In Alaska, fish are the most important food but elsewhere, as in California, sea urchins are favoured. In fact, where sea otters are abundant on the Californian coast the formerly abundant sea urchin Strongylocentrus franciscianus has been nearly exterminated. Abalone fishermen also blame the sea otter for their diminished catches of abalones, but it appears that this is more the fault of increasing numbers of human divers than of sea otters. It does seem, however, that sea otters in a limited area are likely to eat up all their food supplies, and many starve to death in winter when food is very scarce.

When otters become too numerous, starvation keeps the population to a stable ten to fifteen otters per square mile of inshore water. Each animal occupies five to ten miles of coastline and the sexes stay apart except for mating. Breeding takes place at any time of the year, as in common otters; the male and female stay together for only three days. Gestation takes twelve to thirteen months and, although birth has never been witnessed, it probably takes place on land. The single cub is well advanced at birth; it has a thick coat of fur, its eyes are wide open, it is able to float, and it can take some solid food immediately. Its mother is very attentive, carrying the cub on her chest and leaving it to float only when she dives to feed. The cub stays with its mother for at least a year and can catch most of its own food by the end of this period. However, a great many cubs die in stormy weather because their mothers cannot obtain sufficient food for both themselves and the offspring and so desert their young.

Escape from extinction

A slow rate of reproduction – one cub only every two years – is one reason for the drastic decline of the sea otter. Commercial exploitation started when Spanish missionaries bartered for sea otter pelts with Californian Indians in 1733 and in 1779 Captain Cook sold pelts which came from Vancouver Island to China. This started a rush of hunters and, as the species neared extinction in the late nineteenth century, the value of a pelt rose from $150 in 1880 to as much as $1,125 in 1903. In 1911 the United States government took over the management of the remaining stocks by imposing complete protection. By this time only scattered populations remained. From a population of between 100,000 and 150,000 sea otters in 1740, only 1,000 to 2,000 remained in 1911. There were three colonies surviving on the western coast of Canada and the United States, of which only that around Monterey in California remains; otherwise the sea otter survives in Alaska, the islands of the Aleutian chain and the Kurile Islands to the north-east of Japan. Numbers are now increasing by four to five per cent per year, many islands are recolonized, and in 1962 experimental cropping was introduced. By 1965, there were 32,000 to 35,000 sea otters in the world. Their future seems assured although pollution of the sea by oil will probably prevent their return to some of their old haunts.

Right: a sea otter with a haul of clams, among the kelp beds near Monterey in California. Below: the sea otter is among the very few animals which use tools. When feeding it uses a large rock to detach shellfish from the sea bed and as an anvil against which to smash the hard shells

Seals and sealions

Seals are excellent examples of land animals that have become adapted for a life at sea. The Pinnipedia – the flap-footed animals – are, in fact, descended from land-living carnivores and have become adapted for a marine existence through a streamlining of the body, the conversion of the limbs to webbed flippers and by physiological adaptations for diving.

The order Pinnipedia is divided into three natural groups or families. The true or hair seals of the family Phocidae include the familiar common seal *Phoca vitulina* and grey seal *Halichoerus grypus* of European waters, the huge elephant seals *Mirounga leonina* and *M. angustirostris* and the harp seal *Pagophilus groenlandicus*, which has received so much publicity from the slaughter of its white-coated pups. The true seals are well covered with blubber, so as often to appear quite bloated, and they have short foreflippers which they· use to haul themselves with difficulty over the ground. By contrast, the eared seals of the family Otariidae can turn their hindflippers under the body and bound along on all fours. This family includes the fur seals and the sealions of circus fame. They are slender, with less blubber than the true seals, and they rely on a very dense fur to keep them warm. Their heads are distinctly dog-like and they are named after their small external ears, which are missing in the true seals. The eared seals swim by paddling powerfully with the foreflippers, while the true seals propel themselves by pressing together their hind flippers and spreading them out like a fish's tail. The third family, Odobenidae, contains a single species, the walrus *Odobenus rosmarus* of Arctic seas. In general appearance it resembles the eared seals but it is a much bulkier animal.

Although thoroughly at home in the sea, the seals are not as well adapted for a marine life as are the whales and dolphins. Seals have to come to land or onto ice floes to give birth, although common seals do sometimes give birth in water. The single pup which is born to each cow seal spends a short period on land before taking to the water.

Apart from the streamlining and ability to swim well, seals are adapted to a marine life as regards their senses, respiration and blood system. A seal's eyes have a flat cornea that allows them to focus on underwater objects but leaves them shortsighted on land. By way of compensation, the sense of smell is well developed. It is of no use underwater as seals swim with their nostrils shut but their sense of smell does alert them to danger while on land. Even underwater, however, the eyes are of limited use at any great depth where there is little light. Indeed, totally

The Pinnipedia is divided into three families.
Above: an elephant seal, one of the true seals.
Far right: South American sealions, eared seals.
Right: a walrus, sole member of the third family

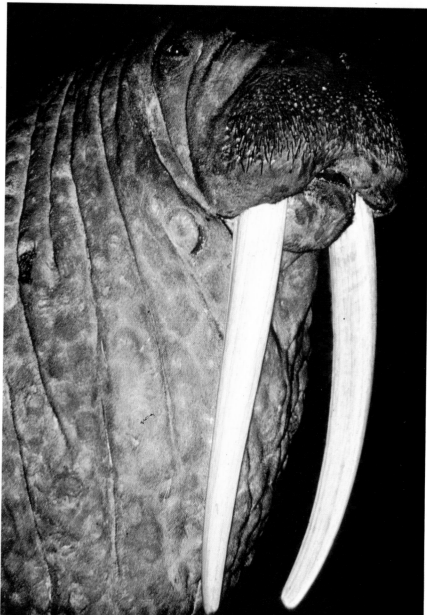

blind seals have been found in perfect health. They probably find their food by means of their sensitive whiskers, although the Californian sealion *Zalophus californianus* uses echo-location. Seals have much the same physiological adaptations for prolonged dives as do the whales. During a dive, the heartbeat slows down and blood is directed to essential organs only. The record diver among seals is the Weddell seal *Leptonychotes weddelli* of the Antarctic. Weddell seals frequently dive to depths of about 1,000 feet, and the deepest dive recorded was 1,950 feet. The longest dive lasted forty-three minutes, 20 seconds.

Seals are catholic feeders, their main diet consisting of fish, crustaceans and squid. A fondness for fish has led them into conflict with fishermen, particularly as the seals take whatever food is most abundant in a particular area. Consequently they gather at the estuaries of salmon rivers and steal salmon from the nets. However, seals do take many other kinds of food, including shrimps and shellfish. Two species of seal are specialist feeders. The crabeater seal *Lobodon carcinophagus* was so named because it was thought to eat crabs; in fact its specially shaped teeth with their interlocking cusps are used in the same way as the 'whalebone' plates of the great baleen whales to strain krill from mouthfuls of water. The leopard seal *Leptonyx hydrurga*, which like the crabeater seal has an Antarctic distribution, is a flesh-eater feeding on penguins and young seals, although it also eats a large amount of fish. Probably only a few leopard seals make a habit of frequenting the beaches near penguin rookeries, a habit also adopted by some fur seals and sealions.

The eared seals
The family Otariidae, or eared seals, comprises twelve species of fur seal and sealions. They are found in waters of the southern oceans and in the North Pacific. Sealions were so named because of the thick lion-like mane of the male. Steller's sealion *Eumetopias jubata* breeds on islands in the North Pacific, from California as far as Japan. It is the largest sealion, much larger than the Californian sealion, which is found mainly in Californian waters but with small populations on the Galapagos Islands and Japan. The remaining sealions live around the shores of South America and Australasia. Of the fur seals, the Pribilof fur seal *Callorhinus ursinus* lives off the islands of the north-western North Pacific with a very new small colony off California. The Guadalupe fur seal *Arctocephalus philippi*, now very rare, lives on the island of Guadalupe off the coast of Lower California. The other five fur seals live in the southern seas. The South American fur seal *A. australis* ranges from the Galapagos Islands to Cape Horn and the Kerguelen fur seal *A. gazella* is found on many subantarctic islands.

To say that a seal is found 'on' a particular island or coast is misleading as its true home is the open sea. The statement strictly relates only to the breeding grounds of that seal. Fur seals and sealions gather on their breeding beaches in vast numbers. As with all seals, the females are ready to breed again shortly after they have given birth, so the males also gather at the same time to mate with them. The colony or 'rookery' of seals is parcelled out among the older bulls, each defending his own territory against his neighbours and against the young bulls who gather around the fringes of the rookery. The cows are free to come and go but, by holding a territory, a bull can mate with any cows that enter it.

The pup is born only two or three days after the cow comes ashore. It is covered with black woolly hair which is moulted after six or seven weeks. The cow stays with her pup for the first few days but later goes back to the sea to feed. She comes ashore at intervals and calls her own offspring out from among the horde of pups that scamper about the beach and swim in the shallows. In a short period of suckling, the pup fills its belly with milk before its mother departs again. The pup is weaned when it is about three months old; from then on it is abandoned to its own devices.

The true seals

Many of the true seals gather in large numbers on the breeding beaches, but only the elephant

Below: the Pribilof fur seal (Callorhinus ursinus) *is found around the shores of Alaska and the Bering Strait. It is the fur seals that have suffered most from commercial exploitation*

seals can rival the sealions and fur seals, which collect in groups numbering tens of thousands. Elephant seals are the largest of the pinnipeds, the biggest bulls weighing up to 8,000 pounds. As with the eared seals, the bulls haul themselves out of the sea a short while before the cows and establish their territories. The huge nose of the bull elephant seal is inflated during the breeding season and acts as a resonator for its roar of defiance when facing a rival. Fights sometimes break out in which two colossal bulls rear up and slam against each other, chest to chest, their blubber wobbling like an enormous jelly.

The majority of true seals are cold- or cool-water animals, the exceptions being the northern elephant seal of California and the monk seals of the Mediterranean, *Monachus monachus*, Hawaii *M. schauinslandi*, and the West Indies, *M. tropicalis*, the last of which is perhaps now extinct. Most of the others breed on the ice floes of polar seas. The harp seal, named after the black marking on its back, gathers in large numbers on the ice off the Gulf of St Lawrence, Newfoundland and elsewhere in the Atlantic sector of the Arctic. It is in the two places just mentioned that the pups are killed in large numbers for their white fur. The appealing sight of the woolly, round-eyed pups is enhanced by the tears running from their eyes. Nevertheless, these tears have nothing to do with the seal's emotions. Seals have no tear duct leading from eye to nose so the natural tears that lubricate and protect the eye spill over.

Another seal that breeds on the ice is the ringed seal *Pusa hispida*, named after the pattern of pale rings bordering dark spots which graces its coat. It is found on both Pacific and Atlantic sides of the Arctic and its pups are born in dens under the snow where they get protection from both the weather and the polar bears. Some ringed seals live in fresh water lakes connected to the Gulf of Finland. It seems most likely that the seals of Lake Baikal *P. sibirica* and the Caspian Sea *P. caspica* are descended from ringed seals that were 'stranded' when these inland seas were cut off from the Arctic Ocean millions of years ago. The common seal *Phoca vitulina*, known as the harbor seal in America, also has freshwater populations. These are in the Seal Lakes near Hudson Bay. Elsewhere, individuals swim up rivers and may even give birth to pups there. The common seal is the most aquatic of all seals in that it sometimes bears its pup in the water. More usually, the pup is born on a sandbank or rock but it still has to swim when the tide rises. Correlated with this is the loss of the white coat before birth; it emerges with its second, adult coat. The only common seals to be born with the white coat are those living on ice floes in the western Pacific.

The pup of the Atlantic grey seal, by contrast, retains its white coat for three to four weeks. It seems likely that all grey seals originally bred on ice floes but they took to breeding on island beaches as the Ice Age waned. They breed in small colonies, the cows waiting offshore and venturing onto the beach only to suckle their pups. The numbers of grey seals in the British Isles, which holds sixty-five per cent of the world's population, have been increasing during the last fifty years, and the cows have taken to giving birth on the tops of islands and to staying with their pups until they are weaned at three weeks of age.

The increase in grey seals has been assisted by the abandonment of islands by their human populations. As the inhabitants have been evacuated from the more remote islands of the Hebrides, Orkneys and Shetlands so the grey seals have colonized the beaches for breeding. The increase affects fishermen whose nets are robbed or damaged by the activities of the seals. Moreover, seals breeding inland gradually destroy vegetation and erode the soil of the islands.

The unique walrus

The walrus, although allied to the eared seals, is a unique animal. In appearance it is grotesque. Old bulls weigh up to 3,000 pounds, their wrinkled skins become almost hairless and the moustache of stiff bristles surrounding the long tusks and their small bloodshot eyes give them a venerable, if dissipated, appearance. Walruses live in the shallow waters of the Arctic and many hundreds crowd together to bask on beaches and ice floes. A few walruses occasionally stray to temperate waters. The tusks are used for stirring up mud to reveal the shellfish on which the walruses feed. The moustachial bristles and thick lips are used to manipulate the shells so that the body of the shellfish can be sucked out and the empty shell discarded. A few walruses take to eating young seals. Another bizarre feature of the walrus is its pair of throat pouches which the animal can blow up with air to a capacity of eleven gallons. The pouches give the walruses buoyancy when they sleep hanging vertically in the water and they also act as resonating chambers for the bell-like sounds which the walruses make during courtship.

Walruses bear a single calf and, unlike seals, which grow up so quickly, young walruses are suckled for over a year. Even after weaning, they stay with their mothers for another year, possibly because they cannot find enough food for themselves. Female walruses seem to make solicitous mothers as they carry their young on their backs, perhaps as a protection against killer whales which, despite the walruses' precautions, are said to surface under the cows and topple the young walruses into the water.

Below: common or harbor seals Phoca vitulina. *This species sometimes enters rivers and in Canada it is found in freshwater lakes. It is unique among seals in that the female may give birth in the water*

The impact of man

The seals, sealions, fur seals and walruses have long been a prime target for human hunters. Some Eskimos and other hunting tribes still rely on seal hunting as an essential part of their economy. One seal carcase provides not only a substantial weight of meat but a variety of other materials with many uses. The blubber is eaten or rendered down to make oil for lighting; the pelt is used for clothing, the coverings of boats and in ropes; the bones are made into various tools; the stomach and intestines make water carriers, clothes and darning thread. Even the stomach contents may be regarded as a delicacy. Finally, the teeth are used for decoration and the tusks of walruses are particularly valued for carving.

Primitive societies have made little impact on seal stocks but from the eighteenth century onwards some populations have been reduced to the brink of extinction, or beyond, by organized hunting. The walrus has disappeared from many parts of its range, although it is now recovering, and the monk seals have also been hard hit. It is the fur seals, however, that have been hardest hit as their pelts have an extremely dense and soft underfur which lies under the long, coarse guard hairs – a striking contrast to the sparse underfur of the sealions. When the huge rookeries of fur seals were discovered in the eighteenth century, the profiteers were quick to move in. At first the skins were shaved to provide material for the manufacture of felt, but later came the invention of a process for removing the guard hairs. These hairs have longer roots than those of the underfur so, if the skin is shaved from the underside, the roots of the guard hairs are cut and they can be withdrawn, leaving the fine underfur untouched.

The market for these furs was insatiable and as fur seals are defenceless on their breeding beaches, they had soon virtually disappeared. Luckily, seal populations are very resilient and the Pribilof fur seals have regained their numbers with United States government protection. Young males are cropped annually by the Aleutian islanders without any overall decrease in numbers. In the southern hemisphere, too, fur seal numbers are rising dramatically. Provided that pollution and disturbance can be avoided, there is no reason why any species of seal should fail to flourish in the future as they did before the eighteenth century.

Right: a young walrus, lacking the tusks of the adult, but displaying the characteristic 'moustache' of stiff bristles.
Below: a harp seal pup. These appealing infants have been slaughtered in large numbers for their white fur. They are born on icefloes in the North Atlantic

Manatees and dugong

There are three species of manatee living today and a single species of dugong. Collectively they are known as sea cows. The name gives an indication of their way of life and a clue to their ancestry, since they are descendants of land-living herbivores. In a parallel way, the seal, which is a descendant of land carnivores, was

Above: a manatee rests on the seabed. Manatees normally surface to breathe every five minutes or so but they may stay underwater for as long as fifteen minutes when they are resting.
Right: a group of Caribbean manatees Trichechus manatus *on the seabed off the coast of Florida.*
Opposite top: the single species of dugong Dugong dugon *is found off coasts of the Indian and Pacific Oceans. Like manatees, dugongs have become rarer in many places due to persecution by hunters.*
Far right: the mouth of the dugong is perfectly adapted for feeding on the sea bed. Its diet is entirely herbivorous

once known as the sea dog or sea bear.

Dugongs and manatees belong to the order Sirenia. It appears that Linnaeus, the Swedish naturalist who invented the modern classification of animals and plants, linked them with the mythical Sirens of ancient Greece. How he could see any resemblance between these ugly beasts and the sweetly singing creatures that tempted Odysseus is a mystery. Yet some three centuries earlier Christopher Columbus had mistaken manatees for mermaids. Evidently sea cows were not well known to either Columbus or Linnaeus and, even today, much about them remains a mystery. Their closest relatives appear to be the elephants, whose tooth patterns are similar.

Elephants of the sea
The three manatees live in tropical Atlantic waters. *Trichechus senegalensis* inhabits the coast and rivers of West Africa and *T. manatus* lives in the Caribbean, from Florida to Cayenne, in French Guiana. *T. inunguis* lives in the fresh waters of the Amazon River basin, and perhaps also in the Orinoco. Manatees look rather like seals with stout, streamlined bodies. The skin is almost hairless, dark grey to black in colour, and the forelimbs are modified as flippers that can be used for steering and grasping food; the hindlimbs are missing and manatees swim by means of a broad paddle-shaped tail. The blunt head lacks external ears, and the eyes are small. The nostrils are placed

high on the pig-like snout and can be shut when the manatee submerges. The bristly upper lip is split, giving the animal a hare-lipped appearance.

The single species of dugong *Dugong dugon* lives in the Indo-Pacific region, and is most numerous off the northern coast of Australia. It is very similar in appearance to the manatees but the tail is divided into two flukes like those of a whale and it has a turned-down rather than a straight snout. Manatees are twelve feet long and weigh up to 1,500 pounds, whereas the dugong is slightly smaller, measuring about ten feet in length. Dugongs are much lighter animals than manatees, weighing up to about 375 pounds only.

Both the dugong and the manatees are placid, inoffensive creatures. They are plant-eaters, living in family parties and never wandering far from the shore. Like the whales they spend their entire lives in the water and are virtually incapable of surviving on land. Dugongs feed entirely on marine plants, such as eel-grass. Parties of dugongs work methodically through strands of vegetation growing on the seabed, surfacing to breathe every few minutes. They tear off leaves and soft stems, using their muscular prehensile lips, and grub up roots. Dugongs have very few teeth; instead there are horny pads on each jaw. Of the five to six pairs of teeth in each jaw, only one pair survives to adulthood. The male also has a pair of tusks in the upper jaw. The manatees have rows of crushing teeth which gradually wear down with constant use, but the wear is not compensated for by continuous growth from the roots as in many other

grazing animals such as cows and horses. The replacement of teeth in manatees follows the pattern found in elephants. The position of the cheek teeth moves slowly forwards – worn teeth fall out at the front of the jaw while new ones erupt at the back. Manatees spend much of the day feeding, like other grazers, but they do not ruminate, or chew the cud. The feeding habits of the dugong and the manatees follow very much the same pattern but manatees have a more catholic diet. They eat a wide variety of marine and freshwater plants and reach up to pull down leaves from overhanging trees. Occasionally, they may hitch themselves half out of the water to take otherwise inaccessible food.

Mermaid mothers

Because sea cows are so wary (their acute hearing gives them early warning of disturbance) they are very difficult to observe. The result is that little is known of their breeding habits. A single calf is born after a gestation period of eleven months in dugongs and up to fifteen months in manatees. Courtship has not often been observed but it appears to be a playful, if brief, affair in manatees. Several pairs gather and swim in circles, the males nuzzling the females. Mating takes place with the pair lying on their sides in shallow water. In dugongs, the male seems merely to follow the female about. Birth takes place underwater and the calf is brought to the surface for its first breath. It has been suggested that dugongs bear their young on land

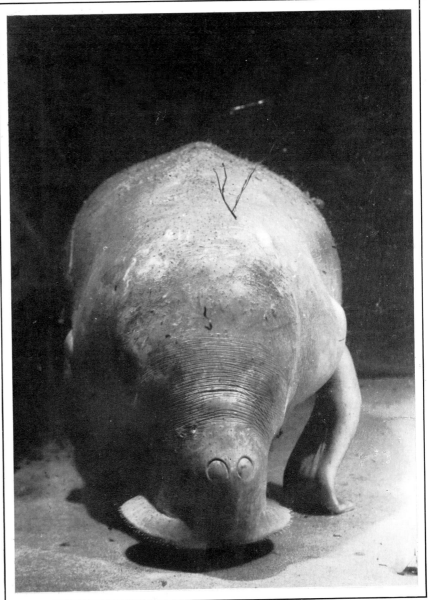

Right: dugongs, with their completely hairless skin, nailless flippers and tails notched like those of whales, are more highly adapted to life in the sea than manatees.

Far right: a manatee breaks the surface to breathe. Scraps of vegetation floating on the surface are a sign of a party of manatees or dugongs feeding below

but as they normally break surface only to breathe, they are difficult to find and observe; also it seems unlikely that they could drag themselves up onto the shore with their small flippers.

The sea cows are solicitous mothers but the males pay no attention to their offspring. It is not known how long the calves stay with their parents. The single pair of mammary glands are prominent and placed high on the female's chest. This is presumably the reason why Columbus mistook the sea cows for mermaids. Certainly, their facial characteristics could not have impressed him. The resemblance to a human mother with her baby has been emphasized by descriptions of the manatee floating vertically and holding her calf to her breast with one flipper. Such a posture seems to be exceptional, however, and suckling normally takes place in a prone position.

Threat of extinction

The numbers of dugongs and manatees have been greatly reduced over the last few hundred years. Only their wariness has saved them from extinction as they are defenceless and their large size makes them a valuable quarry for hunters. At one time manatee meat was a staple food for slaves on Caribbean sugar plantations and manatees have, as a result, disappeared from many parts of that region. Although the dugong spends most of its time underwater and reveals only its nostrils when it comes up to breathe, hunters can locate a feeding party of dugongs by the pieces of torn-off vegetation floating above

the animals. Dugongs were once commercially exploited for oil in Australia but, like the manatees, they have been hunted mainly for food by local people and their thick hides are also valued. The Ark of the Covenant is supposed to have been covered with dugong skin.

Steller's sea cow

Recently attempts have been made to employ manatees to prevent waterways and irrigation ditches from becoming choked with waterweeds. However, manatees will not breed under semi-captive conditions so the plan for combining a system of free weed-clearance with a supply of meat has failed.

As coastal people turn from hunting to other forms of subsistence the pressure on the remaining sea cows is being removed and, hopefully, they will not suffer the fate of another Sirenian – Steller's sea cow *Hydrodamalis stelleri* – which is now extinct. This species was discovered on the Commander Islands in the Bering Sea, when Vitus Bering's expedition was marooned there in 1742, and it was described by the expedition's naturalist Georg Steller. The sea cows, which grew to a length of thirty-five feet, provided the castaways with food and clothing. When news of the find spread after the explorers were rescued, hunters descended on the islands. When they were discovered, there were only a few thousand Steller's sea cows in existence; within thirty years all had been killed. The crew of a Russian ship reported seeing some in 1962 but there has been no confirmation of this observation.

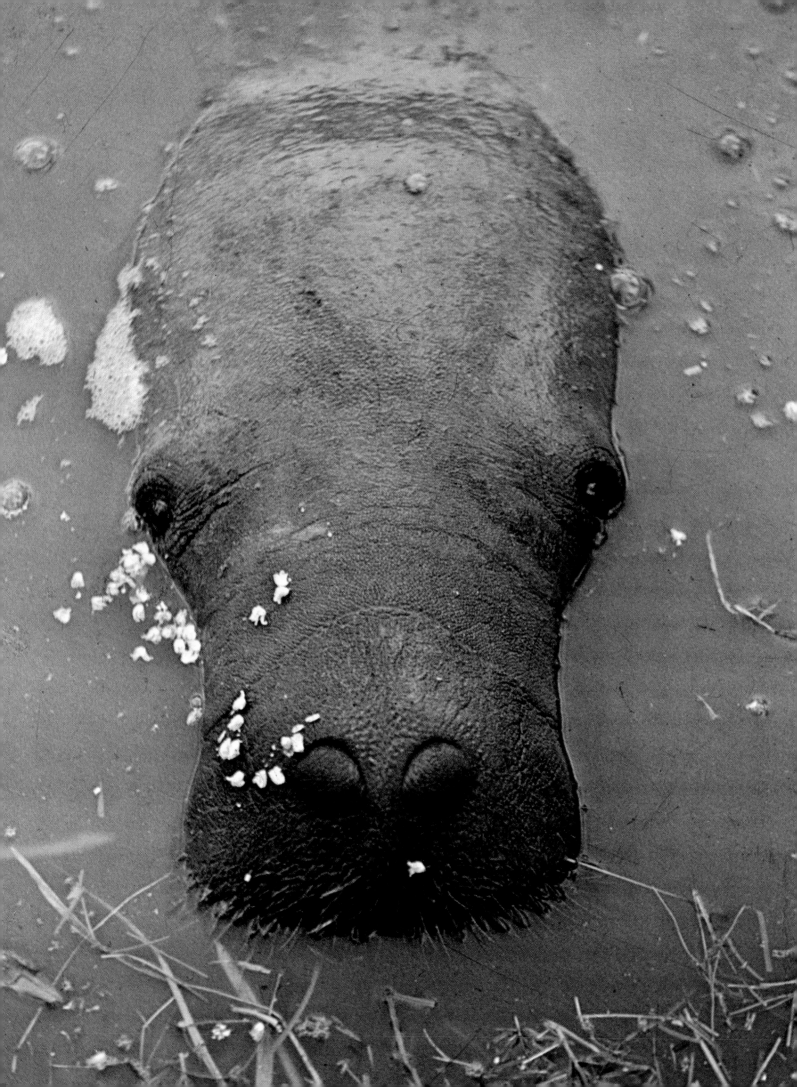

Index

188

Acknowledgments

7 A. Margiocco. 8 D. Faulkner. 8–9 D. Faulkner. 10 D. Faulkner; CEDRI. 11 G. S. Giacomelli; G. Annunziata; © D. P. Wilson. 13 Munschy/Jacana. 14 D. Faulkner. 15 G. Relini. 16 G. Annunziata. 17 Fenaux/Jacana. 18 D. Faulkner; G. Annunziata. 19 D. Faulkner; D. Faulkner; G. Mazza. 20 G. Annunziata; G. Mazza. 21 Bruce Coleman Ltd. 22 R. Maltini – P. Solaini; T. Poggio. 23 G. Mazza. 24 Bruce Coleman Ltd; J. Burton/Bruce Coleman Ltd; J. Six. 24–5 J. Burton/Bruce Coleman Ltd. 25 G. Mazza. 26 J. Burton/Bruce Coleman Ltd. 27 H. Chaumeton/Jacana. 28 G. Relini. 29 D. Faulkner; D. Faulkner; D. Faulkner; D. Faulkner; C. Rives/CEDRI; D. Faulkner. 30 R. Maltini – P. Solaini; C. Rives/CEDRI. 31 ZEFA; G. S. Giacomelli. 32 G. Mazza; C. Rives/CEDRI. 33 R. Maltini – P. Solaini; G. Mazza. 34 D. Faulkner; C. Rives/CEDRI. 35 G. Annunziata; CEDRI. 36 CEDRI; CEDRI; D. Faulkner. 37 P. Orlandi. 38 ICP; E. Dulevant. 39 Seaphot. 40 D. Faulkner; P. Curto. 41 P. Curto. 42 G. Costa. 43 D. Faulkner. 44 A. Margiocco. 44–5 P. Burton/Natural Science Photos; Heather Angel. 45 Heather Angel. 46 J. Burton/Bruce Coleman Ltd. 47 G. Mazza; J. Burton/Bruce Coleman Ltd. 48 Archivio IGDA – Archivio Foto B; Archivio IGDA – Archivio Foto B. 49 J. Burton/Bruce Coleman Ltd. 50 D. Faulkner. 51 H. Chaumeton/Jacana. 53 Heather Angel. 55 C. Rives; P. Curto; © D. P. Wilson; G. Mazza; G. Mazza; A. Margiocco. 56 Marka. 57 D. Faulkner; G. Mazza; D. Faulkner; A. Margiocco. 59 J. Vasserot; D. Faulkner; D. Faulkner; J. Six; R. Maltini – P. Solaini; D. Faulkner. 60 D. Faulkner. 61 Marka. 62 C. Petron/Seaphot. 63 R. Dei. 64 A. Margiocco; Heather Angel. 65 D. Faulkner. 66–7 R. Merlo. 67 J. Harding/Black Star. 68 F. Schulke/Black Star; G. Mazza. 69 D. Faulkner. 70–1 F. Schulke/Seaphot. 70 R. Taylor/Ardea. 71 A. Power/Bruce Coleman Ltd; B. Cropp/Camera Press. 72 R. Merlo. 73 Archivio Puigdengolas. 74 G. S. Giacomelli; G. Mazza; G. S. Giacomelli. 75 G. Mazza; G. Relini. 76 G. S. Giacomelli; D. Faulkner. 77 V. Taylor/Ardea, London; T. McHugh/Photo Researchers; J. G. Harmelin. 78 P. Green/Ardea, London. 79 G. Mazza. 81 P. Morris/Ardea, London. 83–3 Marka. 85 F. Wilderoe. 86 T. McHugh/Photo Researchers. 87 A. Margiocco. A. Margiocco. 89 R. Thompson. 90 Heather Angel. 91 Noailles/Jacana. 92 A. Margiocco; Archivio Puidengolas. 93 Margiocco. 94 D. Faulkner; M. Corsetti. 95 P. Reisere/Bavaria; D. Faulkner. 96 Seaphot. 97 S. Yoff/

Jacana; J. Burton/Bruce Coleman Ltd. 98 T. McHugh/Photo Researchers. 99 © D. P. Wilson. 100 © D. P. Wilson. 101 A. Ferrari. 102 G. Mazza; F. Sauer/Bavaria. 103 G. Mazza. 104 R. Schroeder/Bruce Coleman Ltd; R. Maltini – P. Solaini. 105 G. Annunziata. 106–7 J. George/Seaphot. 107 P. Scoones/Seaphot. 108 P. Scoones/Seaphot. 109 © D. P. Wilson. 110 © D. P. Wilson. 111 A. Rizzi; D. Faulkner. 112 C. Bevilacqua; D. Faulkner; D. Faulkner. 113 D. Faulkner. 114 D. Faulkner. 115 D. Faulkner. 116 G. Mazza. 117 G. Mazza; D. Faulkner. 118 G. Mazza; CEDRI. 119 F. Quilici. 120–1 © D. P. Wilson. 122 J. N. Perrez/Seaphot. 123 T. Micek. 124 G. Annunziata; G. Annunziata. 125 G. Mazza; J. Burton/Bruce Coleman Ltd. 126 D. B. Lewes/Natural Science Photos. 127 J. Burton/Bruce Coleman Ltd. 128 G. Mazza; Marka. 129 P. Reisere/Bavaria. 130 NHPA; H. Lindner/ZEFA. 131 D. Faulkner; D. Faulkner. 132 A. Margiocco. 133 P. M. David; Archivio Puigdengolas. 134 C. Petron/Seaphot. 135 L. Pellegrini. 136 P. Ward/Popperfoto. 137 D. Hughes/Bruce Coleman Ltd. 138–9 R. Schroeder/Bruce Coleman Ltd. 138 Bolla. 139 Bruce Coleman Ltd; G. Annunziata/Jacana. 140 J. Burton/Bruce Coleman Ltd. 141 D. Hughes/Bruce Coleman Ltd. 142 J. Simon/Photo Researchers. 143 L. Pellegrini. 144 R. Merlo. 145 V. Taylor/Ardea, London. 146 A. Power–Bruce Coleman Ltd. 147 A. Margiocco. 148 Soulaire/CEDRI. 149 L. Pellegrini. 154 T. Zuccoli. 155 Photophile – J. Stevenson. 156–7 John Dominis, Life 1963 © Time Inc. 156 Institute of Oceanographic Sciences. 157 R. Giovacchini. 158 World Photo Service. 159 British Antarctic Survey. 160 R. Kinne/Photo Researchers. 161 C. E. Ostman; CEDRI. 152 F. Quilici/Moana 162–3 M. Beebe/Photo Researchers. 163 McHugh/Photo Researchers. 164–5 G. Laycock/Bruce Coleman Ltd. 164 J. H. Tashjian. 165 C. Ray/Photo Researchers. 166 J. Simon/C. E. Ostman 167 Milwaukee/Jacana. 168 Marka. 169 T. McHugh/Photo Researchers. 170 S. G. Costa. 171 R. Kinne/Bruce Coleman Ltd. 172 J. Burton/Bruce Coleman Ltd. 173 T. McHugh/Photo Researchers. 175 J. Foott/Bruce Coleman Ltd. 176 L. Pellegrini; L. Pellegrini. 177 L. Pellegrini. 178 L. Pellegrini. 179 R. Jacques/Photo Researchers. 180 J.-P. Varin/Jacana. 181 Frédéric/Jacana. 182 R. Kinne/Bruce Coleman Ltd. 182–3 Marka. 183 Transworld. 184 Transworld. 185 A. Warren/Ardea. London.